LAN Switching
first-step

Matthew J. Castelli

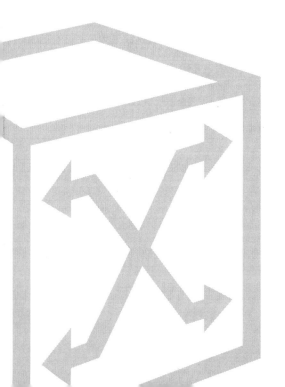

Cisco Press
800 East 96th Street
Indianapolis, IN 46240

LAN Switching
first-step

Matthew J. Castelli

Copyright© 2005 Cisco Systems, Inc.

Cisco Press logo is a trademark of Cisco Systems, Inc.

Published by:
Cisco Press
800 East 96th Street
Indianapolis, IN 46240 USA

Printed in the United States of America 1 2 3 4 5 6 7 8 9 0

First Printing   June 2004

Library of Congress Cataloging-in-Publication Number: 2003107983

ISBN: 1-58720-100-3

Publisher
John Wait

Editor-in-Chief
John Kane

Executive Editor
Brett Bartow

Cisco Representative
Anthony Wolfenden

**Cisco Press
Program Manager**
Nannette M. Noble

Production Manager
Patrick Kanouse

Development Editor
Betsy Henkels

Technical Editors
Heather Bianchi
Jim Doherty
Richard Froom
Matt Lüetjen

Team Coordinator
Tammi Barnett

Book and Cover Designer
Louisa Adair

Compositor
Mark Shirar

Copy Editor and Indexer
Keith Cline

Warning and Disclaimer

This book is designed to provide information about local-area network (LAN) switching. Every effort has been made to make this book as complete and as accurate as possible, but no warranty or fitness is implied.

The information is provided on an "as is" basis. The authors, Cisco Press, and Cisco Systems, Inc. shall have neither liability nor responsibility to any person or entity with respect to any loss or damages arising from the information contained in this book or from the use of the discs or programs that may accompany it.

The opinions expressed in this book belong to the author and are not necessarily those of Cisco Systems, Inc.

Trademark Acknowledgments

All terms mentioned in this book that are known to be trademarks or service marks have been appropriately capitalized. Cisco Press or Cisco Systems, Inc. cannot attest to the accuracy of this information. Use of a term in this book should not be regarded as affecting the validity of any trademark or service mark.

Corporate and Government Sales

Cisco Press offers excellent discounts on this book when ordered in quantity for bulk purchases or special sales.

For more information please contact: **U.S. Corporate and Government Sales** 1-800-382-3419 corpsales@pearsontechgroup.com

For sales outside the U.S. please contact: **International Sales** international@pearsoned.com

Feedback Information

At Cisco Press, our goal is to create in-depth technical books of the highest quality and value. Each book is crafted with care and precision, undergoing rigorous development that involves the unique expertise of members from the professional technical community.

Readers' feedback is a natural continuation of this process. If you have any comments regarding how we could improve the quality of this book, or otherwise alter it to better suit your needs, you can contact us through email at feedback@ciscopress.com. Please make sure to include the book title and ISBN in your message.

We greatly appreciate your assistance.

CISCO SYSTEMS

Corporate Headquarters
Cisco Systems, Inc.
170 West Tasman Drive
San Jose, CA 95134-1706
USA
www.cisco.com
Tel: 408 526-4000
    800 553-NETS (6387)
Fax: 408 526-4100

European Headquarters
Cisco Systems International BV
Haarlerbergpark
Haarlerbergweg 13-19
1101 CH Amsterdam
The Netherlands
www-europe.cisco.com
Tel: 31 0 20 357 1000
Fax: 31 0 20 357 1100

Americas Headquarters
Cisco Systems, Inc.
170 West Tasman Drive
San Jose, CA 95134-1706
USA
www.cisco.com
Tel: 408 526-7660
Fax: 408 527-0883

Asia Pacific Headquarters
Cisco Systems, Inc.
Capital Tower
168 Robinson Road
#22-01 to #29-01
Singapore 068912
www.cisco.com
Tel: +65 6317 7777
Fax: +65 6317 7799

Cisco Systems has more than 200 offices in the following countries and regions. Addresses, phone numbers, and fax numbers are listed on the
Cisco.com Web site at www.cisco.com/go/offices.

Argentina • Australia • Austria • Belgium • Brazil • Bulgaria • Canada • Chile • China PRC • Colombia • Costa Rica • Croatia • Czech Republic
Denmark • Dubai, UAE • Finland • France • Germany • Greece • Hong Kong SAR • Hungary • India • Indonesia • Ireland • Israel • Italy
Japan • Korea • Luxembourg • Malaysia • Mexico • The Netherlands • New Zealand • Norway • Peru • Philippines • Poland • Portugal
Puerto Rico • Romania • Russia • Saudi Arabia • Scotland • Singapore • Slovakia • Slovenia • South Africa • Spain • Sweden
Switzerland • Taiwan • Thailand • Turkey • Ukraine • United Kingdom • United States • Venezuela • Vietnam • Zimbabwe

About the Author

Matthew "Cat" Castelli has 16 years' telecommunications and network experience, in architecture, field and sales, and design engineering. Matthew is currently the deputy network and secure solutions program and product manager with EDS on the NMCI (Navy/Marine Corps Intranet) program, serving as the architecture, engineering, and information assurance lead for the enterprise implementation of the U.S. Navy's classified network. He has been a network architect engineer with a major network carrier, the senior sales engineer for a performance management software company, a principal consultant with a Cisco Preferred Solutions Partner (PSP), and a technical consultant/data network engineer for another major network carrier. Matthew holds CCNA, CCDA, CCNP, and CCDP certifications and is currently pursuing a bachelor of science in management, while learning how to fly private aircraft. Cat is also a regular member of the Farm Creek Poker Club.

Matthew, or "Cat," can be contacted via Cisco Press or directly at mjcastelli@earthlink.net and will reply as promptly as possible.

About the Technical Reviewers

Heather Bianchi is currently the enterprise delivery manager for the U.S. Navy's classified NMCI (Navy/Marine Corps Intranet) implementation, working out of EDS's Network and Secure Solutions Product Management team in Herndon, Virginia. Heather's position enables her to leverage her design, engineering, and client-facing experience in managing a team of engineers and regional delivery managers in creating and facilitating the implementation of solutions for the Navy's classified network requirements. Heather has worked for both small and large companies, thereby developing experience including database development and management, hands-on implementation of the National Guard's video training network, first- and second-level support for the National Guard, and now design and architecture for the NMCI. Along the way Heather has earned her CCDA certification and is now working to be certified as a CCDP.

When not figuring out how to protect the Navy's secrets, Heather keeps busy by taking care of her son and lobbying for a lifetime supply of free Starbucks coffee.

Jim Doherty is a solutions marketing manager with Cisco Systems Enterprise Marketing. Jim coauthored *Cisco Networking Simplified* and authored the Study Notes section of the CCNA Flash Cards and Exam Practice Kits published by Cisco Press.

Richard Froom, CCIE No. 5102, is a technical leader for the storage-area network (SAN) team of the Internet Switching Business Unit Financial Test Lab at Cisco Systems. Richard has been with Cisco for six years, previously serving as a support engineer troubleshooting customers' networks and as a technical leader dealing with Cisco Catalyst products.

Richard, being involved with Catalyst product field trials, has been crucial in driving troubleshooting capabilities of Catalyst products and software. He has also contributed substantially to the Cisco.com LAN Technologies Technical Tips and has written white papers dealing with 802.3 autonegotiation and Hot Standby Router Protocol (HSRP). Richard is currently testing Cisco SAN solutions. Richard is also the coauthor of *CCNP Self-Study: Building Cisco Multilayer Switched Networks (BCMSN),* Second Edition, and *Cisco Catalyst QoS: Quality of Service in Campus Networks* from Cisco Press. He attended Clemson University and completed his bachelor of science in computer engineering.

Matt Lüetjen is currently a senior network engineer for SAIC, working at the National Institutes of Health (NIH) in Bethesda, Maryland. His position in the Engineering Operations section allows him to use his experience in various environments that involve the design, redesign, and implementation of network configurations. He has worked for many different companies, from small companies with a single network to a countrywide upgrade of a large backbone, performing tasks that included switch, router, server, and desktop issues. Some of the customers that have benefited from Matt's assistance are NIH, NexTel, CSX, and multiple government organizations, both military and civilian. Along the way, Matt has obtained his MCSE, CCNA, and CCNP, and continues to teach and learn about all layers of the OSI model.

When not under the hood of a CPU, Matt likes to take out his frustration playing lacrosse and riding anything that has two wheels.

Dedications

To my mother Jayne, who on December 19th, 2003, found her smile.

To my brother Dan, who continues to demonstrate and amaze all with magic that is "out of this world." See you on the World Poker Tour.

To Kim Graves, always my muse and inspiration—I'll find our treasure yet!

RKTTE NERIC RREPQ EHKUA XKSXX

"You can know the name of a bird in all the languages of the world, but when you're finished, you'll know absolutely nothing whatever about the bird.... So let's look at the bird and see what it's doing—that's what counts. I learned very early the difference between knowing the name of something and knowing something."

Richard Feynman (1918–1988)

Acknowledgments

I want to give special recognition to Bob, Lèo, and Jamie O'Conner, Kim, Mike, and Matthew Graves, Jon Hage, Eric Roller and the Chutzpah gang, Deborah Dworanczyk, Heather and Jeffrey II Bianchi, Brian, Aurora, Jason, Curtis, Tom and Amanda White, Muneesh Talwar, Amir Kazemzadeh, Kenny Rodgers, Andre Buckner, Jeff Wolfe, Joe Shannon, and Karla Myers. In addition, I want to recognize, Jeff B., Rachel S., Patti S., Brian W., Mark and Susan K., Matt L., John S., John Sa., Chris S., Joe B., Belinda G., Scott C., Harrison M., Andrea H., Brent D., and many others too numerous to list here.

A big "thank you" goes out to the production team for this book and for their patience with its author. John Kane, Jim Schachterle, Michelle Grandin, Amy Moss, and Christopher Cleveland have been a pleasure to work with. A special "thank you" goes out to my development editor, Betsey Henkels. Betsey believed in my vision for this book and helped me focus the picture during the times when my vision got fuzzy; this book is better now because of Betsey's work and encouragement. I couldn't have asked for a finer team—let's do this again.

I want to thank my technical editors: Heather Bianchi, Matt Lüetjen, Jim Doherty, and Richard Froom. These patient souls had the challenging task of keeping me straight—something I admit is not always an easy thing to do. If any mistakes are found in this book, they are solely my own doing and not theirs.

I want to thank "The Herd": Keyser, Jack, Lola, Ted, Sam, Buzz; and since passed, Spike, Zeke, and Tony; it is this bunch who challenge my sanity on a daily basis and reinforce that it's necessary to let loose once in a while regardless of whether anyone is watching.

Last, but certainly not least, I want to thank John O'Meally for his support, inspiration, and encouragement.

Contents at a Glance

Contents

Icons Used in This Book

Communication
Server

PC

File
Server

Terminal

Modem

Hub

Managed
Object

Management
Database

Router

Bridge

Printer

Laptop

Switch

Multilayer
Switch

ATM
Switch

ISDN/Frame Relay
Switch

RMON Probe

Network Cloud

Line: Ethernet

Line: Serial

Line: Switched Serial

Command Syntax Conventions

The conventions used to present command syntax in this book are the same conventions used in the IOS Command Reference. The Command Reference describes these conventions as follows:

- **Boldface** indicates commands and keywords that are entered literally as shown. In actual configuration examples and output (not general command syntax), boldface indicates commands that are manually input by the user (such as a **show** command).

- *Italics* indicate arguments for which you supply actual values.

- Vertical bars (|) separate alternative, mutually exclusive elements.

- Square brackets [ ] indicate optional elements.

- Braces { } indicate a required choice.

- Braces within brackets [{ }] indicate a required choice within an optional element.

Introduction

The purpose of this book is to provide an introduction to local-area network (LAN) switching. This LAN switching introduction starts with a discussion of network building blocks, moving into designing a switched LAN, managing your switched LAN, and some real-world case studies demonstrating these concepts.

Audience

Want to learn about how bridges and switches work in a local-area network? If so, this book is for you. This book is intended for anyone who desires to learn about LAN switching concepts and implementation, without wading through the sometimes-intense explanations offered in other sources.

How the Book Is Organized

This book is organized almost as if it were a novel, intended to be read the first time cover to cover. This is not saying that you cannot jump right to a particular chapter of interest, far from it; I encourage you to read what is of interest here, keeping in mind that each chapter builds on discussions from previous chapters.

The chapters cover the following topics:

Chapter 1, Networking Basics—This chapter introduces you to the concepts of a network—what it is and what it's made of, such as the physical and logical pieces of a network.

Chapter 2, Network Models and Standards—This chapter discusses network models and network standards. Models are guidelines subject to vendor interpretation and application, often leading to proprietary protocols and the like. Standards are "laws" that all vendors must adhere to if they want their products to interoperate and be useful in a network implementation.

Chapter 3, Local-Area Networking Introduction—This chapter discusses the evolution of local-area networking and its prevalence today in places as varied as the small home local network to the large corporate LAN.

Chapter 4, Traditional LAN Architecture—This chapter discusses the components and infrastructure of a LAN from the ground up, including types of cabling and interfaces, termination points, and the differences of each regarding Token Ring and Ethernet LANs.

Chapter 5, Ethernet LANs—This chapter builds on Chapter 4, applying the Chapter 4 concepts to real-life situations.

Chapter 6, How a Switch Works—This chapter discusses the functions of a switch: what happens inside the switch and how a switch works within a network.

Chapter 7, Spanning Tree Protocol (STP)—This chapter discusses what the Spanning Tree Protocol is and how it works within the LAN environment.

Chapter 8, Virtual LANs (VLANs)— This chapter takes the concept of a physical LAN, throws it against the wall, and puts it back together to look like something a bit different. You are introduced to the "virtual" concept and how to make LANs do some interesting things, such as sharing.

Chapter 9, Switching Security—This chapter discusses how you can put your guard dog Patches to work to guard a network and revisits some of the discussions from Chapter 6. In taking things a step further, the chapter discusses how to restrict access to a switch.

Chapter 10, LAN Switched Network Design—This chapter pulls all the pieces together from the previous chapters and discusses what a switched Ethernet LAN might look like and how it operates in an internetwork. Although there are no case studies here, there are plenty of examples and figures, at least two examples for Layer 2 and Layer 3 switching. The chapter briefly revisits the OSI model discussions from Chapter 2 and Chapter 3. The OSI discussion here sets the stage for the discussions of Layer 2 and Layer 3 switching.

Chapter 11, Switch Network Management— This chapter discusses the monitoring, management, and maintenance of a switched LAN. The OSI model from Chapter 2 is revisited and the FCAPS model is introduced, with an emphasis on the FCAPS model.

Chapter 12, Switching Case Studies—This chapter reviews some LAN switching real-world implementations. One case study here is a typical home network: one (or more) PC(s), DSL/cable modem, and a small Ethernet switch.

After you've finished reading this book, you will know the answer to this question: Should you use a hub, bridge, or a switch? (The answer might surprise you.)

How the Book Can Be Used

This book is designed to be read straight through like a novel. If you prefer to jump right to the chapters that might interest you, however, that is okay as well. If there is a significant point discussed in further detail in another chapter, that is noted.

The book provides a basic foundation on which you can build your learning experience.

Chapter Objectives

Every chapter begins with a list of objectives that are addressed in the chapter.

Highlighted Keywords

Whenever a keyword or term appears for the first time, it is bolded and italicized to indicate that it is defined in the Glossary.

Chapter Summaries

Every chapter concludes with a comprehensive chapter summary that reviews chapter objectives, ensuring complete coverage and discussing the chapter's relation to future content.

Chapter Reviews

Every chapter concludes with a chapter review. In a question-and-answer format, the chapter review tests the basic ideas and concepts covered in each chapter. Answers to the chapter reviews are included in an appendix at the back of the book.

Case Studies

Some chapters include case studies that focus on the real-world implementation of concepts.

Glossary

The Glossary defines essential terms and acronyms.

Feedback

Feedback, as always, is appreciated. As much as I hope you learn from me, I hope to learn from you as well. Although an explanation of something might seem perfectly clear to me, you may think otherwise. In a classroom or lecture environment, audience facial expressions generally indicate to me whether confusion exists; in this current format, however, I don't have that luxury. It is my intention that upon completion of this book you will have gained the knowledge you were seeking. I encourage you to contact me with any feedback you might have.

The Twelve Networking Truths

As one last introductory note, I invite you to read the following RFC 1925 (by Ross Callon), perhaps ironically published April 1, 1996. Whatever your involvement in networking will be, you will find that there are certain inalienable and undeniable truths; herein are the Twelve Networking Truths:

The Twelve Networking Truths

Status of this memo:

This memo provides information for the Internet community. This memo does not specify an Internet standard of any kind. Distribution of this memo is unlimited.

Abstract:

This memo documents the fundamental truths of networking for the Internet community. This memo does not specify a standard, except in the sense that all standards must implicitly follow the fundamental truths.

Acknowledgements

The truths described in this memo result from extensive study over an extended period of time by many people, some of whom did not intend to contribute to this work. The editor merely has collected these truths, and would like to thank the networking community for originally illuminating these truths.

1. Introduction

This Request for Comments (RFC) provides information about the fundamental truths underlying all networking. These truths apply to networking in general, and are not limited to TCP/IP, the Internet, or any other subset of the networking community.

2. The Fundamental Truths

1. It Has To Work.

2. No matter how hard you push and no matter what the priority, you can't increase the speed of light.

2a. (corollary). No matter how hard you try, you can't make a baby in much less than nine months. Trying to speed this up *might* make it slower, but it won't make it happen any quicker.

3. With sufficient thrust, pigs fly just fine. However, this is not necessarily a good idea. It is hard to be sure where they are going to land, and it could be dangerous sitting under them as they fly overhead.

4. Some things in life can never be fully appreciated nor understood unless experienced first-hand. Some things in networking can never be fully understood by someone who neither builds commercial networking equipment nor runs an operational network.

5. It is always possible to agglutinate multiple separate problems into a single complex interdependent solution. In most cases this is a bad idea.

6. It is easier to move a problem around (for example, by moving the problem to a different part of the overall network architecture) than it is to solve it.

6a. (corollary). It is always possible to add another level of indirection.

7. It is always something.

7a. (corollary). Good, Fast, Cheap: Pick any two (you can't have all three).

8. It is more complicated than you think.

9. For all resources, whatever it is, you need more.

9a. (corollary) Every networking problem always takes longer to solve than it seems it should.

10. One size never fits all.

11. Every old idea will be proposed again with a different name and a different presentation, regardless of whether it works.

11a. (corollary). See rule 6a.

12. In protocol design, perfection has been reached not when there is nothing left to add, but when there is nothing left to take away.

What You Will Learn

On completing this chapter, you will be able to:

- ✔ List the basic characteristics of a network

- ✔ List the major physical and logical components of a network

- ✔ Describe three modes of data transmission

- ✔ Describe the three basic types of logical networks

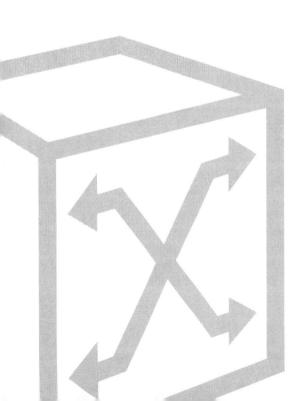

CHAPTER 1

Networking Basics

This chapter discusses the concept of a network—what it is and what it's made of, including its physical and nonphysical (logical) pieces and—uses common transportation networks, such as trains and subways, to illustrate these concepts.

What Is a Network?

A network is a system of interconnecting lines, such as telephone lines for communication or subway tracks for transportation. We use transportation networks during the course of an average day for a number of different purposes: the train or subway for daily expeditions, the roads for commuting to and from work, and the airlines for longer trips. In the computer and Information Technology (IT) environment, a *network* is just defined as a group of computers and connecting circuitry functioning in a specific manner. A transportation network is defined as a system of crossing or interconnecting routes, such as roads or subway tracks. This chapter analogizes transportation systems and computer systems to help you apply computer concepts to a familiar context.

Transportation and Computer Networks

Let's look at these definitions in more detail. Simply stated, a transportation network connects two or more points, enabling the exchange of resources, such as people, goods, or information. These points might be cities connected by railroad lines, buildings within a city connected by streets, or desks within a building connected by hallways and stairwells. The common denominator here is that there is some

sort of connection, or path, between these points—railroad tracks, city streets, or office hallways. These paths provide a way for people or goods to get from one point to another. This originating point, or starting point, is called the sender, originator, or *source*; the second point, or arrival point, is called the receiver, or *destination*.

In transportation networks, an originating (source) and ending point (destination) are two distinct locations in a journey. In addition, the ending point can become the originating point for another part of a journey. Think of a flight from Los Angeles to Cleveland with a two-hour layover in Denver, as shown in Figure 1-1. Denver, in this case, is both a destination and an end point of one trip and the starting point of another trip. Computer networks function in a similar way. Data can be sent to a destination (endpoint) that in turn becomes the originating point for another transmission to the final destination. These sources and destinations are not fixed points, but change depending on the direction of message (data) flow.

Figure 1-1   Source and Destination Relationships

Los Angeles	Denver	Cleveland
Source	Source and Destination	Destination
Your Office Computer	Computer in Denver	Comuputer in Sales Office (Cleveland)

To better understand IT networks, such as data (computer or Internet) or voice (telephone) networks, and the concept of switching within these networks, let's look first at the networks we use daily, such as the subway, railroad, and airline *routes*. As described previously, these are transportation networks that effect the moving of resources (people) from one point to another across an established path. Take, for example, the New York City subway. Figure 1-2 shows a few stops.

Figure 1-2   New York City Subway Stops

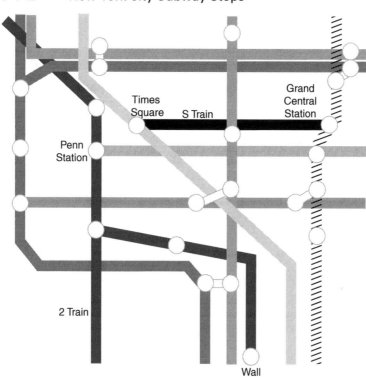

If you are on Wall Street and want to go to Grand Central Station, you cannot take a direct route between these two points. As illustrated in Figure 1-2, you might take the number 2 train to Times Square and the S train from Times Square to Grand Central.

It is the connection of Wall Street to Times Square to Grand Central that enables you to move from Wall Street to Grand Central, and it is the network of these subway connections that enables you to move throughout the city.

The airline and the subway networks connect different points and connect them in differing fashions. In the case of the airlines, cities are connected via preplanned routes in the sky. In the case of the subway, various city points (stations) are connected via subway tracks. A key point here is that just because a network path passes through a city block, in the case of the subway, or over a city, in the case of an airline, that pass-through point cannot be used to get on or off the network. The only way you can join a network is at an origination (starting) or termination (ending) point of the network connection.

While walking along the streets of New York City, for example, you can hear, and sometimes see, the subway trains running under the city sidewalk, but you can't get on the train from that point (unless you happen to be in a Hollywood movie chase scene). To get on that train, you must get to a station on that train's route, a *demarcation point*. A demarcation point is the boundary between two entities; in this case, the demarcation point is the boundary between the street and the train station. This demarcation point is both the point whereby passengers get on the train (originating or source point) or get off the train (terminating or destination point).

It is important to understand that the origination point and the termination point are *interconnected*, meaning they are connected to each other in some fashion. In the New York City subway, Wall Street and Times Square are interconnected via one set of tracks, Times Square and Grand Central Station are interconnected via another set of tracks, and Wall Street and Grand Central Station are interconnected via yet another set of tracks. Times Square is the switching point for passengers between Wall Street and Grand Central, because subway passengers need to disembark the number 2 train (Wall Street—Times Square) in order to board the S train (Times Square—Grand Central).

Each track segment and station is a leg in the subway network. Legs of the network are joined at key locations, where other major arteries carry you to other key locations. These key locations are "distribution" or "hub" points on the network. This is true of airlines, roads, and telephone calls.

Logical Networks

Transportation networks are made up of physical objects that you can hold or touch with your hand, such as railroad ties and subway rails. Logical network elements do not have these same physical properties as physical networks. Just as virtual reality in video games gives you the illusion of driving a tank or firing a weapon (even though you are not really in a tank or pulling the trigger), logical networks are based on elements that you can't really see or hold, but nonetheless they are there.

A network is made up of several pieces and parts that connect the source and destination. These pieces and parts are grouped into two categories: physical and logical components. It is these physical and logical components that make up the infrastructure and end-user pieces of a network, enabling you to communicate with someone else on the network. Suppose, for example, that you are taking the train from Washington, D.C., to San Francisco. There is a physical and logical component to your trip, as illustrated in Figure 1-3.

Figure 1-3   Physical and Logical Journey from Washington, D.C., to San Francisco

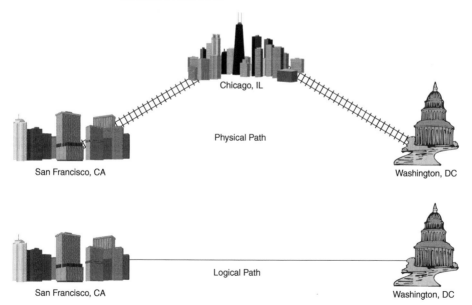

The physical path of your journey takes you from Washington, D.C., to Chicago, where you switch trains to continue to San Francisco. In your mind, however, your trip is logically from Washington, D.C., to San Francisco because you are not staying over in Chicago, merely changing trains. The physical component here are the tracks between the three cities, but the logical component is the starting and ending point of the two cities because you are most concerned with where you start your trip and where your trip ends.

This same physical and logical concept applies to networking and networking components. A brief introduction to these physical and logical components follows.

Network Physical Components

The physical component of a network is a network hardware device, such as a *switch* and the cabling. This collection of devices and cables, carrying the data from source to destination, makes up the complete physical network.

 note
Chapter 5, "Ethernet LANs," discusses switches, bridges, and hubs in more detail.

Switches

If there isn't a straight route from one city to the next, either the train passengers have to disembark from one train and board another, at a demarcation point (train station), or the trains themselves have to change paths at rail switching stations along the way. Network switches work in a similar fashion by connecting network paths together, providing a route for the frame from source to destination. A switch can also connect one machine to another in a straight path and might be the only path that exists, such as for two PCs connected together in the same room, or for a PC and a networked printer.

Figure 1-4 illustrates the function of a switchyard in a railroad network. A train starting at a ***distant-end*** station must go through a railroad switchyard that will change the train's route so that the train can reach its destination train station. In networking, the distant end can be either of the following, depending on the context of the conversation you are having with someone when discussing your network:

- The terminating point of the attached network connection

- The entire path

Figure 1-4   Railroad Switching Point Between Different Tracks

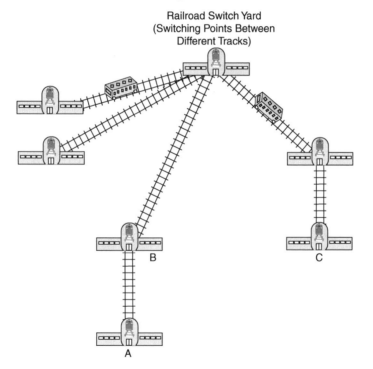

In Figure 1-4, for example, a train leaves from station A, the distant end of the track is station B, and the distant end of the path (ultimate destination of the passengers) is station C. It is important to establish the context when discussing net-

work origination and termination points: Are you discussing the physical connection between two points or the entire path from source to destination?

Figure 1-5 illustrates this same switching concept in a data network, such as you might find in a corporate office.

Figure 1-5   Network Switching Between Paths

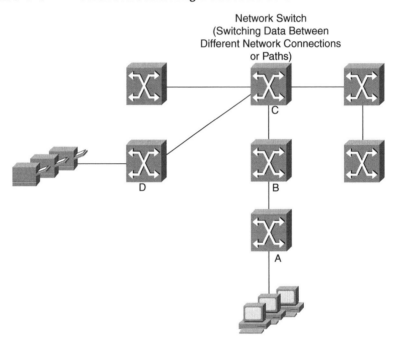

For example, user computers are connected to this network by switch A. To print documents from their computers, the users instruct the application to print. The application then sends the document across the network to the printers connected to switch D. The document to be printed is packaged in a frame and sent out on to the network, where it passes through switch B and switch C and terminates at switch D. Switch D then passes the frame(s) to the printer for the users to retrieve. All this switching, which is transparent to the user, occurs as a result of the user pressing Ctrl-P in a word processor program.

Cabling

To interconnect two or more points, there must be some sort of medium to carry the information from one point to the other, like the railroad tracks between train stations. A *medium* is defined as the physical substance through which something else is transmitted or carried. Different types of *media* are used today for network communication, such as copper cable, fiber-optic cable, and the air. (Yes, the same air that we breathe.)

Copper cabling carries electrical signals, such as those generated by computer *modems* and telephone handsets. Fiber-optic cabling carries light signals, which are transmitted as pulses of light. Imagine turning a flashlight on and off in Morse code. Fiber-optic transmission works in a fashion similar to Morse code, but is much faster and uses a different code. The air carries radio and voice signals, such as the words we speak and the radio broadcasts to which we listen. Simply stated, when people talk, the air between the speaker and the listener is changed, or *modulated*. The listener's eardrum converts the changes, or *demodulates* the signal (in this case the voice), so that the listener can understand the signal.

Network cabling connects network devices, such as computers, much as the railroad tracks connect stations within a city or between cities. Without these tracks, the railroad engines and cars would have no way to go from city to city. Without cabling, network devices would not be able to exchange information. If you are deploying a wireless network, however, the communication principles are the same in that each network device must be connected to a wireless transmitter/receiver, or *transceiver*, for communication to occur).

Network Logical Components

The logical component of a network is the information being carried from source to destination. The user information, which is called *data*, is carried inside a *frame* across the network.

Frames

Frames carry the data across the network and are made up of three parts: the header, the data itself, and the trailer. It is these frames that carry user data, just as railroad cars carry passengers. Whereas railroad passengers have tickets specifying their destinations, frames have destination addresses.

Let's look at the functions of the three components of a frame—header, payload, and trailer—by comparing them to railroads:

- **Frame header**  Train engine carrying source and destination information, such as the source and destination address (identifies the sender of the data and as well as the intended recipient)

- **Frame data**   Train car carrying passengers (user data)

- **Frame trailer**   Train caboose signifying the end of the train (frame)

These components combine to make up a complete frame, as illustrated in Figure 1-6.

Figure 1-6   Complete Frame—Header, Data (Payload), Trailer

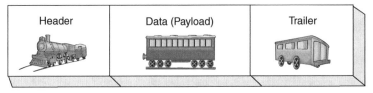

User data moves like passengers on a train—they ride the train to reach a destination. Whereas railroad cars carry passengers, network frames carry data. The physical network moves these frames carrying the data from source to destination across the network.

Data Transmission Modes

Network devices use three transmission modes (methods) to exchange data, or "talk" to each other, as follows: *simplex*, *half duplex*, and *full duplex*.

- **Simplex transmission** is like a one-way street where traffic moves in only one direction. Simplex mode is a one-way-only transmission, which means that data can flow only in one direction from the sending device to the receiving device. Figure 1-7 illustrates simplex transmission.

Figure 1-7   Simplex (One-Way Street)

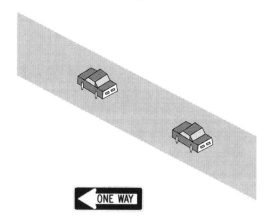

- **Half-duplex transmission** is like the center lane on some three-lane roads. It is a single lane in which traffic can move in one direction or the other, but not in both directions at the same time. Half-duplex mode limits data transmission because each device must take turns using the line. Therefore, data can flow from A to B and from B to A, but not at the same time. Figure 1-8 illustrates half-duplex transmission.

Figure 1-8   Half Duplex (Center Turn Lane)

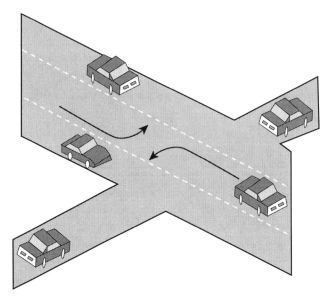

■ **Full-duplex transmission** is like a major highway with two lanes of traffic, each lane accommodating traffic going in opposite directions. Full-duplex mode accommodates two-way simultaneous transmission, which means that both sides can send and receive at the same time. In full-duplex mode, data can flow from A to B and B to A at the same time. Figure 1-9 illustrates full-duplex transmission.

note

Full-duplex transmission is, in fact, two simplex connections: One connection has traffic flowing in only one direction; the other connection has traffic flowing in the opposite direction of the first connection.

Figure 1-9   Full Duplex (Interstate Highway)

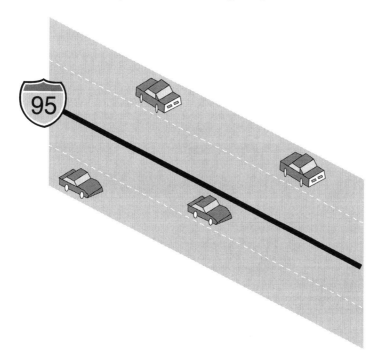

Types of Networks

Three primary types of information networks are in use today:

- **Local-area networks (LANs)** are found in small geographic areas, such as the floor of an office building.

- **Metropolitan-area networks (MANs)** are found in medium-sized geographic areas, such one or several city blocks.

- **Wide-area networks (WANs)** are found in large geographic areas, such as expanses that cross a state or country.

Figure 1-10 illustrates the concept of a LAN covering a small geographic area (in this case, the floor of an office building). For these employees to walk between rooms, they must use one or more of the hallways in the building. In this case, the network of hallways provides the connection between each room, enabling each person to move locally on the floor of this building. You would be hard pressed to find a hallway that stretches across several city blocks (MANs) or several states (WANs).

Figure 1-10   Office Building Floor

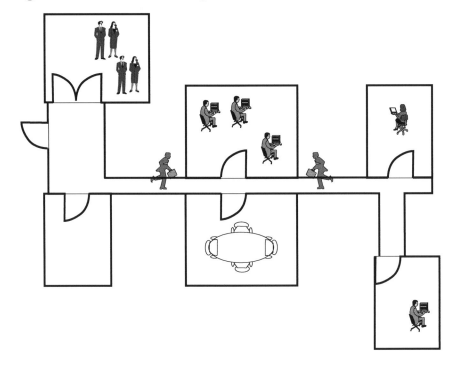

The following characteristics differentiate one network from another:

- **Topology**—The physical or logical geometric arrangement of devices on the network. For example, devices, such as computers, routers, or switches, can be arranged in a ring (Token Ring and Fiber Distributed Data Interface [FDDI]) or in a straight line (Ethernet).

note

Token Ring, FDDI, and Ethernet are all LAN technologies with respective topologies and are discussed in more detail in Chapter 4, "Traditional LAN Architecture."

- **Protocols**—The rules and specifications for communication between two devices, similar to grammar in a spoken or written language. For two people to be able to understand each other, for instance, they must both use not only the same language, but also the same syntax and grammar. Network protocols use these same rules of syntax and grammar to determine the following: how the devices talk with each other; whether the network is a peer-to-peer network, such as for file sharing; whether the network has a client/server architecture, such as used with a corporate database for inventory lookup in a retail store or warehouse.

- **Media**—The physical media carrying the signal between the two network points (source and destination). Examples of media include twisted-pair wire (shielded or unshielded), coaxial cables, fiber-optic cables connecting network devices, and the air. Some networks, such as wireless LANs (WLANs) and radio use the air as their communication media.

note

LAN topologies, protocols, and media are discussed in Chapter 4.

LANs

A local-area network (LAN) is a computer network spanning a small geographic area, such as a single building or floor within a building. One LAN can be connected to other LANs over any distance through media, such as telephone lines or radio waves. A system of LANs connected in this fashion is called a *wide-area network (WAN)*.

There are many different types of LANs, and Ethernet is the most common LAN type used today. Some other common LAN types include Token Ring and FDDI.

note

Ethernet, Token Ring, and FDDI are discussed in more detail in Chapter 4.

Most LANs connect *workstations*, personal computers, and network printers to each other, often for the purpose of resource sharing. Each individual device on a LAN is called a *node*. Most LAN workstations have their own central processing unit (CPU) with which they execute programs, such as a spreadsheet or word processor program. LAN workstations are also capable of accessing data and devices anywhere on the same LAN. This means that many users can share devices, such as printers, as well as data, either through direct file sharing, or through another LAN node called a *file server*. Users can also use the LAN to communicate with each other, by sending e-mail or engaging in chat sessions, such as those provided by instant messenger applications.

note

A *file server* is a central repository for file storage. Instead of several people in an office e-mailing the same file to each other, for example, the file can be kept in a central location and each person can access the file directly to read or write updates. A *print server* is a computer that manages print requests from multiple users and provides printer status information that is available to end users and network administrators.

MANs

A metropolitan-area network (MAN) is a data network designed for a town or city. A MAN can either be built as service provider and leased among multiple customers or a company can build its own private MAN. In terms of geographic breadth, MANs are larger than LANs, but smaller than WANs. MANs are usually characterized by high-speed connections using fiber-optic cable or other digital media and are often used by companies with several offices located within the same city. A corporation can extend the LAN services in each building across a metropolitan region by deploying a MAN to interconnect each corporate office.

An example of a noncomputer MAN in today's world is a city subway system. The subway routes interconnect different points within a metropolitan area, such as a city, as illustrated in Figure 1-11.

Figure 1-11   Subway System Map for Anywhere, USA

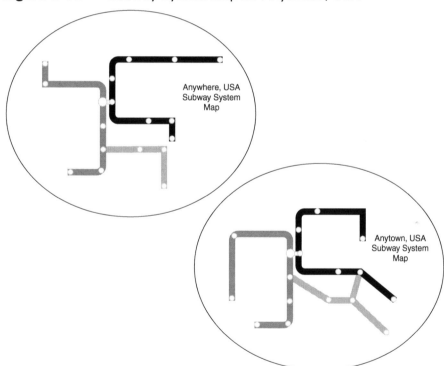

WANs

A wide-area network, or WAN, is a computer network that spans a relatively large geographic area, such as an expanse that crosses several states or countries. Com-

puters connected to a WAN are often connected through public networks, such as the telephone system (through a network service provider). Computers can also be connected through leased lines or satellites, also from a network service provider.

 note

The largest WAN in existence is the Internet.

An example of a noncomputer WAN in today's world is the routes flown by various airlines between cities. These routes span a broad geographic area. Figure 1-12 shows an airline route map; in this case, the geographic area is North America.

Figure 1-12   Airline Route Map

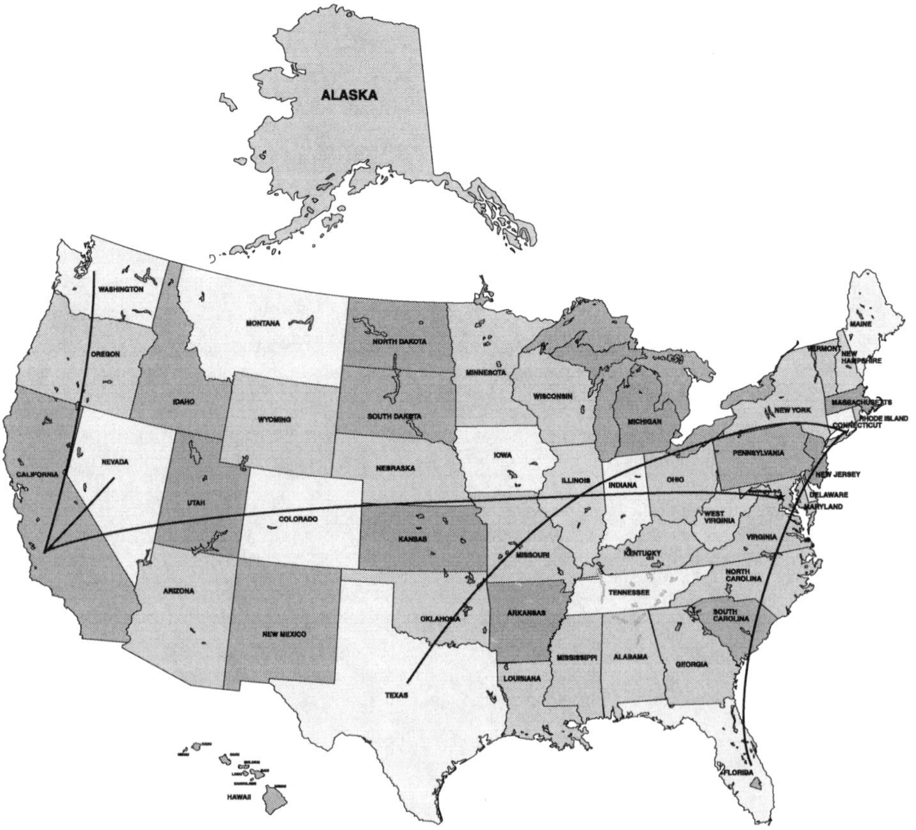

![Airline route map showing North America with airline routes connecting various cities across the United States]

Network Standards and Models

Before delving into network standards, let's look at an analogy. Esperanto was developed in an attempt to create a language that people all over the world could learn with ease. Its proponents believed that it favored no one people or culture and had straightforward grammar and spelling. Network standards were developed with similar ideals in mind.

A network standard normalizes how different pieces of network equipment connect to each other, whereas a network model provides the guiding principles behind the development of these network standards. The most prevalent network model used today is the Open System Interconnection (OSI) model. This chapter presents an overview of standards and models, and Chapter 2, "Network Models and Standards," delves more deeply into these topics.

Standards

A network standard is like a law—it is inviolable. Obviously, if a vendor does not follow network standards, there are no legal penalties. Instead, the use of the equipment produced by that vendor will be limited. Standards are in place to ensure that even the lowest level of communication on the media is possible, so that nodes, networking devices, and applications can all interoperate (or "play well with others"). This is important so that network users can buy equipment from different vendors as their needs dictate, rather than be locked into one specific vendor for the life of the network. The vendors would not mind being the sole equipment provider, but the technology and the user community dictate that these vendors interoperate, and it is network standards that enable this interoperability.

note

Many times, standards are developed through the collaboration of multiple vendors and users, all working toward a common, openly shared goal. The standards body maintains, publishes, and upholds the standard. Two of the best-known standards bodies are the Internet Engineering Task Force (IETF) and the Institute for Electrical and Electronics Engineers (IEEE).

When a vendor implements a feature that does not adhere to network standards, it is called a ***proprietary*** feature. Proprietary features often perform specific functions that pertain only to a particular piece of equipment or vendor implementation of a technology, such as a certain way of using the Internet to carry a telephone or a videoconference call.

To continue the subway analogy, network standards are like different subway routes; different standards use network technologies in different ways. These different standards sometimes use similar pieces but in different ways, just as each subway route uses the same-scale tracks, but those tracks are used in a different fashion (such as for different train routes). In New York City, for example, the number 2 train takes you from Houston Street to Times Square and the number 6 train takes you from Grand Central Station to Lexington Avenue, yet both trains use the same-size tracks on their routes. Standards also govern the vehicles (data) that ride on the subway tracks (networks). For instance, railroad cars must be built to standard size/weight to ride over the rails, just as data must be formatted according to certain standards to be carried over the wires.

Digital Equipment Corporation, Intel, and Xerox (DIX) were the inventors of the Ethernet. DIX used one method to transmit data across unshielded twisted-pair (UTP) cabling. In contrast to DIX, IBM, the inventor of Token Ring, uses a different method to transport data across UTP. DIX and IBM represent different network standards, but share the commonality of operating across the same cable type: UTP. The point to remember is that just because organizations transmit data across the same type of cabling (UTP, for instance), that does not mean they can talk with each other, or interoperate. Think of it in terms of a steam locomotive and an electric-powered train: Both use the same type of track, but do not have compatible engines, and therefore cannot be swapped with one another.

Models

As previously mentioned, network standards are like laws: They regulate how different networks talk with each other. Network models, on the other hand, provide the guiding principles for the development of these network standards and for the implementation of these networks.

The most prevalent network model used is the OSI model. Nearly every network standard centers on how the standard fits into the OSI model.

Imagine that your job is to design and build a car, and you want to design a sports car that no one has ever seen before. At the same time, you want this car to fit on the existing roads and in parking lots. Therefore, the car can be only so wide and so long. Standards provide the guidelines that you and other automobile engineers will follow, so that your car can be used on existing roads.

Chapter Summary

A network is a system, or collection of systems, that facilitates the exchange of resources from one point to another. This is a fancy way of saying that a network is the sum of the parts connecting two or more points. Examples of networks include the subway, the highway system, the telephone system, and the Internet.

A network is made up of physical and logical components. The physical components are the cables and network hardware devices, such as switches. The logical components of a network are the frames and data carried by and across the network.

Networks have two points—the source and destination, also known as the origination and termination points (respectively).

There are three modes of transmission between origination and termination points: simplex (one-way) mode, half-duplex mode (two-way, but not at the same time), and full-duplex mode (two-way, at same time).

There are three major types of networks. The distinguishing characteristic of each network types is the geographic range covered by the network:

- LANs cover a small geographic range—the area within an office building, for instance.

- MANs cover a broader geographic range than LANs—the area of a city, for instance.

- WANs cover a broad geographic range—an expanse across several states or countries, for instance.

The design, engineering, and implementation of a network are based on the application of network models and standards. A network model is a guiding principle in network communications, whereas a network standard is a network communications law. A vendor's special use of a standard is called a proprietary feature or proprietary implementation. Another example of proprietary feature is a product a vendor implements that is not based on a standard at all.

Chapter Review Questions

1. What is the definition of a network?

2. What are network models?

3. What is a network standard, and why are there network standards?

4. What is a proprietary feature?

5. What are the three data transmission modes, and how do they operate?

6. List the major characteristics of a LAN.

7. List the major characteristics of a MAN.

8. List the major characteristics of a WAN.

9. What are the three parts of a frame? What is a function of each part?

10. What function in a network does cabling provide?

11. List some examples of user data.

12. What is the best definition of network topology?

13. What is the best definition of network protocol?

14. What is the definition of network media?

15. What is a network origination point?

16. What is a network termination point?

What You Will Learn

On completing this chapter, you will be able to:

✔ Describe the OSI model and the major function of each of its layers

✔ Explain the process of sending (encapsulating) and receiving (decapsulating) data across a network

✔ Summarize the functions of bodies that create standards, such as ANSI, ITU-T, and the IEEE

✔ List the Ethernet standards that are relevant to today's networking environment

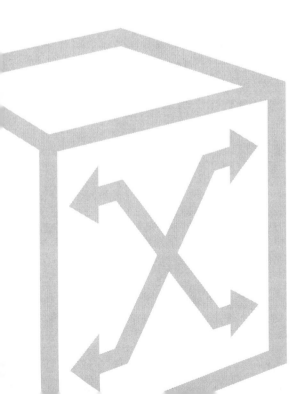

CHAPTER 2

Network Models and Standards

Switches are one piece of the greater network whole, serving in both wide- and local-area environments. The network model helps explain where switches fit into the network. To set the stage for Chapter 3, "Local-Area Networking Introduction," this chapter discusses network models and standards. To understand local-area network (LAN) switching, you must understand the networking rules and how these rules and switching work together. Networking rules are a combination of network models and standards.

As discussed in Chapter 1, "Networking Basics," network models provide the guiding principles behind the development of network standards, much as automobile design standards for different types of cars around the world determine their components: They have four wheels, an engine, and a steering wheel, and use unleaded gasoline.

Remember that a standard is like a law: It is inviolable and not to be messed with. Network standards are in place to ensure that different equipment vendors produce products that work together, much as different automobile standards are in place so that tire manufacturers make standard-size tires for certain car makes and models. In the network environment, standards are important so that network users can buy equipment from different vendors as needs dictate, instead of being locked into one specific vendor for the life of the network.

When utilizing a one-vendor system, users may gain certain vendor-specific, or **proprietary**, features, such as special queuing algorithms for managing how information is stored before it's sent across the network. However, a problem arises when users in such a system attempt to send information to someone who is not using the same vendor features. In such a case, the queuing algorithms benefit neither the sender nor the receiver. However, they can still communicate with each

other, as long as the differing devices use the same standard to communicate, much as DVD players from two different manufacturers can play same-standard DVDs.

The inventors of Ethernet—Digital Equipment Corporation, Intel, and Xerox (*DIX*)—used one method to run data across unshielded twisted-pair (UTP) cabling. The inventor of the Token Ring—IBM—used a different method. Ethernet and the Token Ring are different network standards, but share the commonality of operating across UTP cable. The point here to remember is that even though both technologies run data across the same type of cabling, UTP, that does not mean that these different technologies can talk to each other across the same physical cable.

OSI Model

This general overview of the Open System Interconnection (OSI) model lays the foundation for the rest of this book, but do not consider it exhaustive. The OSI model defines a networking framework in seven layers. Control of the data passes from one layer to the next, starting at the sending station's application layer, and then working down through the model, to the bottom layer. Control of the data then passes across the physical connection between each station along the path and then back up the model layers to the top layer at the receiving (destination) station. Figure 2-1 shows this process.

Figure 2-1   OSI Model Sending and Receiving

Transmit	User	Receive
Data		Data
	Application Layer	
	Presentation Layer	
	Session Layer	
	Transport Layer	
	Network Layer	
	Data Link Layer	
	Physical Layer	
	Physical Link	

In the networking environment, the OSI is the universal model and is made up of seven layers, each layer providing a service to the layer above it and dependent on the layer below. These seven layers are as follows:

- **Layer 7**—Application

- **Layer 6**—Presentation

- **Layer 5**—Session

- **Layer 4**—Transport

- **Layer 3**—Network

- **Layer 2**—Data link

- **Layer 1**—Physical

Layers 1 through 4 are referred to as the lower layers, and Layers 5 through 7 are referred to as the upper layers. Each layer performs a specific function in itself and provides a service to the layer above it. For example, Layer 2 (data link) depends on services provided to it by Layer 1 (physical) and provides services to the layer above it, Layer 3 (network). Each layer of the OSI model performs a specific function, as discussed in more detail in the following sections, starting with the uppermost—Layer 7, the application layer.

Layer 7—Application Layer

The application layer is the user-interaction layer, enabling the software and end-user processes. Everything at this layer is application specific. For example, a web browser application for surfing the Internet would user this layer. The application layer provides application services for file transfers, e-mail, and other network-based software services, such as your web browser or e-mail software.

Layer 6—Presentation Layer

The presentation layer provides for data representation to the user, such as a document (.doc) or spreadsheet (.xls). The presentation layer also "translates" the user data into a format that can be carried by the network, such as the segments and packets required at the lower layers. The presentation layer converts your data into a form that the application layer can accept, such as converting a string of data into a recognizable file format, such as .doc (word processing document) or .jpeg (graphics format). The presentation layer formats and encrypts data (when required by the user's application) to be sent across the network.

note

Encryption is the process by which original data, or *plaintext*, is converted into an unreadable format, or *ciphertext*, that can be read by only its intended recipient. The encryption process is based on a mathematical algorithm, or code, to create the ciphertext.

Layer 5—Session Layer

The session layer establishes, manages, and terminates virtual communications connections between applications. In other words, the session layer starts and stops communication sessions between network devices. When you place a telephone call, for example, you are establishing a communication session with another person. When you are finished with the call, you hang up the telephone, which terminates the session.

Layer 4—Transport Layer

The transport layer provides data transfer between end systems and is responsible for end-to-end error recovery and flow control. Flow control ensures complete data transfer and provides transparent checking for data that might have been dropped along the way from sender to receiver. Error recovery retrieves lost data if it is dropped or suffers from errors while in transit from source to destination.

Layer 3—Network Layer

The network layer provides the routing technologies, creating a forwarding table or a logical path between the source and destination. These logical paths are known as virtual circuits and are considered to be point-to-point network connections. Routing and forwarding are functions of the network layer. Network addressing, error handling, congestion control, and packet sequencing are all functions of the network layer.

note

The network layer is where routers and routing protocols operate.

note

Error handling is the response to an error that advises either the user or another process that an error has occurred. *Error correction* is the action taken to correct the error. Examples of error correction methods include resending the data or the application, or "figuring out" the corrupted data by the use of a checksum (a mathematical operation based on the number of 1s and 0s in the data).

Layer 2—Data Link Layer

At the data link layer, data packets are placed into frames for subsequent transmission across the network. The data link layer provides the transmission protocol knowledge and management and handles physical layer errors, flow control, and frame synchronization.

The data link layer is divided into two smaller sublayers: the Media Access Control (MAC) layer and the logical link control (LLC) layer. The MAC sublayer controls how a computer on the network gains access to the data and permission to transmit it. The LLC layer controls frame synchronization, flow control, and error checking.

Think of the MAC and LLC sublayers as the pilot and copilot of an aircraft. The MAC sublayer prepares the frame for physical transmission, much as the pilot focuses on the physical aspects of flying the aircraft. The LLC sublayer is concerned with the logical aspects of the transmission, not with the physical aspects of the transmission. The LLC layer acts like the copilot, who focuses on navigation, leaving the physical aspects of flying to the pilot.

note

Bridges and traditional switches operate at the data link layer.

Layer 1—Physical Layer

The physical layer carries the bit stream through the network. The bit stream can be carried as an electrical, light, or radio signal. This layer provides the hardware means of sending and receiving data on a carrier, including defining the cables, cards, and physical aspects. Gigabit Ethernet, wireless, dense wavelength-division multiplexing (DWDM), Synchronous Optical Network (SONET), Electronic Industries Alliance/Telecommunications Industry Alliance 232 (EIA/TIA-232; formerly RS-232), and Asynchronous Transfer Mode (ATM) are all protocols with physical layer components.

Table 2-1 outlines the signal type carried by each medium.

Table 2-1   Physical Media Used by Different Signal Types

Medium	Signal Type
Fiber optic	Light
Copper	Electrical
Air	Wireless, radio

note
Hubs and repeaters operate at the physical layer.

Moving Through the OSI Model

To better understand how network switching works, it is vital to understand how the OSI model works and how data moves through the OSI model. How you move through the OSI model depends on whether you are the sender or the receiver. The sending side wraps, or *encapsulates*, the data, much as you enclose a letter in an envelope. The receiving side unwraps, or *decapsulates*, the data, much as the receiver opens an envelope to remove the contents.

Sending, or encapsulating, data requires five steps, as follows:

Step 1   User data (Layers 5–7—application, presentation, session)

Step 2   Segments (Layer 4—transport)

Step 3   Packets (Layer 3—network)

Step 4   Frames (Layer 2—data link)

Step 5   Bits (Layer 1—physical)

To demonstrate the encapsulation of data, let's look at what happens when you write and send a letter (a real, old-fashioned letter, not e-mail), as illustrated in Figure 2-2.

Figure 2-2   Data Encapsulation

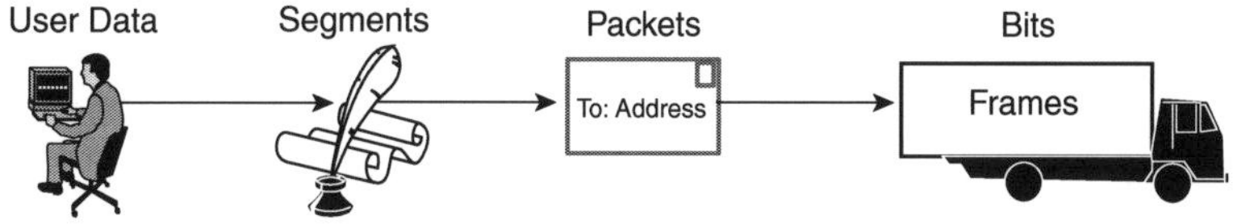

User Data   Segments   Packets   Bits

To: Address   Frames

As shown in Figure 2-2, data (in this case, old-fashioned mail) is sent (or encapsulated) as follows:

- **User data (Layers 5–7)**—You write your words using a specific style, such as Roman characters or script, on a piece of paper, in a certain language, such as English.

- **Segments (Layer 4)**—You fold the paper and place it into an envelope. If your letter is made up of multiple pages, each page, or "segment," is numbered so the letter is reassembled in the correct order by the receiver.

- **Packets (Layer 3)**—You write the sender's and receiver's postal address on the envelope. Like an envelope, a packet contains user information and identifies the sending and receiving address.

- **Frames (Layer 2)**—Your letter is put into a mailbag with other letters to be carried to the same destination. The mailbag here is the frame carrying multiple packets. These frames are put onto a mail truck, in which a truck driver carries the envelope to its destination.

- **Bits (Layer 1)**—The truck is driven across the highways and other roads to reach the receiver.

The following steps demonstrate what happens to the data on the receiving end, where it is opened (decapsulated):

1. The mail truck arrives at its destination, carrying the envelope.

2. The receiving station examines the destination address on the envelope and delivers it to that address.

3. Someone at the receiving address opens the envelope and extracts the paper.

4. The paper's recipient then reads the contents, the words and paragraphs, of the letter.

Hierarchical Design Model

The Cisco Hierarchical Design Model is another network model that is used to design and engineer data communication networks. The Hierarchical Design Model is a three-tiered, or layered, model with a core, distribution, and access layer, as illustrated in Figure 2-3.

Figure 2-3   Three-Tiered Design Model

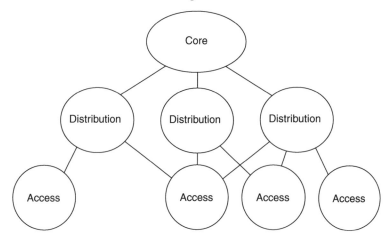

The Hierarchical Design Model is used by network designers, architects, and engineers when designing and implementing scalable and efficient networks. As stated previously, the three tiers of this model (illustrated in Figure 2-4) are the core, distribution, and access layers. The core layer provides high-speed switching between sites and is considered the backbone of the network. The distribution layer provides policy-based connectivity, such as what type of data can and cannot transit across the network. The access layer enables users to access the network and its resources.

Hierarchical design models can also be found in travel. The taxi you take from home to the airport is working at the access layer because the taxi is providing access to the airport resources (in this case, the airplane). At the airport, your ticket determines through which gate you enter. Your ticket provides the routing—that is, it tells you which gate to use to board your airplane.

Figure 2-4 Three-Tiered Model

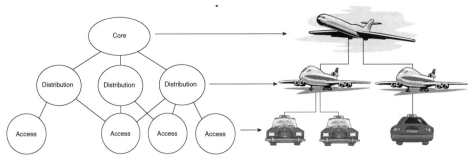

Network Standards

If the different network standards in place today were in print, they would fill volumes upon volumes of text. These network standards serve specific purposes, as defined by the standard itself. For example, there is a standard for you to communicate across the Internet and a different standard for you to talk across the telephone network.

Standards dictate almost everything that surrounds us during the course of a day. The television signal of your TV follows a standard, as does the lid on your "to-go" coffee cup. Some standards, such as the television signal, are regulated by an administering body such as the National Television System Committee (NTSC) or the new High-Definition Television (HDTV) standard developed in part by the Advanced Television System Committee (ATSV), whereas other standards are nonregulated.

These nonregulated standards are known as de facto standards and become standardized over time by their use. For example, no regulating authority is responsible for "to-go" coffee cup lids, but the sizes of cups used are static, meaning that a "to-go" coffee cup from one coffee shop doesn't usually differ from a "to-go" coffee cup from another shop. Hence it is logical that the lids for these cups will be the same, regardless of the manufacturer.

Standards in the network world work the same way. There are regulated standards such as those published by the International Telecommunication Union (ITU), the American National Standards Institute (ANSI), and the Institute of Electrical and Electronics Engineers (IEEE). There are also de facto standards, such as those put forth by network vendors, such as Cisco, and adopted over time by everyone else.

ITU (International Telecommunication Union)

TheInternational Telecommunication Union (ITU) is made up of telecommunication policy makers and regulators, network operators, equipment manufacturers, hardware and software developers, regional standards-making organizations, and financing institutions. The activities, policies, and strategic direction of the ITU are determined and shaped by the industry it serves.

The three sectors of the ITU are Radiocommunication (ITU-R), Telecommunication Standardization (ITU-T), and Telecommunication Development (ITU-D).

- **ITU-R** draws up the technical characteristics of terrestrial and space-based wireless services and systems, and develops operational procedures. It also undertakes the important technical studies, which serve as a basis for the regulatory decisions made at radio communication conferences.

- **ITU-T** experts prepare the technical specifications for telecommunication systems, networks, and services, including their operation, performance, and maintenance. Their work also covers the tariff principles and accounting methods used to provide international service.

- **ITU-D** experts focus their work on the preparation and development of recommendations, opinions, guidelines, handbooks, manuals and reports. These documents provide decision makers with "best business practices" relating to a host of issues ranging from development strategies and policies to network management.

Each of the three ITU sectors works through conferences and meetings at which members negotiate the agreements that serve as the basis for the operation of global telecommunication services. The activities of the ITU cover all aspects of telecommunication: setting standards that facilitate seamless interworking of equipment and systems on a global basis; adopting operational procedures for the vast and growing array of wireless services; and designing programs to improve telecommunication infrastructure in the developing world.

ANSI (American National Standards Institute)

American National Standards Institute (ANSI) serves as administrator and coordinator of the United States private-sector voluntary standardization system. ANSI was founded in 1918 by five engineering societies and three governmental agencies, and is a private, nonprofit membership organization. ANSI ensures each foot-long ruler is accurate in its dimensions, for instance, essentially using a ruler to measure a ruler. ANSI ensures that each inch on the ruler is in fact 1 inch, and that the foot-long ruler is in fact made up of 12 of these inches.

ANSI, like the ITU, regulates telecommunications standards; unlike the ITU, however, ANSI regulates standards in North America, whereas the ITU regulates standards in Europe. For example, ANSI regulates the *T1* telecommunications standard, whereas the ITU regulates the *E1* telecommunications standard in Europe.

IEEE 802 Group

The Institute of Electrical and Electronics Engineers (IEEE, pronounced "eye-triple-E") is a nonprofit, technical professional association in 150 countries. The IEEE is a leading authority in technical areas ranging from computer engineering, to biomedical technology, to telecommunications, to electric power, to aerospace and consumer electronics. The IEEE produces 30 percent of the world's published literature in electrical engineering, computers, and control technology and has nearly 900 active standards with 700 under development.

Some of the best-known IEEE standards are as follows:

- IEEE 802.1 (LAN/MAN)

- IEEE 802.3 (Ethernet)

- IEEE 802.5 (Token Ring)

- IEEE 802.11 (Wireless LAN)

IEEE 802.1 LAN/MAN Standards

The IEEE 802.1 group defined internetworking standards, with IEEE 802.1d and IEEE 802.1q used in the local-area networking environment. The standards are as follows:

- **IEEE 802.1d—Spanning Tree Protocol (STP)**—STP is a link-management protocol that is part of the IEEE 802.1 standard for Media Access Control bridges and is used for Layer 2 redundancy. Using the spanning-tree algorithm, STP provides redundant paths through the LAN while preventing loops in the LAN that are created by multiple active paths between stations. These multiple paths, or loops, occur when there are alternative routes between hosts. To establish path redundancy, STP creates a tree that spans all the switches in an extended network, forcing redundant paths into a standby, or blocked, state. STP allows for one active path at a time between any two network devices, preventing loops, but establishing the redundant links as a backup (in case the primary link fails). If a change occurs in the LAN, such as a network segment becoming unreachable, the spanning-tree algorithm reconfigures the tree topology and reestablishes the link by activating the standby path. Without STP in place, both primary and redundant connections might be simultaneously live, resulting in an endless loop of traffic on the LAN. Chapter 7, "Spanning Tree Protocol (STP)," discusses STP in more detail.

- **IEEE 802.1q—virtual LANs (VLANs)**—A VLAN is a network of computers that behaves as if the computers are connected to the same physical network segment, even though these computers might be physically located on different segments of a LAN. VLANs are configured in software and are not limited by physical location or to specific switch ports. This makes VLANS flexible to use within a network. One of the advantages of VLANs is that when a computer is physically moved to another location, it can stay on the same VLAN without any end-device or protocol reconfiguration. Chapter 9, "Switching Security," discusses VLANs in more detail.

IEEE 802.3 Ethernet Standards

Several Ethernet standards are used in today's network environment. Some of these standards dictate the bandwidth and operation of the Ethernet LAN, such as Ethernet and Fast Ethernet, whereas other standards dictate how these Ethernet networks function, such as the STP.

Ethernet is a half-duplex shared-media LAN in which each station on the segment uses part of the total bandwidth. The total LAN bandwidth for Ethernet is 10 megabits per second (Mbps—Ethernet) or 100 Mbps (Fast Ethernet). Ethernet and Fast Ethernet can operate in either half-duplex or full-duplex mode; half-duplex Ethernet shares the LAN media, whereas full-duplex mode has separate LAN media dedicated to the sending and receiving side of the network interface card (NIC). The 1000 Mbps (Gigabit Ethernet) is not a shared-media LAN implementation because Gigabit Ethernet operates in full-duplex mode only. Hubs enable shared-media LANs, and switches enable dedicated-media LANs. With switched Ethernet, each sender and receiver pair has the full bandwidth available for use, as illustrated in Figure 2-5.

Figure 2-5   Switched and Shared Ethernet Networks

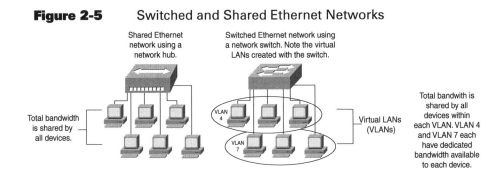

note
Switched Ethernet networks enable the creation of virtual LANs, or VLANs.

The IEEE 802.3 standards define how the Ethernet standard is used in the networking environment. These 802.3 standards are as follows:

- **IEEE 802.3 (Ethernet)**—10-Mbps Ethernet specification developed by Xerox, served as the basis for the IEEE 802.3 standard. This specification describes the use of carrier sense multiple access collision detect (CSMA/CD) in handling the simultaneous demands for network access. Often used in LAN environments.

- **IEEE 802.3u (Fast Ethernet)**—100-Mbps Ethernet specification working at 10 times the speed of 10-Mbps Ethernet. Often used in LAN environments.

- **IEEE 802.3z (Gigabit Ethernet)**—1000-Mbps/1-Gbps Ethernet specification that transfers data at 1 gigabit per second (1000 Mbps). Often used in large LAN environments at the core layer.

- **IEEE 802.3ae (10Gigabit Ethernet)**—10,000-Mbps/10-Gbps Ethernet specification that transfers data at 10 gigabits per second (10,000 Mbps). Often used in metropolitan-area networks (MANs).

note

CSMA/CD is a standard enabling Ethernet hosts to detect a collision. In a half-duplex Ethernet environment, collisions occur when two nodes begin sending traffic at the same time. Collisions do not occur in full-duplex Ethernet environments. After detecting a collision, the host waits a random amount of time and then tries retransmitting the message. If the sending host detects a collision again when trying to send the same frame, the host waits an exponentially increasing amount of time after each transmission attempt before resending.

IEEE 802.5 Token Ring Standards

With Ethernet, any host on the network can send data at any time, as long as no one else is on the line. In contrast, the Token Ring works by passing a token around the network, almost like a relay-race runner passing the baton to the next

runner. When a host has possession of this token, it has the right to send data across the network, just as the relay runner can run only when in possession of the baton. If a host has nothing to send, it passes the token to the next host down the line in the network.

IEEE 802.5 is a related specification and compatible with the Token Ring standard developed by IBM. Token Ring refers to both IBM Token Ring and IEEE 802.5 network implementations. IBM originally developed the Token Ring network in the 1970s; however, IBM gave up on Token Ring in favor of Ethernet several years ago.

Token Ring is a LAN in which all the hosts are arranged in a logical circle. A special frame, called the token, travels around the circle. To send a message, a host catches the token, attaches its data, and then lets it continue to travel around the network. Token Ring is not found in many LANs nowadays because of its slow speed as compared to Ethernet LANs.

note

The IEEE 802.5 specification was modeled after the IBM Token Ring specification.

IEEE 802.11 Wireless LAN (WLAN) Standards

The IEEE 802.11 standard refers to a family of specifications developed for wireless LAN technology. IEEE 802.11 specifies an over-the-air interface between a wireless client and a base station, such as a wireless laptop and a wireless base unit or between two wireless clients, such as between two wireless laptops.

Figure 2-6 illustrates a wireless LAN between a laptop and a base unit, with the base unit connected to the Internet, either in the home or the office. The base unit can enable multiple users to share the same Internet connection as long as each user has a wireless-LAN-capable device. The benefit here is straightforward: no wires to get tangled or cables to be hidden. Wireless LANs raise other issues—the most notable is the broadcast of your data into the open air. Wireless LANs should not be implemented without some sort of encryption to protect your data from being stolen out of the air.

Figure 2-6   Wireless LAN Between a Laptop and a Base Unit

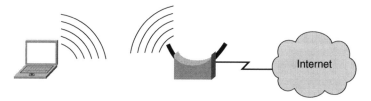

Figure 2-7 illustrates a wireless LAN that might also be found in a home or office. This configuration demonstrates the same sharing concept of the previous example, but this time users are sharing a wireless printer. The benefit here is the same: no wires.

Figure 2-7   Wireless LAN Between a Laptop and a Printer

note
The printer itself does not have to be wireless capable or wireless ready; the printer can be attached to a wireless base unit to enable wireless connectivity.

Chapter Summary

The internetworking environment is governed by two complementary rule sets: standards and models. Standards are the laws that vendors must adhere to if they are to interoperate with other vendors, in turn making themselves available and

useful for the end user. Some vendors develop special features that can be configured and used only on their equipment; these are called proprietary features. Keep in mind, a proprietary implementation can limit itself in its use and therefore is not always an attractive option when implementing a network.

The OSI model is the universal model in the networking environment and is made up of seven layers. Each of the seven layers provides services to the layer above it and depends on the layer below. The seven layers of the OSI model from top to bottom are (7) application, (6) presentation, (5) session, (4) transport, (3) network, (2) data link, and (1) physical.

The application, presentation, and session layers are known as the upper layers; the transport, network, data link, and physical layers are known as the lower layers.

The OSI model uses encapsulation and decapsulation, depending on where data is moving through the model. The sending side wraps, or encapsulates, the data, much like enclosing a letter in an envelope. The receiving side unwraps, or decapsulates, the data, much like opening an envelope and removing the contents.

Another internetworking model used is the Cisco Hierarchical Design Model, made up of three layers: core, distribution, and access. The core layer provides for high-speed connectivity in a network backbone and is the most efficient and direct path between two points. The distribution layer provides for policy routing. This layer controls the answers to network questions such as these: "How can I get there from here?" and "Who can I allow to go there?" The access layer controls access to the network, keeping local connectivity out of the network, such as a local communication between a computer and a network printer that does not need to go across the WAN.

Numerous network standards are in place today, and many new standards are being developed all the time. The three primary standards bodies to note are the ITU-T, ANSI, and the IEEE. The ITU-T (International Telecommunication Union—Telecommunication Standardization Sector), as the name implies, is the international standards body and can be found on the World Wide Web at www.itu.int/ITU-T/. ANSI (American National Standards Institute), as its name also implies, is the governing standards body for North America and can be found on the World Wide Web at www.ansi.org. The IEEE (Institute of Electrical and Electronics Engineers) is a leading technical authority and is responsible for standards across several technology-oriented fields, such as computer and network engineering, and is regarded as the second-leading international standards body, after the ITU-T. The IEEE can be found on the World Wide Web at www.ieee.org.

Chapter Review Questions

1. What is ANSI, and what does it do?

2. What is the ITU-T, and what does it do?

3. What is the IEEE, and what does it do?

4. What does OSI stand for, and what is the OSI model?

5. Describe and name the layers in the OSI model.

6. What are some advantages of a layered model approach to networking?

7. What is the network standard for 10-Mbps Ethernet? 100-Mbps Ethernet? 1000-Mbps/Gigabit Ethernet? 10Gigabit Ethernet?

8. What is encapsulation, and how does it work (in reference to the OSI model)?

What You Will Learn

On completing this chapter, you will be able to:

- ✔ Describe local-area networks (LANs)

- ✔ Explain the functions of wide-area networks (WANs)

- ✔ Describe analog and digital signals

- ✔ Compare characteristics of different network cabling types

- ✔ Draw simple network topologies

- ✔ List the different types of hardware found in a LAN or a WAN

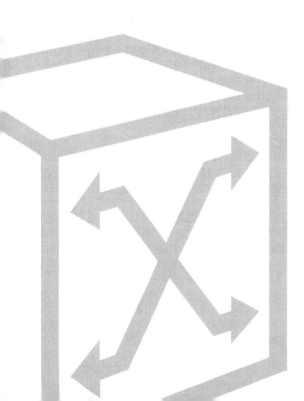

CHAPTER 3

Local-Area Networking Introduction

Local-area networks (LANs) send and receive data at rates much faster than can be transmitted over a telephone line; but the distances are limited, often to a few hundred feet maximum without using costly, long-range technologies, such as Long Reach Ethernet (LRE) or wave-division multiplexing (WDM). Because of distance limitations, LANs are found in small areas such as a floor in your office building or a home network. LANs are used to connect personal computers (PCs), network workstations, routers to the Internet, and other network devices, such as network-capable printers, as illustrated in Figure 3-1.

Figure 3-1   Desktop/Printer Implementation Without a LAN and with a LAN, Respectively

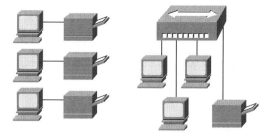

Users connected via a LAN can chat and share files, Internet access, and printer access. The alternative to a LAN is for each user to have his own printer and Internet access.

Three characteristics differentiate one LAN from another:

- LANs can be configured in different topologies. Topology is the geometric arrangement of devices on the network. For example, devices can be arranged in a continuous ring, where each computer is a link in the chain, or in a star, where each computer is connected to the same central device.

- LANs follow different protocols, which are the rules and specifications for sending and receiving data.

- LANs are connected through different media. For example, with LANs, the media through which a signal is transmitted among devices is twisted-pair wire, coaxial cable, fiber-optic cable, or wireless.

Several small LANs can be connected together to create a single larger LAN within a building. If your LANs are in offices across the country, these LANs use connections provided by a network service provider to create a wide-area network (WAN).

Comparing LANs to WANs

Before exploring WANs, let's summarize the characteristics of LANS. As previously stated, a LAN is just what the name implies—a network that is confined to a local geographic area, such as a single office building, a small office in a commercial building, or even a network in your own home. As shown in Figure 3-2, LANs enable you to share resources, such as Internet access or laser printing, with other users on the same network.

Figure 3-2   Local-Area Network (LAN)

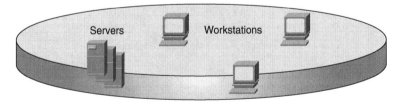

In contrast, WANs cover a much broader geographic range than LANs, as shown in Figure 3-3. WANs are often used to connect LANs across a public network, such as the Public Switched Telephone Network (PSTN). LANs can also be connected through leased lines or satellites to create a WAN.

Figure 3-3   Wide-Area Network (WAN)

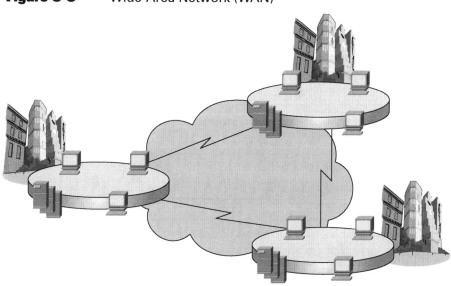

note
Not all WANs require a public network. A WAN can use privately owned connections, such as "dark fiber," to create a wholly owned and dedicated network.

As the name implies, WANs are networks that cover a broad geographic area, such as multiple cities, states, or even countries. The largest WAN in existence is the Internet; it spans the globe.

OSI Model (As It Applies to LANs and the Interrelation Between Layers)

The upper layers of the Open System Interconnection (OSI) model, where user data is found, need the lower layers, like a train needs tracks to get from point A to B. It is these lower layers—physical, data link, and network—that provide the

"railroad tracks" for the user data. They allow the data to ride across the network, such as when sending an e-mail or surfing the Internet.

Layer 1—Physical Layer

The physical layer moves the bit stream (signal) from one point to another across a carrier, such as a network cable, originating from the transmitter (device sending the signal) and terminating at the receiver (device receiving the signal). For example, when you have a telephone conversation with someone, your mouthpiece is the transmitter and the other person's earpiece is the receiver. The signal is either an electrical impulse when carried over copper, light when carried over fiber-optic cabling, or a radio signal when carried through the air.

The physical layer is made up of the following:

- **Signal**—The data being carried in the form of bits (1s and 0s), which are converted into electrical impulses (sine wave), radio signals, or pulses of light

- **Hardware**—A transmitter, receiver, repeater, regenerator, or a hub

- **Media**—Coaxial (coax), fiber-optic, or copper (shielded and unshielded twisted-pair) cabling; and air for wireless signals

In a LAN environment, the physical layer components are the ***network interface card (NIC)*** in your computer, the cable connecting your computer to the network, and the signal being sent by your NIC across the cable.

Signal

The signal, with respect to cabling, is the information being sent across the medium in an electronic or optical (light) fashion.

There are two types of electronic signals: analog and digital. Analog signals are represented as continuous waves, as illustrated in Figure 3-4.

Figure 3-4   Analog Signal Wave

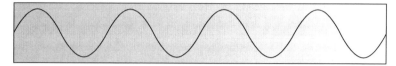

In contrast to the continuous wave of an analog signal, digital signals consist of values measured at discrete intervals, or square waves, as illustrated in Figure 3-5.

Figure 3-5   Digital Signal Wave

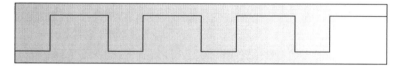

The difference between analog and digital can be best demonstrated by looking at both an analog and a digital watch, as illustrated in Figure 3-6.

Figure 3-6   Analog and Digital Watches

Digital watches display one value (10:54) and then the next (10:55) without show-ing all the intermediate values between the two. Digital watches, therefore, dis-play only a finite number of times of the day, such as every minute. In contrast, the hands of analog watches move continuously around the clock face. As the minute hand goes around, it not only touches the numbers 1 through 12, but also the infi-nite number of points in between, indicating every possible time of day.

We experience the world in an analog fashion; vision is analog because we per-ceive infinitely smooth gradations of shapes and colors. Speech is analog because there are infinite variances in tone and pitch that make up the sounds we hear. Most analog events, however, can be simulated digitally (the photographs in newspapers, for instance). Although these photos are made up of arrays of discrete black or white dots (digital form), when we look at the photographs we perceive lines and shading that appear to flow into each other to form images. In this way, we perceive a digital image as an analog picture. Although digital representations are approximations of analog events, they are useful because they are relatively easy to store and manipulate electronically. As shown in Figure 3-7, the idea here is that analog is free flowing, whereas digital is exact.

Figure 3-7   Analog-to-Digital Conversion

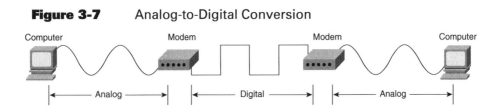

This same principle of digital information being presented as analog is the princi-ple behind compact discs (CDs). The music exists in an analog form as waves in the air, but these sounds are then translated into a digital form that is encoded onto the disc as 1s and 0s. When you play a compact disc, the CD player reads this digital data, translating the 1s and 0s back into a form of music (audio vibrations) that we hear from our stereo giving the perception of the original analog music.

note

The term *bit* (short for *binary digit*) was first used in 1946 by John Tukey (1915–2000), a leading statistician and adviser to five U.S. presidents. (If you win money in a trivia contest for knowing this, please contact me and we can split the winnings.)

To send and receive these signals across a medium, we need network hardware.

Hardware

A transmitter is the device sending the signal, a receiver is the device receiving the signal, and a repeater is a network device used to copy or boost a signal on the path between the transmitter and receiver. Repeaters are used in transmission systems to regenerate analog or digital signals distorted by transmission loss. Analog repeaters amplify the signal, whereas digital repeaters reconstruct the signal to its near-original quality, as shown in Figure 3-8. Analog and digital repeaters amplify any noise on the line as well as the signal. Regenerators amplify the signal but not the noise. However, regenerators are often more costly to implement than repeaters. Repeaters and regenerators can be used for electronic, optical, and wireless signals, and are used extensively in long-distance transmission. Repeaters are used to tie two LANs of the same type together, such as two Ethernet LANs.

Figure 3-8 Repeater

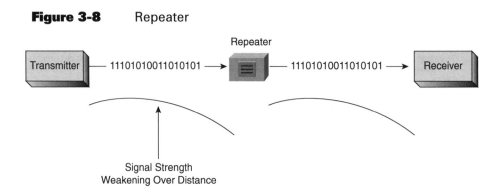

Hubs are often used to connect small LAN segments where the number of devices generally is 24 or fewer. Hubs are multiport repeaters, and when a frame arrives on one port, it is repeated to the other ports so that all segments of the LAN can see all frames, as illustrated in Figure 3-9.

Figure 3-9 Hub

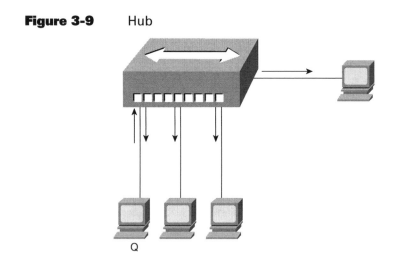

Figure 3-9 shows Host Q sending traffic, in the form of frames, out to the network via a port on the hub. These frames are received by the hosts connected to the same hub, including the host that sent the traffic to begin with, Host Q. Host Q, knowing what it sent, ignores what comes back. The other hosts, however, must read each frame to determine whether they are the intended recipients. If it helps you to understand the process shown in Figure 3-9, you can think of it as being similar to mail arriving for everyone in your office in separate envelopes. Each person receiving an envelope reads the name and address to determine whether the mail is in fact for him. To return to the electronic example—if you are in a small office, with a few people, this is not so bad; in a larger office, however, the process becomes cumbersome because it slows the network down with all the additional traffic.

Each host connects to a network device, be it a hub, bridge, or switch, via some sort of medium, as discussed in the next section.

Media

The network medium provides the physical connection between the sender and the receiver. Air is the medium used for wireless communications, and cabling is the medium used in wireline (nonwireless) communications. The three types of network cabling in use today are as follows:

- Twisted-pair cable, which is illustrated in Figure 3-10, comes in two cabling options—unshielded twisted-pair (UTP) and shielded twisted-pair (STP).

Figure 3-10   Twisted-Pair Cable

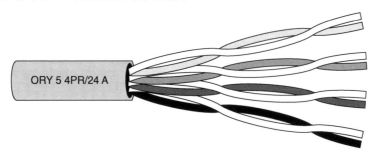

ORY 5 4PR/24 A

— UTP is a popular type of cable made up of two unshielded wires twisted around each other. Due to its low cost, UTP cabling is used for LAN and telephone connections. UTP cabling does not provide for

high bandwidth or good protection from electromagnetic interference (EMI) such as coaxial or fiber-optic cabling provides. EMI is an electrical disturbance caused natural phenomena (such as lightning), low-frequency waves from electromechanical devices, such as disk drives and printers, or high-frequency waves (radio frequency interference, RFI) from chips and other electronic devices, such as central processing units (CPUs).

— STP is a type of copper telephone wiring in which each of the two copper wires is twisted together and coated with an insulating coating functioning as a ground for the wires. The extra covering in STP wiring protects the transmission line from EMI leaking into or out of the cable, resulting in signal degradation or loss.

■ Coaxial cable, illustrated in Figure 3-11, is a type of wire carrying electrical impulses that consists of a center wire surrounded by insulation and then a grounded shield of braided wire. The shield minimizes EMI and RFI and is the primary cabling type used in the cable television (CATV) industry.

Figure 3-11   Coaxial Cable

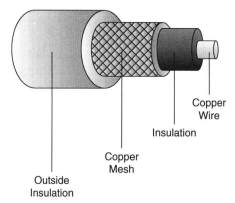

Copper
Wire

Insulation

Copper
Mesh

Outside
Insulation

■ Fiber-optic cable is a type of cable using glass or plastic threads (fibers) to transmit data. As illustrated in Figure 3-12, fiber-optic cable consists of a bundle of glass threads, each of which transmits messages via light waves. This glass is encased in cladding and coating, reinforced by strengthening fibers and further wrapped within a cable jacket.

Figure 3-12   Fiber-Optic Cable

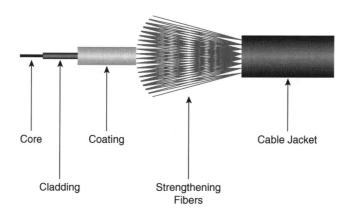

Fiber Optic Cable Construction

Core   Coating   Cable Jacket

Cladding   Strengthening
Fibers

Layer 2—Data Link

So far, this chapter has discussed the types of signal and media that are found at Layer 1 of the OSI model, but you might be asking yourself, "What are these signals carrying?" The signals are carrying user data in the form of frames. Frames are found at Layer 2 and move data around the network. It is the network topology that determines which devices these frames can be exchanged among.

Have you ever bought a "one size fits all" hat that you couldn't squeeze onto your head? The arrangement, or topology, of a network is much the same; there is no "one size fits all." Each topology serves its own purpose, and it is this purpose that determines what size fits. For example, let's revisit the railroad from Chapter 2, "Networking Models and Standards," for a moment. If all the cities needed to be directly connected with one another, a full mesh topology might be used because a direct path between each city would be available. A star topology might also be used in which each city would directly connect to a central place where the trains would switch tracks.

This same connectivity concept applies to data networks. If hosts on the network need to communicate directly with each other, a full-mesh topology is the answer.

(For a description of full-mesh topology, see Table 3-1.) However, this is not often the case; instead, it is more common to see each host communicate through a central point, as in a star topology.

Table 3-1   LAN and WAN Topologies

Topology	Description	Figure	When to Use
Full mesh	Devices are connected with many redundant interconnections between network nodes. In a true mesh topology, every node has a connection to every other node in the network.		Hosts need to talk directly with each other. This topology might be used in a peer-to-peer environment where frequent file sharing is required. The challenge here is the number of connections each host has to maintain. A formula used to determine the number of links required in a full-mesh network: $(n * (n - 1))/2$ or $(n^2 - n)/2$ n is number of nodes. In a WAN environment, a full-mesh topology might be used in virtual private network (VPN) environments where it is easy to configure multiple sites connected to each other.

Table 3-1   LAN and WAN Topologies (continued)

Topology	Description	Figure	When to Use
Star	All devices are connected to a central hub. Nodes communicate across the network by passing data through the hub.		This is a common LAN topology. In a star topology, all LAN devices connect to a centralized point, such as a hub or a switch. This central point enables each host to talk to the other hosts but not in the direct fashion afforded in the full-mesh topology. The advantage of the star over the full-mesh is that each host has one connection to maintain, not several. One drawback to this topology is that the central point is a single point of failure; if this point fails, all connected devices are also down. A formula used to determine the number of links required in a star network: $n - 1$, where n is the number of nodes. In a WAN environment, a star topology might be used to provide connectivity to multiple remote locations, such as remote offices in a corporate network.

continues

Table 3-1   LAN and WAN Topologies (continued)

Topology	Description	Figure	When to Use
Ring	All devices are connected to one another in the shape of a closed loop, so that each device is connected directly to two other devices, one on either side of it.		The ring topology is often used when there is a redundancy requirement. Therefore, if a network segment fails, each network device can continue to communicate with the others around the ring. A ring topology might be used to provide metropolitan-area network (MAN) connectivity, possibly using WDM.
Tree	A hybrid topology. Groups of star-configured networks are connected to a linear bus backbone.		The tree topology is used when a hierarchical network is desired to group users together, such as by geographic location or by function, such as accounting or sales. This topology is often seen in WAN environments.

Remember the OSI model? We're never very far from it during any network discussion, and topology discussions are no different. Each layer of the OSI model could have its own topology. For example, each network device could be physically connected in a star topology to a central device but logically work as a ring topology. This type of Token Ring implementation is illustrated in Figure 3-13 and Figure 3-14.

Figure 3-13   Token Ring Physical Topology

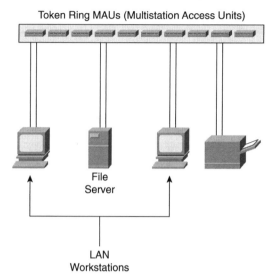

Figure 3-14   Token Ring Logical Topology

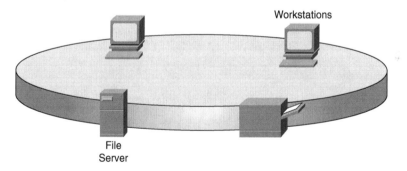

Frames

Recall the discussion of frames from Chapter 1, "Networking Basics." Frames carry data across the network and are made up of three parts: the ***header***, the ***payload*** itself, and the ***trailer***. It is these frames that carry user data (packets) just as railroad cars carry passengers. Whereas railroad passengers have tickets that specify their destinations, data-link frames have destination addresses specifying

where the frame should go. The following table outlines the three components of a frame and their respective functions.

Table 3-1   Frame Components and Functions

Frame Component	Function
Header	Signifies the start of the frame and carries Layer 2 source and destination address information
Payload	Carries data from Layer 3, such as packets from the network layer containing user data
Trailer	Signifies the end of the frame and carries error-detection information in the form of a cyclic redundancy check (CRC)

The three frame components—header, payload, and trailer—combine in making up a complete frame, as was illustrated in Figure 1-6 in Chapter 1.

Much as a train consists of the engine, passenger/cargo car, and caboose, the frame is made up of a header, payload, and trailer. Whereas the train engine determines which track, or path, the train takes, the frame header determines which path through the network the frame follows. The data (payload) carries the information just as the passengers are carried by the train. The trailer identifies the end of the frame, just as the caboose identifies the end of the train.

Just as the railroad train moves around the country, so too do frames move around the network across the tracks. These tracks are often interconnected with bridges, connecting track segments to form longer rail lines; and railroad switches provide a way for each train to change tracks, or direction. Network bridges and switches work in much the same fashion as the bridges and switches in the railroad and are discussed in more detail in the next section.

Hardware

As mentioned earlier in this chapter, repeaters work at Layer 1 (physical) by repeating the signal received from the transmitting side out to the receiver and vice versa. This type of repeater has two ports—one for each direction.

If multiple devices need the benefits of a repeater, however, a hub is used because a hub is a multiport repeater. Recall that with a hub, a signal received on one port is repeated out all ports. Much as a hub is a multiport repeater, a bridge is a multiport hub. Bridges connect two LANs or two segments of the same LAN using the same protocol, such as Ethernet. Bridges learn from experience and build and maintain address tables of the nodes on the network, called *Media Access Control (MAC) tables*. By monitoring the LAN, the bridge learns which hosts belong to which segment and builds a table using the source MAC address of the frames, as they come in to the bridge.

Bridges work at the data link layer (OSI Layer 2) and are protocol independent. Bridges with more than two ports (multiport bridges) perform switching functions. Switches also work at the data link layer and, like bridges, are protocol independent.

A bridge is considered a multiport hub, whereas a switch is considered to be a multiport bridge with multiple network segments that might, or might not, communicate with each other. Switches also build tables based on the MAC address received on each switch port and forward frames based on these tables.

Figure 3-15 illustrates the use of bridges and switches in a data network and in a railroad network.

Figure 3-15   Network Bridges and Switches

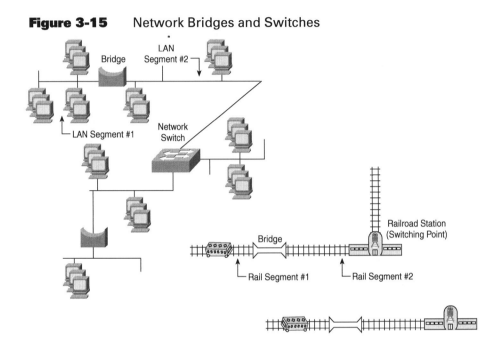

In a railroad network, bridges connect separate track segments to create a single "network" of tracks from the smaller track segments. Sometimes these trains change tracks at a railroad switchyard or station, with the passengers still on board. Other times the trains go back and forth between stations with the passengers switching between trains. If the passengers are not at their intended destination and need to continue their journey, they do not stay on the same train and try to convince the engineer to keep going. They change trains at the train station.

The train stations provide a switching point for the passengers riding these trains and sometimes the trains themselves. If a passenger needs to ride several trains to get from the originating (starting) point to the terminating (ending) point, the passenger switches trains at the railroad station. How does the passenger know which train to board at the railroad station? The answer is found in the train ticket, which states the originating and terminating points (start and destination).

When you arrive at the train station, with ticket in hand telling you where you are going (in case you forgot), you look at the train departure board to determine from which track your train is departing. When you know which track, you go to the gate, board the train, and continue your journey, repeating these steps until you arrive at your intended destination.

A train switching tracks with the passengers still aboard is similar to frames being switched between LAN segments (Layer 2 switching). When the passengers disembark and board another train at the train station, with ticket in hand telling them where to go, this is similar to packets being routed between network segments (Layer 3 routing).

note
Chapter 5, "Ethernet LANs," discusses Layer 2 hardware and operation in more detail.

Layer 3 and Above

The logical topology at Layer 3 (network) is made possible by the logical topology at Layer 2 (data link) and the physical topology at Layer 1 (physical) underneath it all. A packet has to and from addresses (destination and origination), much as a letter has sending (return) and receiving addresses. The letter does not concern itself (as much as a letter is "concerned") with how it gets from sender to receiver because it has a logical "straight line." The letter, or packet, is not aware of the lower logical and physical layers that comprise the line of direction, just that the letter has a path to get to its intended destination, as illustrated in Figure 3-16.

Figure 3-16 Logical and Physical Topology of a Letter's Travels

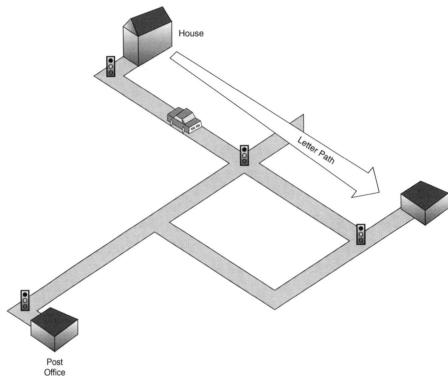

The physical topology is illustrated by the roads between the house and the post offices. This physical topology is broken down into segments by the traffic lights at various points along the way. The logical topology here is the straight line from the house to the post office, unaffected by the roads traveled or the traffic signals along the way. The letter's transmission from house to post office is affected here when there is no physical path at all, such as all available roads closed or blocked.

Packets

Because packets and frames work at different layers (Layer 3 and Layer 2 respectively), they involve different aspects of the network. Think of a frame as a train engineer—he needs to know where to go and how to get there and is not concerned with where the train has just left. A ***packet*** needs to know where it is going and from where it came, much as a letter needs to have the recipient's address and the sender's address. The recipient in turn uses the return address to send a reply.

note

A packet is a fixed block of data sent as a single entity across a network. Commonly when LANs are discussed, the terms *frame* and *packet* are used synonymously. However, packets are found in the network layer (Layer 3 of the OSI model), and frames are at the data link layer (Layer 2 of the OSI model).

Packets are only affected by the underlying physical and logical topology if a failure results in the path being broken. For example, suppose you have three roads between home and work and at any time you can take any one of those roads. One morning one of those roads is closed for construction; the physical path is unavailable for use. The physical topology for your drive has changed because now two roads are available rather than the original three. You are not concerned here because you still have a way to get from home to work. Your logical path has not changed; it is still home to work, but the physical topology has changed in that now you have to take a different road. Network packets work in the same way. It is the routers and Layer 3 switches that decide over which path the packets move, making the decisions just as you would behind the wheel of the car.

Hardware

Hubs and repeaters are found at Layer 1, bridges and switches and found at Layer 2, and routers are found at Layer 3. A router is a network device that receives and forwards data packets along a network. A router connects two or more networks together; often these are WANs, but routers can also be used to connect two or more LANs. The most common placement of a router is between a LAN and a WAN, such as the Internet, as illustrated in Figure 3-17.

Figure 3-17   Router Connecting a LAN and the Internet

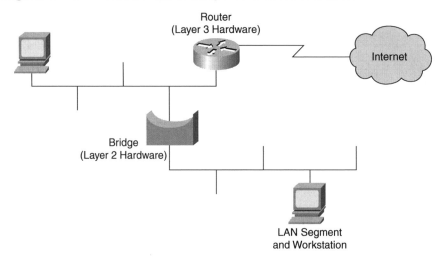

Routers work at Layer 3 of the OSI model to examine the header of each packet. From the header the router determines the path on which the packet must be forwarded. This is similar to the decision you make when you look at an arrival and departure board in the train station to determine on which track your train departs. Routers determine pathways for packets based on routing tables.

The common theme here is that you make a determination based on a table of information, and routers make a determination based on a similar table of information, called a routing table.

Chapter Summary

Local-area networks (LANs) are confined to small geographic areas, such as your home or office building. Wide-area networks (WANs) span broad geographic areas, such sections of a country or continents. WANs interconnect LANs and create what appears to users as a single network.

Information sent across media is called a signal and is in electronic (analog or digital), optical (light), or radio (wireless or cellular) form. Analog signals are measured as continuous waves with a certain frequency, whereas digital signals are measured as square waves with discrete values: 1 or 0. Optical signals are light pulses and are also measured as square waves with the same values as digital signals. Radio signals are measured like analog signals, in continuous waves with a specified frequency.

Recall the physical topology of a network is its layout; the logical topology determines where the devices are placed in the network and how these devices communicate with each other. It is the topology that also determines how network devices talk with each other, either in a direct path or through another device. A full-mesh topology enables every network device to talk with every other device—each device has a direct path to every other device. A star topology provides a central point in the network for communication from each device to pass through.

The physical (OSI model Layer 1) topology of a network represents how each device is interconnected by media or equipment. The logical (OSI model Layers 2 and 3) topology of a network represents the conceptual view of how devices are interconnected, often, but not always, bearing a resemblance to the physical topology.

Hubs carry bits, switches carry frames, and routers carry packets. They all connect physical segments together to create a larger network. Frames are moved around the network by Layer 2 hardware, such as bridges or switches. Bridges and switches use the frame header to determine to which network segment the frame must be forwarded. Bridges and switches determine forwarding decisions for frame movement based on a forwarding table in a MAC table.

The packet, a Layer 3 data unit, is carried by the frame inside its payload section. Packets are the concern of Layer 3 hardware, such as routers. The difference is that whereas a bridge or switch just forwards the frame out a specified port, routers decide the disposition of the packet, such as through which port to forward the packet and if the router is to forward the packet at all. A router can make a more intelligent decision because it knows the source and destination and has capacity to make a decision about paths that are several hops downstream from the router.

Chapter Review Questions

1. What the three components of a frame?

2. What is a bit?

3. What are the main characteristics and differences between a LAN and a WAN?

4. How does a repeater work?

5. How does a hub work?

6. How does a bridge or switch work?

7. What is the difference between a bridge and a switch?

8. What is the difference between a physical topology and a logical topology?

What You Will Learn

On completing this chapter, you will be able to:

- ✔ Identify the components of a LAN

- ✔ Identify three types of LAN topologies

- ✔ Describe three LAN topology implementations

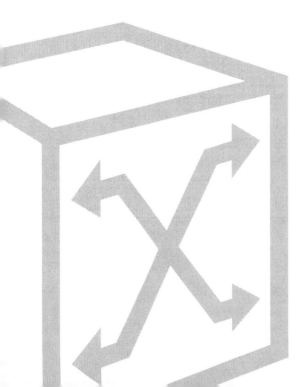

CHAPTER 4

Traditional LAN Architecture

This chapter details the physical components of a local-area network, or LAN, including the different cabling types, the network termination points, and the interfaces at these termination points. Just as railroad ties and rails enable trains to move passengers and cargo between cities, the interconnection of LAN physical components makes up the infrastructure enabling communication among the attached devices, such as your workstation and a network printer.

Components of a LAN

By simple definition, a LAN is two or more devices connected to each other by some type of medium, such as a cable. With the exception of wireless LANs, which are beyond the scope of this book, if there is no cable connection between devices, no connection can occur. These network cables attach to LAN devices via the network interface card (NIC) or network interface port, such as found on a switch.

Cabling

Chapter 3, "Local-Area Networking Introduction," outlined different cabling types. This chapter now details more fully the two most popular types of LAN cabling: twisted pair and fiber optic.

Twisted-Pair Cabling

Twisted-pair cable is a thin-diameter copper wire used for voice and data network cabling. The wires are twisted around each other to minimize interference from other twisted pairs in the cable. Twisted-pair cabling, illustrated in Figure 4-1, enables the use of less bandwidth than required for coaxial cable or optical fiber.

Figure 4-1   Twisted-Pair Cable

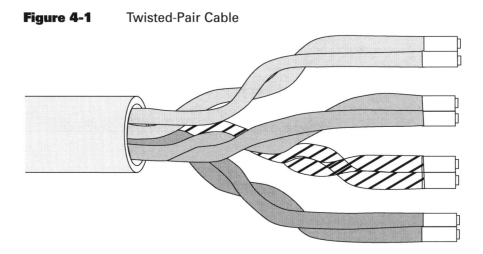

Two types of twisted-pair cabling are found in LANs: shielded twisted-pair (STP) and unshielded twisted-pair (UTP).

Shielded Twisted-Pair (STP)

Shielded twisted-pair (STP) is a type of copper wiring in which each of the two copper wires is twisted together and coated with an insulating coating that functions as a ground for the wires. The extra covering in STP wiring protects the transmission line from electromagnetic interference (EMI) leaking into or out of the cable that could result in signal degradation or loss.

STP is used for most Ethernet cabling requirements, especially Fast Ethernet connections, such as 100 megabits per second (Mbps). STP cabling is also used when emission security concerns exist, such as with a classified network (protecting national security information, for instance).

Unshielded Twisted-Pair (UTP)

Unshielded twisted-pair (UTP) is a popular cable type made up of two unshielded wires twisted around each other. Because UTP is not expensive, it is the prevailing choice for LAN and telephone connections. UTP cabling differs from STP in that UTP does not provide the high bandwidth and good protection from EMI that coaxial and fiber-optic cabling provides.

UTP cabling is available in seven standard categories defined by the *Telecommunications Industry Association 568 (ANSI/EIA/TIA-568)* and are listed in Table 4-1.

Table 4-1   UTP Cable Categories

Category	Number of Wires	Transmission Rate
1	Two	Voice (telephone cable)
2	Four	Up to 4 Mpbs
3	Four	Up to 10 Mbps
4	Four	Up to 16 Mbps
5	Four	Up to 1 gigabit per second (Gbps)
5e	Four	Up to 1 Gbps
6	Four	Up to 10 Gbps

The cable category indicates the number of twists per inch. The more twists in the cabling, the more immune the cable from interference, the faster the cable can transmit, and the greater the bandwidth.

Fiber-Optic Cabling

An optical fiber is a thin glass or plastic strand designed for light transmission and capable of transmitting trillions of bits per second. Optical fiber offers many advantages over copper wire because the light pulses carried by fiber are not affected by random radiation in the environment, and its error rate is significantly lower. Fiber enables longer distances to be spanned before the signal has to be

regenerated by repeaters, as required for the electrical signal carried by copper wire. Fiber is also more secure than copper because wire taps in the fiber line can be detected.

A *fiber-optic cable* is essentially a glass or plastic strand encased in a metal and plastic sheath. Light is transmitted across the fiber strands via lasers. To understand how the laser light moves down the strand, imagine shining a flashlight down a poster tube. The tube prevents the light from spreading in all directions; instead, the tube contains the light and provides a path for the light to travel across. The laser is sent from a laser diode at the sending end of the fiber and travels down the strand to the receiver; and no, you cannot set the laser to stun in the laser diode.

Figure 4-2 illustrates the two primary types, or modes, of fiber used in optic transmission: multimode and single mode.

Figure 4-2   Multimode and Single-Mode Fiber

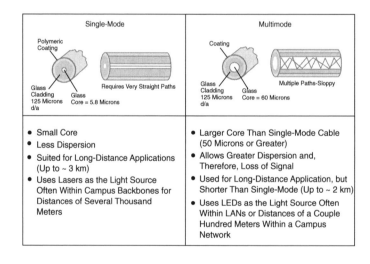

Single-mode fiber is used to span longer distances, and multimode fiber is common for short distances.

Single-mode fiber (SMF) is an optical fiber used for high-speed transmission over long distances. SMF provides a higher-quality cable that allows for a cleaner, stronger signal, and therefore provides more bandwidth than multimode. However, the smaller core of SMF makes it more difficult to align the light source at the receiver.

Multimode fiber (MMF) is an optical fiber with a larger core than single-mode fiber and is the most common fiber used for short distances, such as for LANs. Light can enter the core at different angles, making it easier to transmit light from the source to a broader receiver. This broader scope permits the use of a light emitting diode (LED) rather than the precise laser required by single-mode fiber. This is comparable to the difference between using a flashlight and a laser pointer as a pointing device during a lecture; the flashlight is somewhat broad in its coverage, whereas the laser pointer is more precise.

Cable Termination

Cabling between two devices serves no purpose if there is no way to attach the two together—and although duct tape certainly has its purposes in this world, this is not one of them. Cables, whether copper or fiber optic, are clamped at the ends with a jack connection, known as a ***registered jack***, or ***RJ***.

Several types of RJ connectors are used in networking today, and each type is identified by a number. For example, most telephone handset and wall ports use RJ-11 connectors. Ethernet uses RJ-21 and RJ-45 jack types, and T1 lines use RJ-48.

The RJ-21 (Registered Jack-21) is an Ethernet cable using a 50-pin telco connector on one end. On the other end, the cable branches out to 12 RJ-45 (Registered Jack-45) connectors. The RJ-45 is a connector that holds up to eight wires, as illustrated in Figure 4-3.

Figure 4-3   RJ-45 Plug and Socket (Jack)

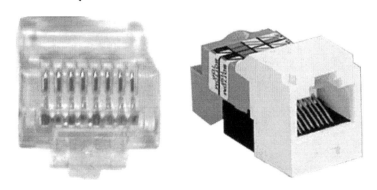

These RJ-45 plugs and sockets (jacks) are used in Ethernet and Token Ring devices, as illustrated in Figure 4-4.

Figure 4-4   LAN User Cable Termination Points

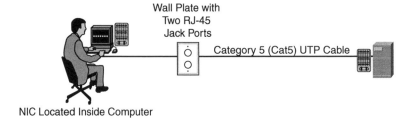

The NIC found inside the user's desktop computer or other network device, such as a mail server or network printer, is connected via the network cable to the network interface jack.

Wall Plates and Wall Boxes

Wall plates and wall boxes serve the aesthetic purpose of hiding holes in the wall and visible wires. Wall plates and wall boxes help protect the cable from being pulled out, cut, or damaged. They also help with providing a place to label cables. Further, a box can be organized to centralize multiple services for a user in a single location (for example, phone and data together). Figure 4-5 and Figure 4-6 illustrate a wall plate and a wall box that are often used in LAN implementations.

Figure 4-5 Wall Plates

Figure 4-6 Wall Box

The wall plate is mounted onto the wall with an opening for the RJ connection, and a wall box is a freestanding box that can be, but is not always, mounted to a wall. Behind these wall plates and wall boxes is the cabling that runs back to the LAN switch, often sitting in a communications closet somewhere within the building.

Network Interface Card (NIC)

Much as your driveway is an interface to the main road, the network interface card is your interface to the network. With one end of the network cable connected to a port in the wall, the other end needs to connect to a device to complete the circuit. This device is the *network interface card*, or *NIC*. NICs are circuit boards that plug into your desktop, laptop, or network servers, such as a web or e-mail server. The NIC controls the sending and receiving of data across the physical Open System Interconnection (OSI) model Layer 1 and data link OSI model Layer 2.

LAN Topologies

In Chapter 3, the implementation of the previous network topologies was discussed. This chapter discusses the more common *topologies*: the star, ring, and tree topologies. The chapter describes when use of one topology is better than another as well as the role (if any) that switches play in each topology.

There are differences between physical and logical topologies, just as there are differences between physical and logical networks. A physical topology is determined by the cabling that connects the network devices together, whereas a logical topology is determined by the traffic flow across the network.

Star Topology

The defining aspect of the star or hub-and-spoke topology is that all network devices are connected to a central point, such as a hub or a switch. The topology resembles a star, as illustrated in Figure 4-7. Star topologies best reflect the difference between a physical and logical topology in that the star topology is wired in a physical star, but your data, such as a print request, moves around the network in a circle.

Figure 4-7   Star or Hub-and-Spoke Topology

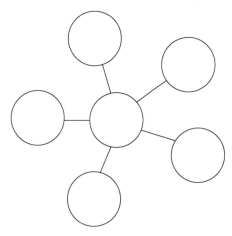

The central point of a star topology plays the role of traffic cop in that it directs traffic to its intended destination rather than to everyone on the network. In a LAN implementation, the traffic cop is often the switch. A star topology with a single switch at its central point might look something like the illustration in Figure 4-8.

Figure 4-8   Single-Switch LAN

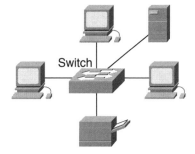

This topology might be found in small office/home office (SOHO) networks or small- to medium-sized corporate networks. A switch is central to the LAN, providing a connection between all devices, such as desktop workstations, servers for file sharing or e-mail, or network-attached shared printers.

Ring Topology

In a physical ring topology, all devices are connected to one another in a closed loop, so that each device is connected to two other devices, one on either side of it. Ring topologies are used in Token Ring and Fiber Distributed Data Interface (FDDI) LANs because of the inherent redundancy in a ring network. For example, if the connection on one side of your machine goes down, the connection on the other side of your machine remains up so you are still connected to network resources.

Figure 4-9   Ring Topology

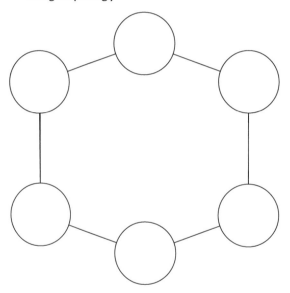

Ring topologies do not use switches but rather *multistation access units*, or MAUs, enabling connection from each device to the LAN. These MAUs enable your data to travel around the ring in either a clockwise or counterclockwise fashion with each device connected to the ring acting as a repeater.

Tree Topology

The tree topology is a multitiered hierarchical star topology, in which the endpoint of one spoke in a star is the hub of another, as illustrated in Figure 4-10.

Figure 4-10   Tree Topology

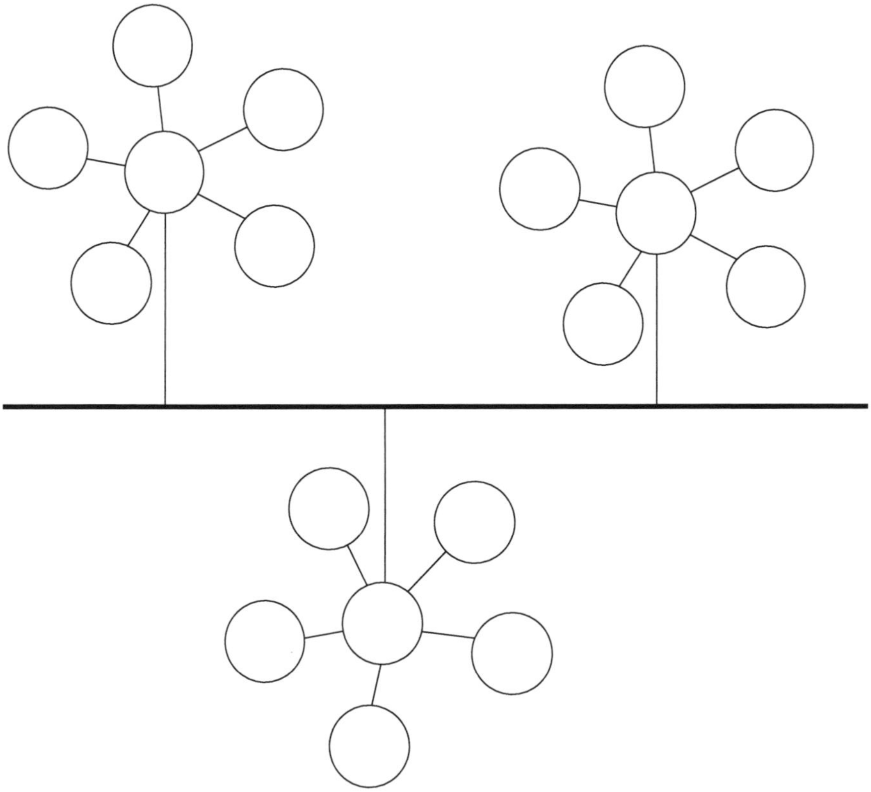

This physical topology is made possible with multiple switches and might be used in an office building where each floor has its own switch, or branch off the tree, connecting to a backbone switch, which provides connectivity between floors, as illustrated in Figure 4-11.

Figure 4-11   Multiswitch LAN

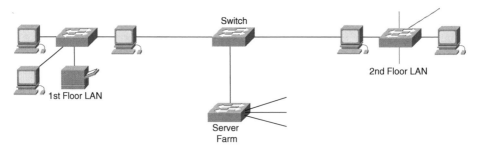

Figure 4-11 shows that the users on the first or second floor LAN can use the server farm resources by the connection provided by the backbone switch. These *server farm* resources might be web servers, e-mail servers, file servers, network printer servers, or any other server on which multiple users need to share information. For example, compare these two methods for sharing files with someone else in your office: E-mail the file back and forth until all changes are complete; or share and edit the file as it sits on a shared file server. You will likely choose the latter, because editing a shared file is easier to manage than multiple e-mails and revisions. In a medium or large LAN, these servers might be grouped together in one place or distributed across the LAN. For example, each floor could have its own shared file and print server.

Local-Area Networks (LANs)

The topology of the LAN is determined by the technology. (For example, a ring topology is implemented by Token Ring or FDDI, and a star or tree topology is implemented by Ethernet.)

Token Ring

Token Ring is a technology developed by IBM and standardized by the Institute of Electrical and Electronics Engineers (IEEE) 802.5 committee for implementation in a LAN environment. Token Ring uses a special frame, called a token, to designate the authoritative speaker for that LAN segment. This technology can connect up to 255 nodes in a physical star or ring connection that can sustain 4 or 16 Mbps. Each node on a Token Ring LAN connects to a central wiring hub called the multistation access unit (MAU) using a twisted wire cable, such as UTP.

Token Ring is more deterministic than Ethernet, which means that it ensures that all users get regular turns at transmitting their data. With Ethernet, all users have to compete for network access to get on to the network. In a Token Ring network, a token is passed around the network from one workstation to the next, giving each workstation equal access to the network. Unlike an Ethernet workstation, which can send data if the line is idle, a Token Ring workstation cannot send data across the network unless it is in possession of the token.

FDDI

Fiber Distributed Data Interface, or FDDI (pronounced "fiddy"), is a LAN and metropolitan-area network (MAN) access method. It is a token-passing network, similar to Token Ring, and uses optical fiber cabling to transmit at 100 Mbps up to 10 kilometers. FDDI provides network services at the same OSI model layers as Ethernet and Token Ring (Layer 1 and Layer 2).

FDDI provides the option of a dual counter-rotating ring topology. This dual-ring topology is used for redundancy so that if one ring fails the other ring carries the traffic. Traffic on these rings travels in opposite directions: The traffic on one ring travels clockwise, whereas the traffic on the other ring travels counterclockwise.

Ethernet

Ethernet is the most widely deployed LAN access method, defined by the IEEE as the 802.3 standard. Ethernet has become popular such that a specification for a LAN connection or network card implies the use of Ethernet even if not explicitly stated. A 10/100 Ethernet port supports both 10BASE-T at 10 Mbps and 100BASE-T at 100 Mbps.

Ethernet is often considered to be a shared-media LAN, which means that all stations on the segment share the total bandwidth—10 Mbps (Ethernet), 100 Mbps (Fast Ethernet), or 1000 Mbps (Gigabit Ethernet). When Ethernet is deployed in a switched environment, it is no longer considered to be shared. Therefore, each sender and receiver pair has the full Ethernet bandwidth available for use.

Ethernet uses *carrier sense multiple access collision detect* (*CSMA/CD*) technology, broadcasting each frame onto the physical medium (wire, fiber, and so on). All stations attached to the Ethernet listen to the line for traffic, and the station with the matching destination *MAC address* accepts the frame and checks for errors before doing anything further with the frame. If the frame is error free, it is handed to the network layer (Layer 3) of the OSI model and ultimately the data is presented to the user, such as an e-mail. If the frame has errors, however, it is discarded.

note
Chapter 5, "Ethernet LANs," discusses Ethernet in more detail.

Chapter Summary

A LAN is just two or more network-capable devices connected to each other over a small area through a medium, such as a cable. LAN architecture is the set of rules and design principles that define the LAN. A LAN is made up of three components: physical media, such as the cabling and network interfaces; the topology, such as a star or ring topology; and the protocols, or LAN technologies, such as Token Ring or Ethernet.

The topology of a LAN is characterized by its logical form and its physical shape, such as the shape of a star, ring, or a tree. A star topology is also known as a hub-and-spoke because the connecting point of all devices is at the center of the star, much as the hub of a wheel is the center of the wheel spokes. A ring topology is shaped like a circle, in which each device has a connection on both sides to attached devices, so that all devices are connected in a ring.

The topology of the LAN is based in part on the technology used, such as Token Ring, FDDI, or Ethernet. A ring topology is enabled by either a Token Ring or FDDI LAN implementation with an inherent redundancy against failure. This redundancy provides two paths across the LAN from the workstation: one on each side of the workstation. A workstation in a Token Ring or FDDI LAN can send data across the network only when its turn for the token has come around. A star or tree topology is enabled by an Ethernet LAN implementation with no inherent redundancy. Unlike a Token Ring or FDDI workstation, an Ethernet workstation can send data across the network at any time as long as the network is idle, meaning no other workstations are sending data at the same time.

Chapter Review Questions

1. What determines the category of a cable?

2. Describe a star topology.

3. Describe a ring topology.

4. Describe a tree topology.

5. Which LAN topologies usually use switches?

6. When would you use a star (hub-and-spoke) or a ring topology?

7. When would you use a tree topology?

What You Will Learn

On completing this chapter, you will be able to:

- ✔ List the different Ethernet LAN types

- ✔ Describe the addressing used in Ethernet LANs

- ✔ Describe half- and full-duplex Ethernet LAN operation

- ✔ List the different hardware types found in Ethernet LANs

- ✔ Describe how each hardware device works in an Ethernet LAN

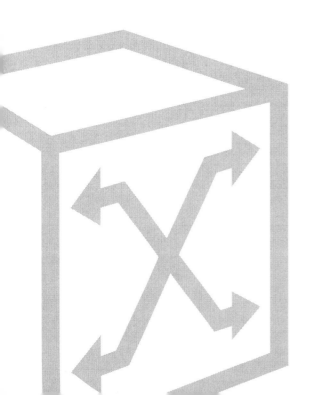

CHAPTER 5

Ethernet LANs

The most widely used local-area network (LAN) access method, defined by the Institute of Electrical and Electronics Engineers (IEEE), is the 802.3 standard. Ethernet has become so popular that most Apple computers and many PCs come with 10/100 Ethernet ports for home use. These ports enable you not just to create a small home network but to connect to the Internet via a Digital Subscriber Line (DSL) or cable modem, which requires an Ethernet connection. A 10/100 port means that the network interface supports both 10BASE-T at 10 megabits per second (Mbps) and 100BASE-T at 100 Mbps.

Ethernet is often a shared-media LAN, which means that all stations on the segment use part of the total bandwidth. Depending on the type of Ethernet implemented, this total bandwidth is a 10 Mbps (Ethernet), 100 Mbps (Fast Ethernet), or 1000 Mbps (Gigabit Ethernet). In a shared Ethernet environment, each device has to contend for network bandwidth using the *carrier sense multiple access with collision detect (CSMA/CD)* mechanism. In a switched Ethernet environment, each sender and receiver pair has the full bandwidth available for use.

Ethernet LANs use the Media Access Control, or MAC, address to determine how traffic is moved between network segments. Ethernet hubs, defined by the Open System Interconnection (OSI) model physical layer (Layer 1), repeat only the physical signal; the hub does not look at a source or destination address. Ethernet bridges and switches use the source and destination MAC address, defined by the OSI data link layer (Layer 2) to build an interface table and to determine which segment should receive the frame. Routers use the network address, found at the OSI network layer (Layer 3) to build a routing table.

This chapter discusses how the MAC address, the Layer 2 and Layer 3 operations, and the Ethernet hardware fit into an Ethernet LAN environment.

Media Access Control (MAC) Addressing

The MAC address is the unique serial number burned into each network adapter that differentiates the network card from all others, just as your house number is unique on your street and identifies your home from all others. To be a part of any network, you must have an address so that others can reach you. Two types of addresses are found in a network: the logical (OSI model Layer 3, network) and the physical (OSI model Layer 2, data link). For this discussion of LAN environments, the physical address (also known as the *Media Access Control [MAC] address*) is relevant.

A MAC address is the physical address of the device. It is 48 bits (6 bytes) long and is made up of two parts: the organizational unique identifier (OUI) and the vendor-assigned address, as illustrated in Figure 5-1.

Figure 5-1   MAC Address

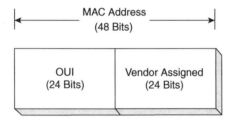

The MAC address on a computer might look like this: 00-08-a1-08-c8-13. This MAC address is used for the Fast Ethernet adapter on the computer in question. The OUI is 00-08-a1, and the vendor-assigned number is 08-c8-13.

The OUI is administered by the IEEE and identifies the vendor of the network adapter. The vendor-assigned portion of the MAC address is just that, the alphanumeric identifier assigned by the vendor. It is the combination of the OUI and the vendor-assigned number that ensures that no two network adapters have the same MAC address.

note
MAC addresses are represented as ***hexadecimal*** *(hex)* numbers.

With the hexadecimal numbering system, each half byte (4 bits) is assigned a hex digit, which is listed in Table 5-1, with its decimal and binary equivalents. Hex values are identified with an *h* or dollar sign, so $3E0, 3E0h, and 3E0H all stand for the hex number 3E0.

Table 5-1   Hexadecimal, Decimal, and Binary Conversion Table

Hexadecimal (Base 16)	Decimal (Base 10)	Binary (Base 2)
0	0	0000
1	1	0001
2	2	0010
3	3	0011
4	4	0100
5	5	0101
6	6	0110
7	7	0111
8	8	1000
9	9	1001
A	10	1010
B	11	1011
C	12	1100
D	13	1101
E	14	1110
F	15	1111

Carrier Sense Multiple Access with Collision Detect (CSMA/CD)

Have you been in a meeting in which everyone has had something to say? It's difficult to get anything done when everyone is talking at the same time. When this happens, everyone eventually stops talking and lets one person talk. Ethernet works much the same way when using CSMA/CD.

With CSMA/CD, when an Ethernet device attempts to access the network to send data, the network interface on the workstation or server checks to see if the network is quiet. When the network is clear, the network interface knows that transmission can begin. If it does not sense a carrier, the interface waits a random amount of time before retrying. If the network is quiet and two devices try sending data at the same time, their signals collide. When this collision is detected, both devices back off and wait a random amount of time before retrying, much like two people starting to talk at the same time—both stop and wait a random amount of time before trying to speak again.

CSMA/CD Operation

In a half-duplex environment, Ethernet operates with CSMA/CD, such as found in 10BASE-T (10 Mbps) Ethernet LANs. *Half-duplex Ethernet operation* means that each device can send and receive data, but not at the same time.

In the framework of CSMA/CD, the computers on a network operate as follows.

- **Carrier sense**—Each computer on the LAN is always listening for traffic on the wire to determine when gaps between frame transmissions occur.

- **Multiple access**—Any computer can begin sending data whenever it detects that the network is *quiet*. (There is no traffic.)

- **Collision detect**—If two or more computers in the same CSMA/CD network *collision domain* begin sending at the same time, the bit streams from each sending computer interfere, or *collide*, with each other, making each transmission unreadable. If this collision occurs, each sending computer must be able to detect that a collision has occurred before it has finished sending its frame.

Each computer must stop sending its traffic as soon as it has detected the collision and then wait some random length of time, called the ***back-off algorithm***, before attempting to retransmit the frame.

Collisions

Collisions are used by Ethernet to control network access and shared bandwidth among connected stations that are trying to transmit at the same time on a shared medium, such as the network segment. Because the network medium is shared, a mechanism must exist whereby the network stations can detect network availability so that they do not transmit at the same time; this mechanism is ***collision detection***.

Collisions occur when two frames try to use the same network segment at the same time and both frames are lost, not unlike two people trying to talk at the same time. As you might suspect, collisions in networks and conversations are best avoided. However, collisions in a shared environment cannot be avoided, whether that shared environment is a network segment or the air of a conversation.

Figure 5-2 illustrates what happens when a collision occurs on a network segment.

Figure 5-2   Ethernet Collision

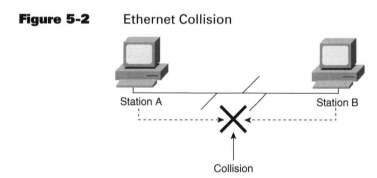

- Station A attempts to send a frame across the network. First, Station A checks to see if the network is available *(carrier sense)*. If the network is not available, Station A waits until the current sender on the medium has finished.

- Let's suppose that Station A believes the network is available and tries sending a frame. Because the network is shared (multiple access), other stations on the same network segment might also attempt to send at the same time (Station B, for instance).

- Shortly after Station B attempts to send traffic across the line, both Station A and Station B realize that another device is attempting to send a frame (collision detection). Each station waits a random amount of time before sending again. The time after the collision is divided into time slots; Station A and Station B each pick a random slot for attempting a retransmission.

- Should Station A and Station B attempt to retransmit at the same time, they extend the amount of time each waits before trying again, decreasing the chance of resending data in the same time slot.

note

The maximum number of retransmissions for the same data frame is 16; if the transmission fails 16 consecutive times, the network is considered unavailable.

Reducing the number of collisions in a LAN is essential to the design and operation of the network just as reducing the amount of traffic in the city is crucial to reducing delays. Increased collisions result from too many users and devices on the network contending for network bandwidth. This contention slows the performance of the network from the user's point of view, yielding the most frequent call to the help desk: "The network is slow today." Breaking up, or segmenting, the network is the common way of reducing this network contention. ***Network segmentation*** occurs when a network is divided into different pieces joined together logically with a bridge, switch, or router.

Ethernet LAN Equipment

Chapter 3, "Local-Area Networking Introduction," discussed the different types of hardware found in a LAN environment. The following discussion addresses the suitability for different environments of various types of hardware—hubs, bridges, and switches—and how each piece of hardware functions specifically in an Ethernet environment.

Repeaters—Layer 1 Devices

To begin this discussion, it is useful to review the definition presented in Chapter 3: A repeater is a network device used to regenerate or replicate a signal. Repeaters are used in transmission systems to regenerate analog or digital signals distorted by transmission loss. Repeaters are used in both local- and wide-area networking environments to extend the distance a signal can reach. For example, you might use a third person repeating your words to carry your message across a large room, as shown in the Figure 5-3.

Figure 5-3   Two-Person Conversation with a Third Person Repeating

In the LAN environment, you would use a ***repeater*** to extend the distance a data signal can travel on a cable, as illustrated in Figure 5-4.

Figure 5-4   Repeater Operation

Workstation   Server

If you are in a large building and you are connecting two network devices that are several hundred feet apart (a server and a workstation, for example), a single 25- or 50-foot cable segment is obviously not going to be long enough. You can use a repeater to connect multiple cables together to make a single cable length long enough for your requirement.

Hubs—Layer 1 Devices

As mentioned in Chapter 3, a hub is often used to connect small LAN segments in which the number of devices is generally 24 or fewer, and hubs are multiport repeaters. *Hubs* are used to create collision domains, in which all devices on the network can see each other. In larger designs, signal quality begins to deteriorate as segments exceed their maximum length, often a couple hundred feet. Hubs provide the signal amplification required to allow a segment to be extended a greater distance. A hub takes an incoming signal on any one port and repeats it out all ports to enable users to share the Ethernet network resources.

Ethernet hubs create star topologies in 10-Mbps or 100-Mbps half-duplex Ethernet LANs. It is the hub that enables several point-to-point segments to be joined together into one single network, and it is this network of hubs that makes up a shared Ethernet, just as several point-to-point roads join together into the single large network of roads you use to get around town.

A shared Ethernet LAN means that all members of the network are contending for transmission of data onto a single network (collision domain); individual members of a shared network get only a percentage of the available network bandwidth, as illustrated in Figure 5-5.

Figure 5-5   Shared Ethernet (Total Bandwidth Shared Among Attached Hosts)

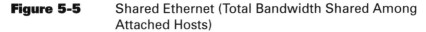

Single "shared Ethernet" network made up of two hubs.

Point-to-point links between the hub and the network device.

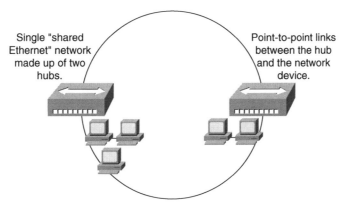

One end of the point-to-point link is attached to the hub, and the other is attached to the network device, such as a computer or printer. Connecting multiple hubs together expands the shared Ethernet segment but puts more stress on the line's bandwidth because now more users are trying to use the same bandwidth. This is similar to building a new neighborhood without adding roads and thus putting stress on existing roads. As you and your car sit stuck in traffic, so might your data suffer in network *congestion*.

Network bridges are one way to prevent this congestion. *Network bridges* function like hubs in that bridges provide a network connection; however, bridges preserve the separation of these network segments by keeping network traffic local to its respective segment instead of repeating it all to the world. Bridge operation is discussed in detail in the following section.

Bridges—Layer 2 Devices

Repeaters and hubs have no intelligence; they just repeat whatever signal is received from one port out all ports without looking at what is being sent or received. Bridges add a level of intelligence to the network by using the MAC address to build a table of hosts, mapping these hosts to a network segment and containing traffic within these network segments. For example, Figure 5-6 illustrates a bridged network with two network segments.

Figure 5-6   Bridge Connecting Two Ethernet Segments

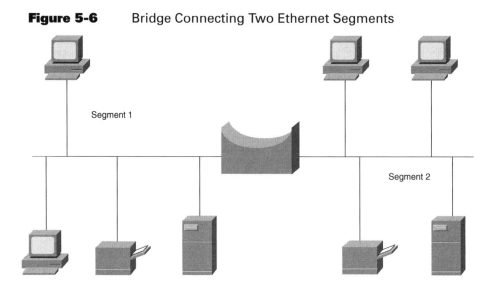

Segments 1 and 2 contain two workstations each, a file server (for file sharing) and a network printer. Suppose that your engineering and financial teams share a floor in an office building and that Segment 1 is made up of your engineering team and Segment 2 is made up of your financial team. If a hub were used to connect these teams to your corporate network, each team would be contending for the total network bandwidth, causing slowdowns on the network. The engineering team might be using all the bandwidth at the moment that someone in finance is trying to process the payroll.

As you might surmise, using a hub in this scenario is not the preferred method because of the contention for the network bandwidth. In this scenario, a **bridge** is a better choice than a hub because the bridge segments the network into two smaller parts—an engineering team segment and a financial team segment—keeping traffic local to its respective segment.

Ethernet bridges map the MAC addresses of the network devices, or **nodes**, residing on each network segment. Bridges allow only necessary traffic to pass through the bridge, such as traffic destined for a segment other than the source. When a frame is received by the bridge, the bridge looks at the frame header and reads the source and destination MAC addresses, determining the frame sender and destination. If the frame's source and destination segments are the same, the frame is *dropped*, or filtered by the bridge; if the segments differ, the bridge forwards the frame to the correct segment.

Figure 5-7 illustrates a small bridged network with three network segments.

Figure 5-7   Bridge Connecting Three LAN Segments

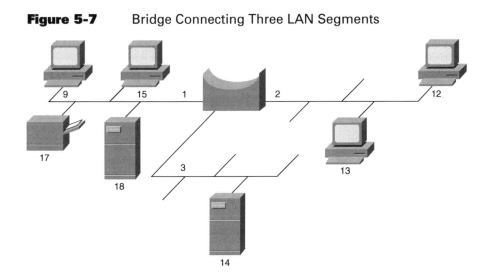

If the bridge sees a frame arrive on port 1 from Host 9, the bridge concludes that Host 9 can be reached through the segment connected to port 1. If the same bridge sees a frame arrive on port 2 from Host 12, the bridge concludes that Host 12 can be reached through the network segment connected to port 2, as illustrated in Figure 5-8. Through this learning process, bridges build a table, such as shown in Table 5-2.

Table 5-2 Bridge Table

Host Address	Network Segment
15	1
17	1
12	2
13	2
18	1
9	1
14	3

This filtering or forwarding function is similar to what an organization's mailroom does on receipt of an envelope; if the destination of the envelope is the same as the source (within the building), the mailroom attendant filters this envelope from any outgoing mail being forwarded to the post office. If this envelope is for a destination outside of the building, the mailroom attendant forwards it to the network, and in this case, the network is the post office.

Bridge Operation

The most frequently used bridge in Ethernet LANs is the transparent bridge. The bridge is called "transparent" because the computers using a bridge are unaware of its presence in the network, and traffic passes "transparently" over the bridge. Think how often you barely notice a small bridge you drive across; if it weren't for the view, you would not know you passed over a bridge because the road continued onward.

LAN bridges forward frames from one LAN to another. For example, as illustrated in Figure 5-8, the bridge forwards all traffic originating from LAN A to destinations found in LAN B, such as Computer C.

Figure 5-8   Bridge Connecting Two LAN Segments (A and B)

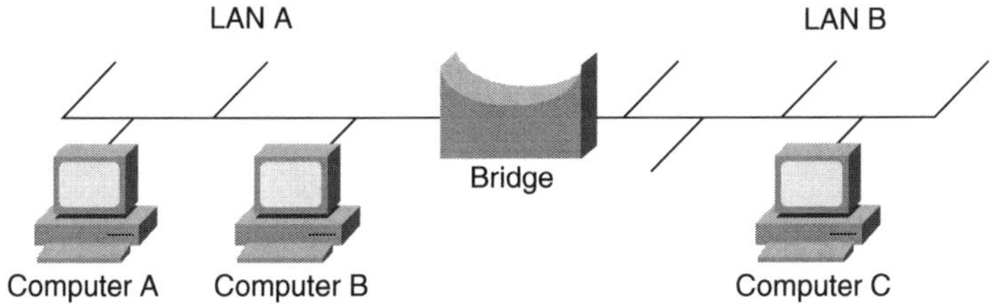

The bridge could forward all frames it receives but in doing so it acts as a repeater, not a bridge. The desired operation is for the bridge to forward only frames that need to travel from one LAN to another, such as from LAN A to LAN B and vice versa (as shown in Figure 5-8). In forwarding traffic between LAN segments the bridge learns the following: which computers are connected to which LANs, which addresses to use when forwarding traffic on to another LAN segment, and which addresses to filter or not forward.

To learn which addresses are used and by which ports, the bridge examines the headers of received Ethernet frames on each port in use. The bridge is looking specifically at the source MAC address of each received frame and recording the port on which it was received. A bridge stores the hardware addresses observed from frames received by each interface and uses this information to learn which frames need to be forwarded by the bridge. Figure 5-9 shows this bridge-learning process.

Figure 5-9   Operation of a Bridge Filter Table

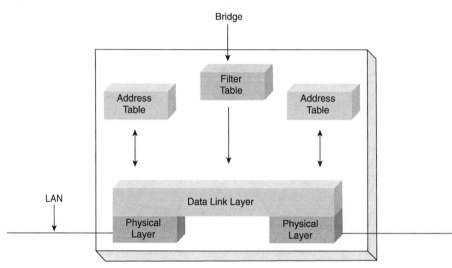

The learned addresses are stored in the interface address table associated with each port (interface). As this table is being built, the bridge examines the destination MAC address of all received frames. As it examines the frames, the bridge searches the interface table to see whether a frame has been previously received from the same address, such as a frame with a source address matching the current destination address.

The bridge's search of the interface table can encounter the following circumstances:

- If the address is not found, no frames have been received from the source.

- The source may not exist, or it may not have sent any frames using this address. (The address may also have been deleted by the bridge because the bridge was restarted or ran short of address entries in the interface table or the address was too old.)

Because the bridge does not know which port to use to forward the frame, it sends the frame out all ports, except that port from which the frame was received; this is called *flooding*.

note

It is unnecessary to send the frame back to the same cable segment from which it was received, because any other computer/bridges on this cable will already have received the frame.

- If the address is found in the interface table and is associated with the port on which it was received, the frame is discarded because it is considered to already have been received by the destination.

- If the address is found in the interface table and is not associated with the port from which it was received, the bridge forwards the frame to the port associated with the address.

note

Interface Table Management

A bridge might implement an interface table using a software data structure or use a content-addressable memory (CAM) chip. In either case, the size of the table is finite. In a large LAN, this limit might be a problem in that there could be more hosts and addresses than there is space in the table. To help keep the table small, most bridges maintain a check of how recently each address was used. Addresses that have not been used for a long period of time (minutes) are deleted. This has the effect of removing unused entries; if the address is used again, however, before a frame is received from the same source, it requires the frame to be flooded to all ports.

A useful side effect of deleting old addresses is that the bridge interface table records only working MAC addresses. If a *network interface card (NIC)* stops sending, its address is deleted from the table. If the NIC is subsequently reconnected, the entry is restored; if the connection is made to another port (the cable is changed), however, a different (updated) entry is inserted that corresponds to the actual port associated with the address. (The bridge always updates the interface table for each source address in a received MAC frame. Therefore, even if a computer changes the point at which it is connected without first having the interface table entry removed, the bridge still updates the table entry.)

Switches—Layer 2 Devices

Hubs create a network environment in which each connected device shares the available network bandwidth with other devices contending for the same network resources, as illustrated in Figure 5-10.

Figure 5-10   Shared Network

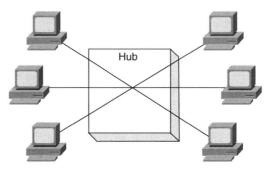

The hub is connecting six workstations together, each sharing the network bandwidth. A finite amount of network bandwidth is available. For example, 10BASE-T Ethernet provides 10 Mbps, and the more workstations added to this network, the less bandwidth available for each. Switches address the shared bandwidth issue and eliminate contention by dedicating a path between the source and the destination, as illustrated in the Figure 5-11.

Figure 5-11   Dedicated Network

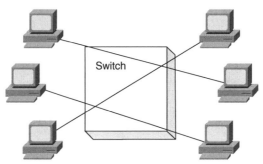

Network switches replace shared-media hubs, increasing network bandwidth. For example, a 16-port 100BASE-T hub shares the total 100-Mbps bandwidth with all 16 attached nodes. By replacing this hub with a switch, each source (sender) and destination (receiver) pair has access to the full 100-Mbps capacity of the network. Each port on the switch can give full bandwidth to a single server or client station or each can be connected to a hub with several stations, as illustrated in Figure 5-12.

Figure 5-12   Switch with Dedicated and Hubbed Nodes

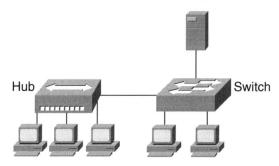

Dedicating ports on *Ethernet switches* to individual nodes is another way to speed access for critical computers. Servers and power users can take advantage of a full segment for one node, so some networks connect high-traffic nodes to a dedicated switch port.

Switches sit in the same place in the network as hubs. Unlike hubs, however, switches examine each frame and process the frame accordingly instead of just repeating the signal to all ports. Switches map the MAC addresses of the nodes residing on each network segment and then allow only the necessary traffic to pass through the switch. A switch performs the same functions as a bridge; so when the switch receives a frame, it examines the destination and source MAC addresses and compares them to a table of network segments and addresses. If the segments are the same, the frame is dropped, or filtered; if the segments differ, the frame is forwarded to the proper segment.

The filtering of frames and regeneration of forwarded frames enables switches to split a network into separate collision domains. Frame regeneration enables greater distances and more network devices, or nodes, to be used in the total network design, and lowers the overall collision rates. In switched networks, each segment is an independent collision domain, whereas in shared networks all nodes reside in one, big, shared collision domain.

Switch Operation

Remember that a bridge with more than two ports can also be called a switch. The difference between a hub and a bridge/switch is the number of frames they forward. Figure 5-13 illustrates how a hub forwards a frame received from Node A that is destined for Node F.

Figure 5-13   A Hub Repeating a Frame from A to F

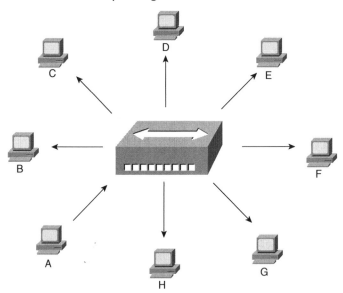

Recall that a hub is a multiport repeater and repeats any signal received on one port out all ports. When the hub receives a signal from Node A, it repeats, or forwards, this received frame out all the ports, so that the frame reaches all connected equipment, even though the frame might be destined for a device connected to one specific port interface (Node F, for example, in the case of Figure 5-13).

Instead of repeating the frame out every port, the switch forwards the frame to only the required interface, as illustrated in Figure 5-14.

Figure 5-14   Switch Forwarding a Frame from A to F

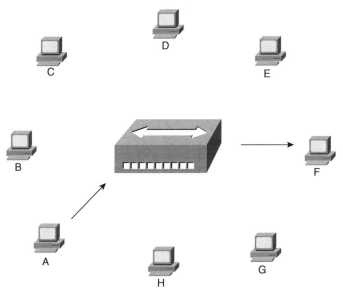

The switch learns the association between the node's MAC address and the interface port in the same way a bridge learns—by listening to which MAC addresses enter the switch and from which port. By sending the frame only where it needs to go, the switch reduces the number of frames on the other LAN segments, in turn reducing the load on these segments and increasing the performance of the connected LANs.

If the switch does not have an entry in its forwarding table and forwards a frame out every port, this is known as a ***broadcast***. This scenario makes it possible to have a flood that is similar to a flood in a hub-based environment. A switch will

perform a directed transmission, if it knows the port, and therefore does reduce broadcasts, but a switch does not remove all broadcasts. Because a switch does not remove all broadcasts, a router is used in network designs because a router breaks up broadcast domains and reduces broadcast storms.

Switching Methods

Ethernet switches are an expansion of Ethernet bridging in that switches can link several LANs together. In linking several LANs together, switches forward frames between these LAN segments using one of two basic methods: cut through and store and forward.

Cut-through switches examine only the frame's destination MAC address before forwarding it on to its destination segment. Cut-through switching is comparable to the postmen taking each piece of mail received at a post office, looking at the address, and then sending the mail on to its destination.

Store-and-forward switches accept the entire frame, analyze it for errors, look at the destination MAC address, and then forward the frame on to its destination. Store-and-forward switching is comparable to postmen taking each piece of mail received at the post office, opening it, checking the contents for spelling, grammar, and ensuring no contents are missing, before sending the mail on to its destination. It takes more time to examine the entire frame, but store-and-forward switching enables the switch to catch certain frame errors and keep them from propagating through the network.

Both cut-through and store-and-forward switches separate networks into collision domains, allowing network design rules to be extended. Each of the segments attached to a switch has a full bandwidth shared by fewer users, resulting in better performance, in contrast to the bandwidth sharing that is characteristic of a hub-based environment. A network composed of a number of switches linked together is called a *collapsed backbone network*.

note

Connecting Bridges and Switches Together

A special rule controls bridge and switch interconnection. The rule says that a bridge/switch/hub LAN must form a tree, and not a ring. This means there must be only one path between any two computers. If more than one parallel path exists, a loop would be formed, resulting in endless circulation of frames over the loop. This network loop would result in network overload. To prevent this from happening, the IEEE has defined the spanning-tree algorithm (STA) in IEEE 802.1d, which detects loops and disables one of the parallel paths. The STA might also be used to build fault-tolerant networks, because if the chosen path becomes invalid due to a cable/bridge/switch fault and an alternative path exists, the alternative path is enabled automatically.

Switches address OSI model Layer 2 (data link) networks, moving frames around based on the hardware, or MAC, address, but switches are limited in their use in that they are LAN devices. Switches do not provide wide-area network (WAN) connectivity. To connect your LAN to another LAN through some outside network, such as the Internet or corporate WAN, a router is needed.

Routers—Layer 3 Devices

Routers are devices that forward data packets from one LAN or WAN to another. Based on routing tables and routing protocols, routers read the network address in the packet contained within each transmitted frame. Routers then select a sending method for the packet based on the most expedient route. This most expedient route is determined by factors such as traffic load, line quality, and available bandwidth. Routers work at Layer 3 (network) in the protocol stack, whereas bridges and switches work at Layer 2 (data link).

Routers segment LANs to balance traffic within workgroups and to filter traffic for security purposes and policy management. Routers also can be used at the edge of the network to connect remote offices, across WANs or the Internet, as illustrated in Figure 5-15.

Figure 5-15   Router Connecting Two LANs to the Internet

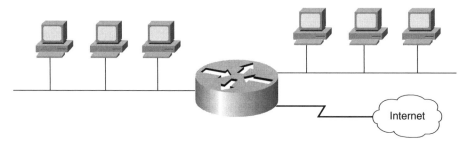

Because routers must examine the network address in the packet, they do more processing and add more overhead than bridges and switches, which both work at the data link (MAC) layer.

Router Operation

A *router* is essentially a computer with two or more NICs supporting a network protocol, such as the Internet Protocol (IP). The router receives packets from each network interface and forwards these received packets to an appropriate output network interface. Received packets have all data link layer (OSI Layer 2) protocol headers removed, and transmitted packets have a new link protocol header added before transmission.

The router uses the information held in the network layer header, such as an IP address, to decide whether to forward each received packet, and which network interface to use to send the packet. Most packets are forwarded based on the packet's network destination address, along with routing information held within the router in a routing table, as illustrated in Figure 5-16.

Figure 5-16   Router Architecture

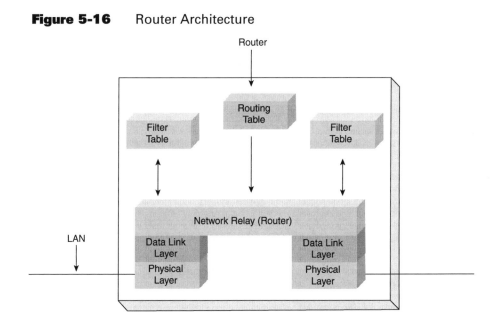

The routing and filter tables found in a router are similar to the tables used by bridges and switches. The difference between routing and switching tables is that instead of specifying link hardware (MAC) addresses, the router table specifies network addresses. The routing table lists known IP destination addresses with the appropriate network interface used to reach that destination. A default entry is used for all addresses not explicitly defined in the table, such as packets destined for the Internet. It's more manageable to have a single entry in the table for the Internet than to have an entry for each Internet site you might visit.

Chapter Summary

At the heart of LAN operation is the MAC address. The MAC address is the unique network adapter serial number distinguishing that network card from all others on the network. The MAC address is made up of two parts: the OUI and the vendor-assigned serial number.

Half-duplex Ethernet uses CSMA/CD as the LAN access method. When an Ethernet device wants to gain access to the network, it checks to see whether the network is quiet; if the network is not quiet, the device waits a random amount of time before retrying. If the network is quiet and two devices access the line at exactly the same time, their signals collide. When the collision is detected, they both back off and each waits a random amount of time before retrying

Table 5-3 lists LAN hardware and the layer in the OSI model at which each piece of hardware operates.

Table 5-3   LAN Hardware

Device	OSI Layer
Repeater	Layer 1 (physical)
Hub	Layer 1 (physical)
Bridge	Layer 2 (data link)
Switch	Layer 2 (data link) or Layer 3 (network)
Router	Layer 3 (network)

Repeaters regenerate signals in the cable line and are used in both local- and wide-area networking environments to extend the distance a signal can reach. Ethernet hubs are multiport repeaters because each signal that is received by the hub is repeated out all hub ports and is received by any device connected to the hub.

Ethernet bridges are essentially multiport hubs. Instead of repeating the incoming signal out all ports, however, the bridge maps the MAC address to a port. This map keeps track of the MAC addresses of each node that resides on each network segment and allows only necessary traffic to pass through the bridge, such as traffic destined for a segment other than the source. If the frame's source and destination network segments are the same, the frame is filtered; if the segments differ, the frame is forwarded by the bridge to the appropriate segment.

A LAN switch is a network device that cross-connects stations or LAN segments. Network switches replace shared media hubs, increasing network bandwidth. Each port on the switch can give full bandwidth to a single server or client station or each can be connected to a hub with several stations. The switch also forwards a frame out all ports if the destination MAC address is unknown.

Routers are basically computers with two or more NICs supporting one or more network protocols, such as the Internet Protocol (IP). A switch receives frames and makes filtering and forwarding decisions based on the hardware MAC address, whereas the router opens these frames and examines the packets contained therein. The router looks at the destination network address in these packets and makes a forwarding decision based on this address. If the router does not know how to reach the destination network, the packet is dropped. The router then forwards the packet to the appropriate LAN or WAN network segment.

Chapter Review Questions

1. What is a MAC address?

2. What are the components of a MAC address?

3. How is a MAC address represented?

4. How does Ethernet operate?

5. What is a collision, and what happens when a collision occurs on an Ethernet network segment?

6. Describe a repeater and how it operates.

7. Describe a hub and how it operates.

8. Describe a bridge and how it operates.

9. Describe a switch and how it operates.

10. Describe a router and how it operates.

11. What is a backoff algorithm?

12. What Ethernet technologies operate in half-duplex mode? Full-duplex mode?

13. Given the MAC address 00-aa-00-62-c6-09, identify the OUI and vendor-assigned serial number.

14. How does a bridge determine whether a frame is forwarded or filtered?

15. What is the difference between cut-through and store-and-forward switching?

16. In what LAN environment are routers most commonly used?

What You Will Learn

On completing this chapter, you will be able to:

- ✔ Differentiate among unicast, multicast, and broadcast transmission methods

- ✔ Describe store-and-forward, cut-through, and fragment-free switching mechanisms

- ✔ Describe Layer 2 and Layer 3 switching operation

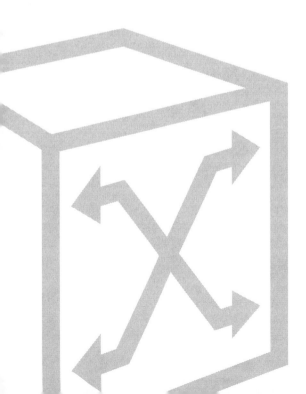

CHAPTER 6

How a Switch Works

Up to this point, frames going in and out of the LAN switch have been discussed, but not what those frames are doing while in the switch and what the switch is doing with the frames. As you might have surmised by now, this chapter discusses these very points, and a few more. To understand how a switch processes the frames that it receives and forwards, you will first learn about the three types of transmission methods found in a local-area network (LAN): unicast, multicast, and broadcast.

Frames Revisited

Recall from Chapter 1, "Networking Basics," that frames carry data across the network and are made up of three parts: the header, the data itself (payload), and the trailer, as illustrated in the Figure 6-1.

Figure 6-1   Complete Frame (Header, Data [Payload], Trailer)

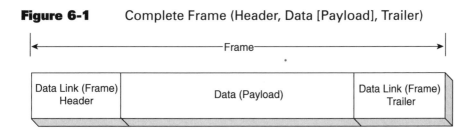

These three frame components—the header, data, and trailer—combine in making up a complete frame. The header identifies the destination data-link address of the

frame, the payload is data from upper-layer protocols (such as packets from the network layer), and the trailer signifies the end of the frame.

Recall from Chapter 5, "Ethernet LANs," that the MAC address (Media Access Control address or physical address) is the unique serial number burned into network adapters that differentiates that network card from all others on the network. To be a part of any network, you must have an address so that others can reach you. There are two types of addresses found in a network: the logical network address and the physical data-link address. In LAN bridging and switching environments, you are concerned with the physical address (MAC address), and the MAC address is found in the frame header.

A MAC address is the physical address of the device and is 48 bits (6 bytes) long. It is made up of two parts: the organizational unique identifier (OUI) and the vendor-assigned address, as illustrated in Figure 6-2.

Figure 6-2   MAC Address

```
              |◄─────── MAC Address ───────►|
              |          (48 Bits)          |

        ┌───────────────┬───────────────┐
        │      OUI      │ Vendor Assigned │
        │   (24 Bits)   │   (24 Bits)    │
        └───────────────┴───────────────┘
```

Recall that the MAC address on a computer might look like this: 00-06-0f-08-b4-12. This MAC address is used for the Fast Ethernet adapter on the computer in question—the OUI is 00-06-0f, and the vendor-assigned number is 08-b4-12.

Transmission Methods

LAN data transmissions at Layer 2 fall into three classifications: unicast, multicast, and broadcast. In each type of transmission, a single frame is sent to one node on the network. If the frame is to be sent to more than one node on the network, the sender must send individual unicast data streams to each node.

In a *unicast* transmission, a single frame or packet is sent from a single source to a single destination on a network. In a *multicast* transmission environment, a single data frame or a single source to multiple destinations packet is copied and sent to a specific subset of nodes on the network. In a *broadcast* transmission environment from a single source to all nodes, a single data frame or packet is copied and sent to all nodes on the network.

Unicast

Unicast is a one-to-one transmission method in which the network carries a message to one receiver, such as from a server to a LAN workstation. In a unicast environment, even though multiple users might ask for the same information from the same server at the same time, such as a video clip, duplicate data streams are sent. One stream is sent to each user, as illustrated in the Figure 6-3.

Figure 6-3   Unicast Operation

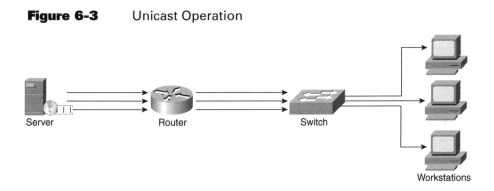

Unicast sends separate data streams to each computer requesting the data, in turn flooding the network with traffic. Unicast might be compared to an after-work gathering. You and several of your co-workers might be going to the same destination, but each taking his own vehicle, flooding the streets with cars. (So the next time you go to an after-work gathering, and each person drives his own car, tell them you're "unicasting.")

Multicast

Multicast is a one-to-many transmission method in which the network carries a message to multiple receivers at the same time. Multicast is similar to broadcasting, except that multicasting means sending to a specific group, whereas broadcasting implies sending to everybody, whether they want the traffic or not. When sending large amounts of data, multicast saves considerable network bandwidth because the bulk of the data is sent only once. The data travels from its source through major backbones and is then multiplied, or distributed out, at switching points closer to the end users (see Figure 6-4). This is more efficient than a unicast system, in which the data is copied and forwarded to each recipient.

Figure 6-4   Multicast Operation

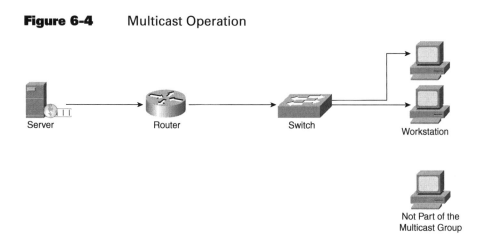

Multicast conserves network bandwidth by sending a single data stream across the network, much as you and others might carpool to and from work, thereby reducing the traffic on the roads. For example, a few of you might ride together to some point, such as a drop-off point in the city, and then disperse from there. Multicasting works in the same way by using the concept of shared transmission across a network. Multicasting sends the data to a predetermined endpoint, such as a switch, where the traffic is sent to each intended recipient, instead of each traffic stream being sent from start to finish across the network, independent of others.

Broadcast

Broadcast is a one-to-all transmission method in which the network carries a message to all devices at the same time, as illustrated in Figure 6-5.

Figure 6-5   Broadcast Operation

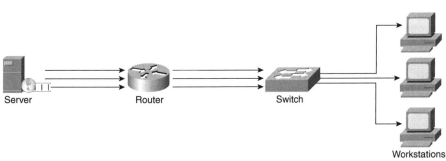

Broadcast message traffic is sent out to every node on the network where the broadcast is not filtered or blocked by a router. Broadcasts are issued by the *Address Resolution Protocol (ARP)* for address resolution when the location of a user or server is not known. For example, the location could be unknown when a network client or server first joins the network and identifies itself. Sometimes broadcasts are a result of network devices continually announcing their presence in the network, so that other devices don't forget who is still a part of the network. Regardless of the reason for a broadcast, the broadcast must reach all possible stations that might potentially respond.

Frame Size

Frame size is measured in bytes and has a minimum and maximum length, depending on the implemented technology. For example, the minimum frame size for an Ethernet LAN is 64 bytes with a 4-byte *cyclic redundancy check (CRC)*, and the maximum frame size is 1518 bytes. The minimum/maximum for a Token Ring LAN is 32 bytes/16 kilobytes (KB), respectively.

Why is it important to know the minimum and maximum frame sizes your network can support? Knowing the sizes enables you to ensure that your users' message traffic gets to where it needs to go quickly and accurately.

Suppose your corporate mailroom is equipped only to handle letter- and business-sized envelopes and is not equipped to handle postcards or larger legal-sized envelopes. The letter-sized envelope is the minimum size, and the business-sized envelope is the maximum sized "frame" allowed by your mailroom. Anything smaller than the letter-sized envelope, such as a postcard, might be considered a *runt*, and anything larger than the business-sized envelope might be considered a *giant*.

Figure 6-6 illustrates the concept of a minimum and maximum frame size, and the result, in a corporate mailroom. (Let's hope this doesn't really happen, although it might explain a few missing pieces of mail.)

Figure 6-6   Mailroom in Action

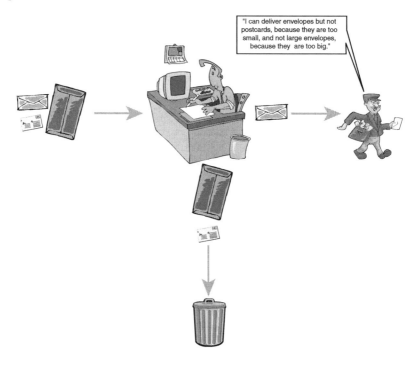

In this mailroom (switch) scenario, both the postcards (runts) and legal-sized envelopes (giants) would not be accepted by the mailroom (the switch) and therefore would be dropped into the trash.

note
The maximum frame size is also known as the maximum transmission unit, or MTU. When a frame is larger than the MTU, it is broken down, or fragmented, into smaller pieces by the Layer 3 protocol to accommodate the MTU of the network.

Layer 2 Switching Methods

LAN switches are characterized by the forwarding method that they support, such as a store-and-forward switch, cut-through switch, or fragment-free switch. In the store-and-forward switching method, error checking is performed against the frame, and any frame with errors is discarded. With the cut-through switching method, no error checking is performed against the frame, which makes forwarding the frame through the switch faster than store-and-forward switches.

Store-and-Forward Switching

Store-and-forward switching means that the LAN switch copies each complete frame into the switch memory buffers and computes a cyclic redundancy check (CRC) for errors. CRC is an error-checking method that uses a mathematical formula, based on the number of bits (1s) in the frame, to determine whether the received frame is errored. If a CRC error is found, the frame is discarded. If the frame is error free, the switch forwards the frame out the appropriate interface port, as illustrated in Figure 6-7.

Figure 6-7   Store-and-Forward Switch Discarding a Frame with a Bad CRC

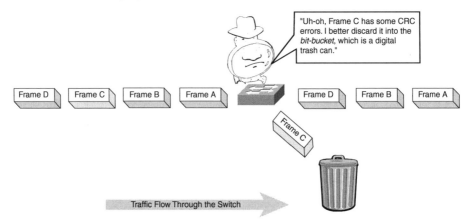

An Ethernet frame is discarded if it is smaller than 64 bytes in length, a runt, or if the frame is larger than 1518 bytes in length, a giant, as illustrated in Figure 6-8.

 note
Some switches can be configured to carry giant, or jumbo, frames.

If the frame does not contain any errors, and is not a runt or a giant, the LAN switch looks up the destination address in its forwarding, or switching, table and determines the outgoing interface. It then forwards the frame toward its intended destination.

Store-and-Forward Switching Operation

Store-and-forward switches store the entire frame in internal memory and check the frame for errors before forwarding the frame to its destination. Store-and-forward switch operation ensures a high level of error-free network traffic, because bad data frames are discarded rather than forwarded across the network, as illustrated in Figure 6-9.

Figure 6-8   Runts and Giants in the Switch

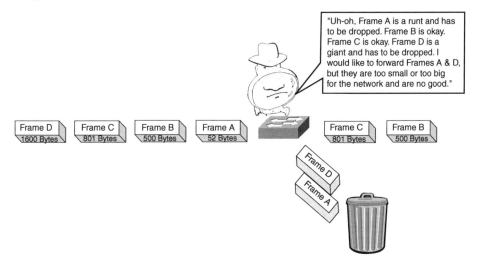

Figure 6-9   Store-and-Forward Switch Examining Each Frame for Errors Before Forwarding to Destination Network Segment

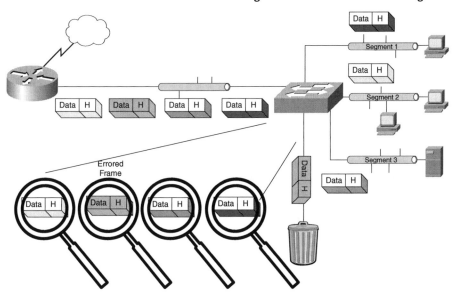

The store-and-forward switch shown in Figure 6-9 inspects each received frame for errors before forwarding it on to the frame's destination network segment. If a frame fails this inspection, the switch drops the frame from its buffers, and the frame is thrown in to the proverbial bit bucket.

A drawback to the store-and-forward switching method is one of performance, because the switch has to store the entire data frame before checking for errors and forwarding. This error checking results in high switch latency (delay). If multiple switches are connected, with the data being checked at each switch point, total network performance can suffer as a result. Another drawback to store-and-forward switching is that the switch requires more memory and processor (central processing unit, CPU) cycles to perform the detailed inspection of each frame than that of cut-through or fragment-free switching.

Cut-Through Switching

With cut-through switching, the LAN switch copies into its memory only the destination MAC address, which is located in the first 6 bytes of the frame following the preamble. The switch looks up the destination MAC address in its switching table, determines the outgoing interface port, and forwards the frame on to its destination through the designated switch port. A cut-through switch reduces delay because the switch begins to forward the frame as soon as it reads the destination MAC address and determines the outgoing switch port, as illustrated in Figure 6-10.

The cut-through switch shown in Figure 6-10 inspects each received frame's header to determine the destination before forwarding on to the frame's destination network segment. Frames with and without errors are forwarded in cut-through switching operations, leaving the error detection of the frame to the intended recipient. If the receiving switch determines the frame is errored, the frame is thrown out to the bit bucket where the frame is subsequently discarded from the network.

Figure 6-10 Cut-Through Switch Examining Each Frame Header Before Forwarding to Destination Network Segment

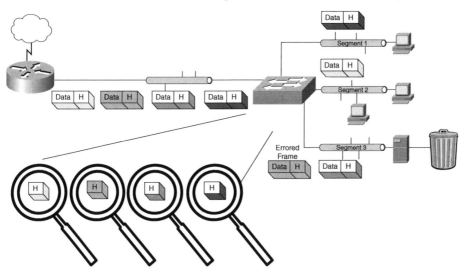

Cut-through switching was developed to reduce the delay in the switch processing frames as they arrive at the switch and are forwarded on to the destination switch port. The switch pulls the frame header into its port buffer. When the destination MAC address is determined by the switch, the switch forwards the frame out the correct interface port to the frame's intended destination.

Cut-through switching reduces *latency* inside the switch. If the frame was corrupted in transit, however, the switch still forwards the bad frame. The destination receives this bad frame, checks the frame's CRC, and discards it, forcing the source to resend the frame. This process wastes bandwidth and, if it occurs too often, network users experience a significant slowdown on the network. In contrast, store-and-forward switching prevents errored frames from being forwarded across the network and provides for *quality of service (QoS)* managing network traffic flow.

note

Today's switches don't suffer the *network latency* that older (legacy) switches labored under. This minimizes the effect switch latency has on your traffic. Today's switches are better suited for a store-and-forward environment.

Cut-Through Switching Operation

Cut-through switches do not perform any error checking of the frame because the switch looks only for the frame's destination MAC address and forwards the frame out the appropriate switch port. Cut-through switching results in low switch latency. The drawback, however, is that bad data frames, as well as good frames, are sent to their destinations. At first blush, this might not sound bad because most network cards do their own frame checking by default to ensure good data is received. You might find that if your network is broken down into workgroups, the likelihood of bad frames or collisions might be minimized, in turn making cut-through switching a good choice for your network.

Fragment-Free Switching

Fragment-free switching is also known as *runtless switching* and is a hybrid of cut-through and store-and-forward switching. Fragment-free switching was developed to solve the late-collision problem.

note

Recall that when two systems' transmissions occur at the same time, the result is a collision. Collisions are a part of Ethernet communications and do not imply any error condition. A late collision is similar to an Ethernet collision, except that it occurs after all hosts on the network should have been able to notice that a host was already transmitting.

A late collision indicates that another system attempted to transmit after a host has transmitted at least the first 60 bytes of its frame. Late collisions are often caused by an Ethernet LAN being too large and therefore needing to be segmented. Late collisions can also be caused by faulty network devices on the segment and duplex (for example, half-duplex/full-duplex) mismatches between connected devices.

Fragment-Free Switching Operation

Fragment-free switching works like cut-through switching with the exception that a switch in fragment-free mode stores the first 64 bytes of the frame before forwarding. Fragment-free switching can be viewed as a compromise between store-and-forward switching and cut-through switching. The reason fragment-free switching stores only the first 64 bytes of the frame is that most network errors and collisions occur during the first 64 bytes of a frame.

note

Different methods work better at different points in the network. For example, cut-through switching is best for the network core where errors are fewer, and speed is of utmost importance. Store-and-forward is best at the network access layer where most network problems and users are located.

Layer 3 Switching

Layer 3 switching is another example of fragment-free switching. Up to now, this discussion has concentrated on switching and bridging at the data link layer (Layer 2) of the Open System Interconnection (OSI) model. When bridge technology was first developed, it was not practical to build wire-speed bridges with large numbers of high-speed ports because of the manufacturing cost involved. With improved technology, many functions previously implemented in software were moved into the hardware, increasing performance and enabling manufacturers to build reasonably priced *wire-speed* switches.

Whereas bridges and switches work at the data link layer (OSI Layer 2), routers work at the network layer (OSI Layer 3). Routers provide functionality beyond that offered by bridges or switches. As a result, however, routers entail greater complexity. Like early bridges, routers were often implemented in software, running on a special-purpose processing platform, such as a personal computer (PC) with two network interface cards (NICs) and software to route data between each NIC, as illustrated in Figure 6-11.

Figure 6-11 PC Routing with Two NICs

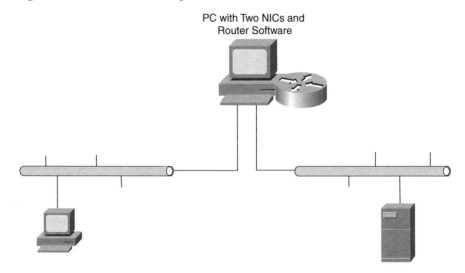

The early days of routing involved a computer and two NIC cards, not unlike two people having a conversation, but having to go through a third person to do so. The workstation would send its traffic across the wire, and the routing computer would receive it on one NIC, determine that the traffic would have to be sent out the other NIC, and then resend the traffic out this other NIC.

note

In the same way that a Layer 2 switch is another name for a bridge, a Layer 3 switch is another name for a router. This is not to say that a Layer 3 switch and a router operate the same way. Layer 3 switches make decisions based on the port-level Internet Protocol (IP) addresses, whereas routers make decisions based on a map of the Layer 3 network (maintained in a routing table).

Multilayer switching is a switching technique that switches at both the data link (OSI Layer 2) and network (OSI Layer 3) layers. To enable multilayer switching, LAN switches must use store-and-forward techniques because the switch must receive the entire frame before it performs any protocol layer operations, as illustrated in Figure 6-12.

Figure 6-12 Layer 3 (Multilayer) Switch Examining Each Frame for Error Before Determining the Destination Network Segment (Based on the Network Address)

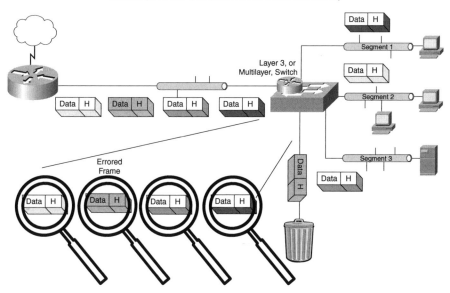

Similar to a store-and-forward switch, with multilayer switching the switch pulls the entire received frame into its memory and calculates its CRC. It then determines whether the frame is good or bad. If the CRC calculated on the packet matches the CRC calculated by the switch, the destination address is read and the frame is forwarded out the correct switch port. If the CRC does not match the frame, the frame is discarded. Because this type of switching waits for the entire frame to be received before forwarding, port latency times can become high, which can result in some latency, or delay, of network traffic.

Layer 3 Switching Operation

You might be asking yourself, "What's the difference between a Layer 3 switch and a router?" The fundamental difference between a Layer 3 switch and a router is that Layer 3 switches have optimized hardware passing data traffic as fast as Layer 2 switches. However, Layer 3 switches make decisions regarding how to transmit traffic at Layer 3, just as a router does.

note

Within the LAN environment, a Layer 3 switch is usually faster than a router because it is built on switching hardware. Bear in mind that the Layer 3 switch is not as versatile as a router, so do not discount the use of a router in your LAN without first examining your LAN requirements, such as the use of *network address translation (NAT)*.

Before going forward with this discussion, recall the following points:

- A switch is a Layer 2 (data link) device with physical ports and that the switch communicates via frames that are placed on to the wire at Layer 1 (physical).

- A router is a Layer 3 (network) device that communicates with other routers with the use of packets, which in turn are encapsulated inside frames.

Routers have interfaces for connection into the network medium. For a router to route data over the Ethernet, for instance, the router requires an Ethernet interface, as illustrated in Figure 6-13.

A serial interface is required for the router connecting to a wide-area network (WAN), and a Token Ring interface is required for the router connecting to a Token Ring network.

A simple network made up of two network segments and an internetworking device (in this case, a router) is shown in Figure 6-14.

Figure 6-13   Router Interfaces

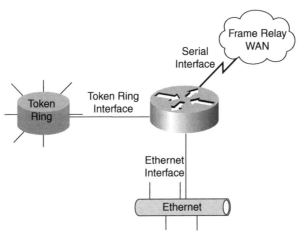

The router in Figure 6-14 has two Ethernet interfaces, labeled E0 and E1. The primary function of the router is determining the best network path in a complex network. A router has three ways to learn about networks and make the determination regarding the best path: through locally connected ports, static route entries, and dynamic routing protocols. The router uses this learned information to make a determination by using routing protocols. Some of the more common routing protocols used include Routing Information Protocol (RIP), Open Shortest Path First (OSPF), Interior Gateway Routing Protocol (IGRP), and Border Gateway Protocol (BGP).

Figure 6-14   Two-Segment Network with a Layer 3 Router

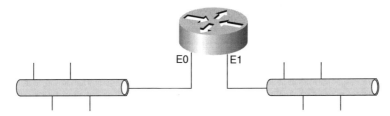

note

Routing protocols are used by routers to share information about the network. Routers receive and use the routing protocol information from other routers to learn about the state of the network. Routers can modify information received from one router by adding their own information along with the original information, and then forward that on to other routers. In this way, each router can share its version of the network.

Packet Switching

Layer 3 information is carried through the network in packets, and the transport method of carrying these packets is called packet switching, as illustrated in Figure 6-15.

Figure 6-15 Packet Switching Between Ethernet and Token Ring Network Segments

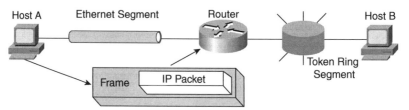

Figure 6-15 shows how a packet is delivered across multiple networks. Host A is on an Ethernet segment, and Host B on a Token Ring segment. Host A places an Ethernet frame, encapsulating an *Internet Protocol (IP)* packet, on to the wire for transmission across the network.

The Ethernet frame contains a source data link layer MAC address and a destination data link layer MAC address. The IP packet within the frame contains a source network layer *IP address* (TCP/IP network layer address) and a destination network layer IP address. The router maintains a routing table of network paths it has learned, and the router examines the network layer destination IP address of the packet. When the router has determined the destination network from the destination IP address, the router examines the routing table and determines whether a path exists to that network.

In the case illustrated in Figure 6-15, Host B is on a Token Ring network segment directly connected to the router. The router peels off the Layer 2 Ethernet encapsulation, forwards the Layer 3 data packet, and then re-encapsulates the packet inside a new Token Ring frame. The router sends this frame out its Token Ring interface on to the segment where Host B will see a Token Ring frame containing its MAC address and process it.

Note the original frame was Ethernet, and the final frame is Token Ring encapsulating an IP packet. This is called media transition and is one of the features of a network router. When the packet arrives on one interface and is forwarded to another, it is called Layer 3 switching or routing.

Routing Table Lookup

Routers (and Layer 3 switches) perform table lookups determining the next hop (next router or Layer 3 switch) along the route, which in turn determines the output port over which to forward the packet or frame. The router or Layer 3 switch makes this decision based on the network portion of the destination address in the received packet.

This lookup results in one of three actions:

- **The destination network is not reachable**—There is no path to the destination network and no default network. In this case, the packet is discarded.

- **The destination network is reachable by forwarding the packet to another router**—There is a match of the destination network against a known table entry, or to a default route if a method for reaching the destination network is unknown. The first lookup tells the next hop. Then a second lookup is performed to determine how to get to the next hop. Then a final determination of the exit port is reached. The first lookup can return multiple paths, so the port is not known until after the determination of how to get there is made. In either case, the lookup returns the network (Layer 3) address of the next-hop router, and the port through which that router can be reached.

■ **The destination network is known to be directly attached to the
router**—The port is directly attached to the network and reachable. For
directly attached networks, the next step maps the host portion of the destination network address to the data link (MAC) address for the next hop or
end node using the ARP table (for IP). It does not map the destination network address to the router interface. It needs to use the MAC of the final end
node so that the node picks up the frame from the medium. Also, you are
assuming IP when stating that the router uses the *ARP table*. Other Layer 3
protocols, such as Internetwork Packet Exchange (IPX), do not use ARP to
map their addresses to MAC addresses.

Routing table lookup in an IP router might be considered more complex than a
MAC address lookup for a bridge, because at the data link layer addresses are 48-
bits in length, with fixed-length fields—the OUI and ID. Additionally, data-link
address space is flat, meaning there is no hierarchy or dividing of addresses into
smaller and distinct segments. MAC address lookup in a bridge entails searching
for an exact match on a fixed-length field, whereas address lookup in a router
looks for variable-length fields identifying the destination network.

IP addresses are 32 bits in length and are made up of two fields: the network identifier and the host identifier, as illustrated in Figure 6-16.

Both the network and host portions of the IP address can be of a variable or fixed
length, depending on the hierarchical network address scheme used. Discussion of
this hierarchical, or subnetting, scheme is beyond the scope of this book, but suffice to say you are concerned with the fact that each IP address has a network and
host identifier.

The routing table lookup in an IP router determines the next hop by examining the
network portion of the IP address. After it determines the best match for the next
hop, the router looks up the interface port to forward the packets across, as illustrated in Figure 6-17.

Figure 6-16   IP Address Space

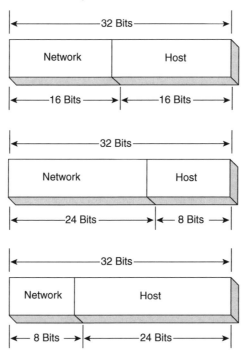

Figure 6-17 shows that the router receives the traffic from Serial Port 1 (S1) and performs a routing table lookup determining from which port to forward out the traffic. Traffic destined for Network 1 is forwarded out the Ethernet 0 (E0) port. Traffic destined for Network 2 is forwarded out the Token Ring 0 (T0) port, and traffic destined for Network 3 is forwarded out Serial Port 0 (S0).

note

In terms of the Cisco Internet Operating System (IOS) interface, port numbers begin with zero (0), such as serial port 0 (S0). Not all vendors, including Cisco, use ports; some use slots or modules, which might begin with zero or one.

Figure 6-17   Routing Table Lookup Operation

Net: 1	Net: 1	Net: 3	Net: 2

Data Flow

Routing Table

Destination Network	Port
1	E0
1	E0
3	S0
2	T0

The host identifier portion of the network address is examined only if the network lookup indicates that the destination is on a locally attached network. Unlike data-link addresses, the dividing line between the network identifier and the host identifier is not in a fixed position throughout the network. Routing table entries can exist for network identifiers of various lengths, from 0 bits in length, specifying a default route, to 32 bits in length for host-specific routes. According to IP routing procedures, the lookup result returned should be the one corresponding to the entry that matches the maximum number of bits in the network identifier. Therefore, unlike a bridge, where the lookup is for an exact match against a fixed-length field, IP routing lookups imply a search for the longest match against a variable-length field.

For example, a network host might have both the IP address of 68.98.134.209 and a MAC address of 00-0c-41-53-40-d3. The router makes decisions based on the IP address (68.98.134.209), whereas the switch makes decisions based on the MAC address (00-0c-41-53-40-d3). Both addresses identify the same host on the network, but are used by different network devices when forwarding traffic to this host.

ARP Mapping

Address Resolution Protocol (ARP) is a network layer protocol used in IP to convert IP addresses into MAC addresses. A network device looking to learn a MAC address broadcasts an ARP request onto the network. The host on the network that has the IP address in the request replies with its MAC (hardware) address. This is called ARP mapping, the mapping of a Layer 3 (network) address to a Layer 2 (data link) address.

note

Some Layer 3 addresses use the MAC address as part of their addressing scheme, such as IPX.

Because the network layer address structure in IP does not provide for a simple mapping to data-link addresses, IP addresses use 32 bits, and data-link addresses use 48 bits. It is not possible to determine the 48-bit data-link address for a host from the host portion of the IP address. For packets destined for a host not on a locally attached network, the router performs a lookup for the next-hop router's MAC address. For packets destined for hosts on a locally attached network, the router performs a second lookup operation to find the destination address to use in the data-link header of the forwarded packet's frame, as illustrated in Figure 6-18.

After determining for which directly attached network the packet is destined, the router looks up the destination MAC address in its ARP cache. Recall that ARP enables the router to determine the corresponding MAC address when it knows the network (IP) address. The router then forwards the packet across the local network in a frame with the MAC address of the local host, or next-hop router.

Figure 6-18   Router ARP Cache Lookup

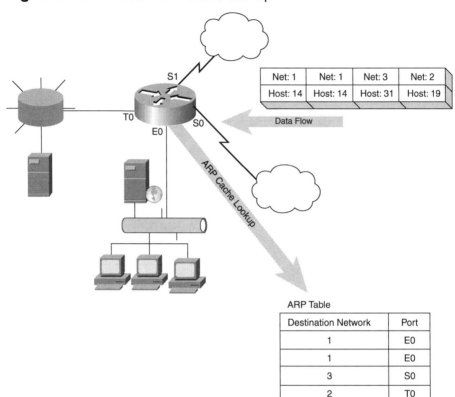

ARP Table

Destination Network	Port
1	E0
1	E0
3	S0
2	T0

note

Note in Figure 6-18 that Net 3, Host: 31 is not part of the ARP cache, because during the routing table lookup, the router determined that this packet is to be forwarded to another, remote (nonlocally attached) network.

The result of this final lookup falls into one of the three following categories:

■ **The packet is destined for the router itself**—The IP destination address (network and station portion combined) corresponds to one of the IP addresses of the router. In this case, the packet must be passed to the appropriate higher-layer entity within the router and not forwarded to any external port.

- **The packet is destined for a known host on the directly attached network**—This is the most common situation encountered by a network router. The router determines the mapping from the ARP table and forwards the packet out the appropriate interface port to the local network.

- **The ARP mapping for the specified host is unknown**—The router initiates a discovery procedure by sending an ARP request determining the mapping of network to hardware address. Because this discovery procedure takes time, albeit measured in milliseconds, the router might drop the packet that resulted in the discovery procedure in the first place. Under *steady-state* conditions, the router already has ARP mappings available for all communicating hosts. The address discovery procedure is necessary when a previously unheard-from host establishes a new communication session.

note

The current version of Cisco IOS (12.0) Software drops the first packet for a destination without an ARP entry. The IOS does this to handle denial of service (DoS) attacks against incomplete ARPs. In other words, it drops the frame immediately instead of awaiting a reply.

Fragmentation

Each output port on a network device has an associated maximum transmission unit (MTU). Recall from earlier in this chapter that the MTU indicates the largest frame size (measured in bytes) that can be carried on the interface. The MTU is often a function of the networking technology in use, such as Ethernet, Token Ring, or Point-to-Point Protocol (PPP). PPP is used with Internet connections. If the frame being forwarded is larger than the available space, as indicated by the MTU, the frame is fragmented into smaller pieces for transmission on the particular network.

Bridges cannot fragment frames when forwarding between LANs of differing MTU sizes because data-link connections rarely have a mechanism for fragment reassembly at the receiver. The mechanism is at the network layer implementation, such as with IP, which is capable of overcoming this limitation. Network

layer packets can be broken down into smaller pieces if necessary so that these packets can travel across a link with a smaller MTU.

Fragmentation is similar to taking a picture and cutting it into pieces so that each piece will fit into differently sized envelopes for mailing. It is up to the sender to determine the size of the largest piece that can be sent, and it is up to the receiver to reassemble these pieces. Fragmentation is a mixed blessing; although it provides the means of communication across different link technologies, the processing accomplishing the fragmentation is significant and could be a burden on each device having to fragment and reassemble the data. Further, pieces for reassembly can be received out of order and may be dropped by the switch or router.

As a rule, it is best to avoid fragmentation in your network if at all possible. It is more efficient for the sending station to send packets not requiring fragmentation anywhere along the path to the destination, instead of sending large packets requiring intermediate routers to perform fragmentation.

note

Hosts and routers can learn the maximum MTU available along a network path through the use of MTU discovery. MTU discovery is a process by which each device in a network path learns the MTU size that the network path can support.

Chapter Summary

One of three transmission methods is used to move frames from source to destination: unicast, multicast, or broadcast. Unicast transmission occurs when there is a direct path from source to destination, a "one-to-one" relationship. Multicast has a one-to-many relationship in which the frame is delivered to multiple destinations that are identified as part of a multicast group. Broadcast is a one-to-all relationship in which the frame is delivered to all the hosts on the network segment, whether or not they want the traffic.

Frame size is measured in bytes and has a minimum and maximum length, depending on the implemented technology, such as Ethernet, Token Ring, or with WAN technologies (such as Frame Relay or IP VPN). The maximum frame length supported by a technology is called the maximum transmission unit, or MTU, and is measured in bytes. A frame received by the switch that is less than the minimum frame length for that technology is called a runt, and a frame greater than the maximum frame length is called a giant. Giant frames must be fragmented into smaller frames, smaller than the acceptable MTU, before these frames can be forwarded across the switch's or router's network interface.

There are two common categories of switches: store-and-forward switches and cut-through switches. Store-and-forward switching accepts the complete frame into the switch buffers for error checking before forwarding on to the network. Cut-through switching reads just the destination MAC address (the first 6 bytes of the frame following the preamble) to determine the switch port to forward the traffic. Store-and-forward switching adds some delay to the time it takes for the frame to get from source to destination; unlike cut-through switching, however, store-and-forward switching does not forward a frame with errors. The delay added by store-and-forward switching is minimal and should not be a determining factor when deciding between using cut-through and store-and-forward switching. Store-and-forward has an advantage over cut-through switching by virtue of its error-handling mechanisms.

A third switching category is fragment-free switching, which accepts the first 64 bytes of the frame and checks for errors. Fragment-free switching works on the precept that if there are any errors on the line, they are detectable within the first 64 bytes of the frame.

The fundamental difference between Layer 2 and Layer 3 switch operation is the layer at which each forwarding decision is made. Layer 2 switches make their forwarding decisions based on tables that store the mapping between MAC addresses and switch ports. Layer 3 switches build a table of network addresses and switch

ports, making the forwarding decisions based on the network address information found in Layer 3, rather than just the MAC address found in Layer 2. Layer 3 switches function like routers because of the similar Layer 3 forwarding decision handling. However, Layer 3 switches tend to have better throughput because of the hardware processing of the address tables rather than the software.

Chapter Review Questions

1. What is unicast and how does it work?

2. What is multicast and how does it work?

3. What is broadcast and how does it work?

4. What is fragmentation?

5. What is MTU? What's the MTU for traditional Ethernet?

6. What is a MAC address?

7. What is the difference between a runt and a giant, specific to traditional Ethernet?

8. What is the difference between store-and-forward and cut-through switching?

9. What is the difference between Layer 2 switching and Layer 3 switching?

10. What is the difference between Layer 3 switching and routing?

What You Will Learn

On completing this chapter, you will be able to:

✔ Describe the function of the Spanning Tree Protocol (STP)

✔ List the five states of the STP

✔ Draw a spanning-tree topology

✔ Describe root bridges, root ports, and designated ports

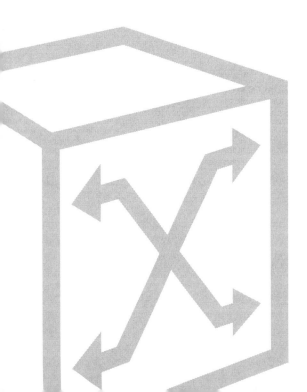

CHAPTER 7

Spanning Tree Protocol (STP)

Recall that in the networking world, a protocol is a standard set of rules and formats for data transmission between computers, similar to the rules of grammar in the English language. If two people put commas and periods in different places and use them for different purposes, for example, communication between the two would be difficult, if not impossible. In this same way, communication is impossible if two computers use different protocols when trying to communicate with one another. This chapter explains the protocol, or grammar, of communication between switches—specifically the Spanning Tree Protocol (STP).

The *Spanning Tree Protocol*, or *STP*, is a link-management protocol that is part of the Institute of Electrical and Electronics Engineers (IEEE) 802.1 standard for bridges and switches. STP uses the spanning-tree algorithm and provides path redundancy in the network. STP also prevents network loops created by multiple active paths between stations.

 note
A bridge loop occurs when two or more paths exist between network segments.

The spanning-tree algorithm is used in bridge- and switch-based networks and determines the best path for traffic to move across the network from source to destination. The algorithm creates a hierarchical tree spanning the entire network, including all bridges and switches. The spanning-tree algorithm determines all redundant paths and makes only one of them active at any given time, much as you might consider alternative routes from your home to your office before taking one.

Figure 7-1   Multiple Routes Between Home and Work

If you tried one morning using more than one route from your home to work, you could end up going around in circles and never getting to work. In a network, loops create broadcast storms and constant table changes, which cause damage to your network because your data will time out before it ever reaches its intended destination.

Loops occur when more than one route, or path, exists between nodes in a network. Establishing path redundancy, STP creates a tree spanning across all the switches in an extended network and forces redundant paths into a standby, or blocked, state. STP allows only one active path at a time between any two network devices, preventing loops, but establishes redundant links as a backup if the primary link fails. If a network segment becomes unreachable for whatever reason, the spanning-tree algorithm reconfigures the logical topology, reestablishing the link by activating the standby path. Without a spanning tree in place, it is possible that both connections might be considered the primary path, resulting in an endless loop of traffic on the local-area network (LAN).

Root Bridge or Switch Port

STP has a root and branches like a tree. The primary decision-making switch in an STP environment is called the root bridge. The network flows out from the root bridge to form a logical branched network. All switches in a LAN participating in STP branch from the root switch port or bridge. In Figure 7-2, Bridge 1 is the root bridge, and all connected segments branch from this root.

Figure 7-2   Five-Bridge Network with Root Bridge (Bridge 1)

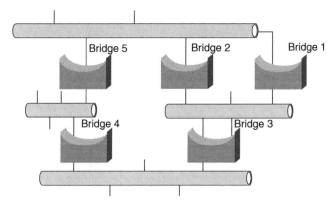

The first task of the STP is determining where the spanning tree begins—the root bridge or switch port. The root bridge is used to build a reference point in the network so that the spanning-tree algorithm can be calculated. All paths from all bridges and switches must be traceable back to the root bridge or root switch, much as all roads lead to or from your hometown, regardless of how many other towns you travel through to reach your destination, as illustrated in the Figure 7-3.

Figure 7-3   Multiple Routes Between the Source and Destination

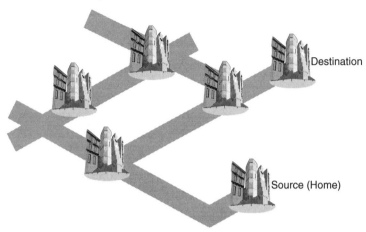

The root switch is elected as part of the STP and is necessary to build a reference point for the spanning-tree algorithm calculations. All paths not needed to reach the root switch network are placed in backup mode. Each switch in the network gathers information about other switches in the same network through an exchange of data messages called bridge protocol data units, or BPDUs.

Bridge Protocol Data Units (BPDUs)

Bridge protocol data units, or BPDUs, are data messages exchanged between the switches and bridges within an extended LAN using the STP. BPDU frames contain information regarding the originating switch port, Media Access Control (MAC) address, switch port priority, and the switch port cost. The cost of a switch port is based on the number of network segments the frame crosses before reaching its destination.

BPDU messages are also exchanged across bridges and switches to detect loops in the network topology. Any loops found are removed by shutting down the selected bridge and switch interfaces and placing the redundant switch ports in a backup, or blocked, state.

The topology of a switched LAN is determined by the following:

- **The unique switch identifier or bridge ID associated with each switch—** The bridge ID is made up of the MAC address and the bridge priority. As your home telephone number is unique so that you can be reached by anyone looking for you, so must the identifier of each switch be unique so that it can be found in the network.

note
The MAC address is the 48-byte hardware address of the network interface.

- **The port cost associated with each switch port—**The port cost is for communication between the switch port and the root port. This is true whether it is a financial cost, as in your long-distance telephone calls, or a logical cost, as in how fast (maximum bandwidth) each network segment is that the frame must cross on its way from source to destination.

One BPDU is superior to another if it has a lower

- Root bridge ID

- Path cost to the root

- Sending bridge ID

- Sending port ID

Each switch originates, but does not forward, configuration BPDUs that are used to compute the spanning-tree topology. The BPDU frame is sent across the LAN, and all connected bridges and switches receive this BPDU. The receiving switch uses the information in the BPDU to determine changes in the network topology. If there is a change, the receiving switch sends a new BPDU across all attached network segments.

BPDUs contain information about the sending switch and its ports, including the following:

- **Switch and port MAC address**—This is the MAC address of each switch and bridge port that is part of the tree.

- **Switch and port priority**—When switches and bridges are running the STP, each has a bridge or switch port priority associated with it. By default, all STP switches are configured with a bridge priority value of 32,768. After the exchange of BPDUs, the switch with the lowest priority value becomes the root bridge.

- **Port cost**—Cost is determined according to the speeds that the ports support; the faster the port, the lower the port cost. Switches use port costs in determining the root port for each and every switch.

The exchange of BPDUs results in the following:

- One bridge or switch port is elected as the root bridge/switch port. This election is similar to a bunch of switches going to a voting booth and choosing their favorite switch. The BPDUs are used as a voter information guide, or ballot, to select the correct candidate. The purpose of this election is to determine which switch has the lowest identifier.

- The shortest distance to the root switch is calculated for each switch. Recall that the shortest distance between two points is a straight line, and the exchange of these BPDUs determines the direction of the straight line between bridge/switch ports.

- A *designated switch* is selected. This designated switch is the closest switch to the root switch through which frames will be forwarded to the root. There is only one designated switch per segment or VLAN.

- A designated port for each switch is selected, providing the best path to the root switch. Every LAN segment needs to know which switch is its entry/exit point to the rest of the network; otherwise, frames would wander aimlessly around the same network segment, never getting anywhere.

- Ports included in the STP are selected. Because all ports might not be part of the spanning tree, the exchange of BPDUs determines which ports have an invitation to the spanning tree (forwarding) and which ports do not. (Those that don't are disabled.) If STP is not running on some ports or switches, loops can occur on those non-STP ports, which then circumvent the STP blocks.

note

All bridge/switch ports are included in the STP BPDU message. The ports not turned on are not included as part of the spanning tree.

- Loops in the switched network are removed. Loops are detriments to networks because traffic on a network containing loops goes around in circles—stuck on the proverbial hamster wheel—and can shut down the network. These network loops are prevented by each switch placing redundant switch ports in a backup state as directed by the STP.

The following figure illustrates how BPDUs enable a spanning-tree topology based on the STP. Bridge A sends out a BPDU across the network that is received by Bridge B and Switch C.

Figure 7-4　BPDU Exchange Establishing the Spanning-Tree Topology

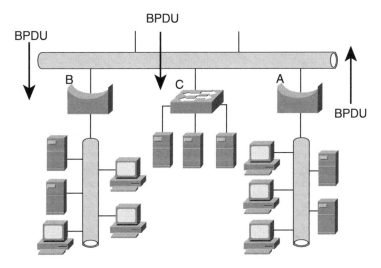

Spanning Tree Protocol Configuration

Before you can understand how a network topology is built and managed using the STP, you need to understand the five states of the spanning tree. If geography isn't your strong suit, that's okay; there are no maps involved when discussing these states.

Spanning-Tree Port States

Because of network delay caused by large LAN segments, topology changes can take place at different times and at different places in the switched network. When a switch port transitions directly from nonparticipation to an active, or forwarding, state, temporary data loops can be created. Ports must wait for new topology information to spread throughout the LAN before frames can be forwarded. Switches must also allow the frame lifetime to expire for frames that have been forwarded using the old topology.

Each port on a switch using STP is in one of the following five states:

- Blocking

- Listening

- Learning

- Forwarding

- Disabled

Each of these states is discussed in more detail in the following sections. A switch does not enter any of these states immediately, except the blocking state, which is entered on power up. Spanning-tree switch ports move through these five states in the timeframe described as follows:

- Initialization to blocking (0 seconds)

- Blocking to listening (20 seconds)

- Listening to learning (15 seconds)

■ Learning to forwarding (15 seconds)

■ Disabled

note

The network administrator can disable a switch port at any time.

Figure 7-5 illustrates a bridge or switch port moving through the five STP states.

Figure 7-5   Spanning Tree Protocol States

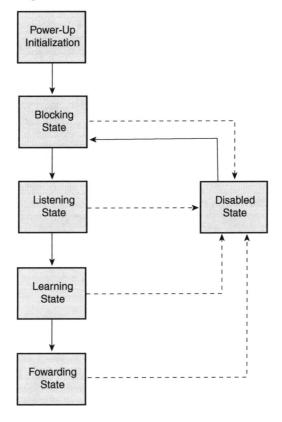

When the STP is enabled, every bridge and switch in the network starts in the blocking state and transitions to the listening and learning states. If properly configured, the ports then stabilize to the forwarding or blocking state until a change in the network is made.

When the spanning-tree algorithm determines that a port is to be in the forwarding state, the following happens:

- The port is put into the listening state while waiting for protocol information suggesting it should go to the blocking state.

- The port waits for the expiration of a protocol, or *forward delay*, timer that moves the port to the learning state.

- In the learning state, the port continues to block frame forwarding as it learns network host location information for the forwarding database.

- The expiration of a protocol (forward delay) timer moves the port to the forwarding state. Both learning and forwarding are enabled while the port is in the forwarding state.

Blocking

A port in the blocking state does not participate in frame forwarding, and after initialization, a BPDU is sent to each port in the switch. A switch assumes it is the root until it exchanges BPDUs with other switches in the network. This BPDU exchange establishes which switch in the network is the root switch. If only one switch resides in the network, no exchange occurs, and after the forward delay timer expires, the ports move to the listening state.

note
A switch always enters the blocking state following switch initialization.

A port in the blocking state

- Discards frames received from the attached network segment.

- Discards frames switched from another port for forwarding.

- Does not incorporate a host location into its address database; because there is no learning at this point, there is no address database to update.

- Receives BPDUs from the network segment and directs them to the switch system module for processing.

- Unlike ports in the listening, learning, and forwarding state, a port in the blocking state does not process BPDUs received from the switch system module.

- Receives and responds to network management messages, such as a network administrator disabling the port.

After 20 seconds, the switch port moves from the blocking state to the listening state.

Listening

The listening state is the first transitional state for a port after the blocking state. The listening state is where the STP determines that the port should participate in frame forwarding. The switch does not perform any learning or forwarding functions while in the listening state, and it therefore does not incorporate station locations into its address database as it would if the switch were in a blocking state, because there is no address table to update (while in a blocking state). In the listening state, a switch performs the following functions:

- Discards frames received from the attached network segment.

- Discards frames switched from another port for forwarding.

- Receives BPDUs from the network segment and directs them to the switch system module for processing.

- Processes BPDUs received from the switch system module.

- Receives and responds to network management messages, such as a network administrator disabling the port.

After 15 seconds, the switch port moves from the listening state to the learning state.

Learning

In the learning state, the switch port prepares to participate in the network by forwarding frames. Learning is the second transitional state through which a port moves toward the end goal: frame forwarding. It is the STP that moves the port from the listening to the learning state.

A port in the learning state

- Discards frames received from the attached network segment.

- Discards frames switched from another port for forwarding.

- Incorporates LAN host location information into its address database.

- Receives BPDUs from the network segment and directs them to the switch system module for processing.

- Receives, processes, and transmits BPDUs received from the system module.

- Receives and responds to network management messages, such as a network administrator disabling the port.

After 15 seconds, the switch port moves from the learning state to the forwarding state.

Forwarding

A port in the forwarding state forwards frames across the attached network segment. The forwarding state is the last state a port enters during the creation of the network topology.

A port in the forwarding state

- Forwards frames received from the attached network segment.

- Forwards frames switched from another port for forwarding.

- Incorporates LAN host location information into its address database.

- Receives BPDUs from the network segment and directs them to the switch system module for processing.

- Processes BPDUs received from the switch system module.

- Receives and responds to network management messages, such as a network administrator disabling the port.

A port stays in the forwarding state until a change occurs in the network topology, such as the addition of a new bridge or switch, a new bridge or switch port, or the failure of a bridge, switch, or port. When a change in the topology is detected, all switches recompute the network topology; this process is called *convergence*.

Disabled

A port in the disabled state does not participate in frame forwarding or the operation of STP because a port in the disabled state is considered nonoperational.

A disabled port

- Discards frames received from the attached network segment.

- Discards frames switched from another port for forwarding.

- Does not incorporate LAN host location information into its address database.

■ Receives BPDUs, but does not direct them to the switch system module.

■ Does not receive BPDUs for transmission from the switch system module.

■ Receives and responds to network management messages, such as notification of a network administrator enabling a port.

Spanning-Tree Operation

Just as a spanning-tree switch has a value, so do the individual ports on the switch, called the *port cost*. As discussed earlier, the port cost is determined based on the network bandwidth, or speeds that the port supports; the faster the port, the lower its cost.

Table 7-1 lists the default IEEE costs associated with common port speeds.

Table 7-1   Default Port Cost

Link Speed	Port Cost
Gigabit Ethernet	4
Fast Ethernet (100 megabits per second [Mbps])	10
Ethernet (10 Mbps)	100

A switch uses the port cost to determine the root port for each switch in the network. All nonroot bridges have one root port that is used as the link over which data traffic is forwarded across the network.

note
The root port represents a switch's lowest-cost path to the root bridge, and, by default, all ports on the root bridge are also root ports and have a cost of 0. Because root ports are directly connected to the root bridge, their cost to reach the root bridge is 0.

Figure 7-6 shows a network with three bridges. Bridge A has been made root bridge 7 because it has the lowest MAC address; because all bridge priorities are equal, the bridge with the lowest MAC address is elected the root.

Figure 7-6   Network with Three Bridges

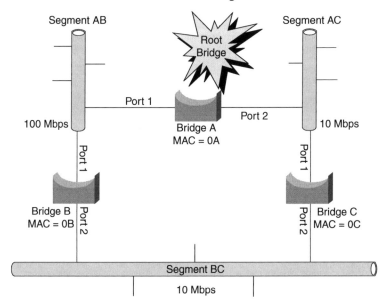

The following three items characterize the network topology shown in Figure 7-6:

- Bridge B is connected to Bridge A via a 100-Mbps link, and Bridge C is connected to Bridge A via a 10-Mbps link.

- Bridges B and C are connected to one another at 10 Mbps via Segment BC.

- Segment BC creates a loop in this network.

Because this network has a loop, the STP determines which links remain in a forwarding mode and which enter a blocking mode.

Bridge A is elected as the root bridge because it has the lowest MAC address based on the STP information exchanged by the BPDUs between bridges in this

network. In this case, the root bridge sends out BPDUs with a port cost of 0; and because it is the root bridge, there is no cost for its own ports to reach it. Therefore, the port cost is 0. These BPDUs will be received on port 1 on Bridge B and Bridge C.

When these BPDUs are received by Bridge B, it (Bridge B) adds its own port cost to the cost provided by the root bridge; because the cost associated with a 100-Mbps port is 19, Bridge B port 1 determines that it can reach the root bridge with a total cost of 19. Port 1 of Bridge C, connected at 10 Mbps, determines that it can reach the root bridge with a total cost of 100 (100 + 0).

note

By default, BPDUs are sent across the network every two seconds.

Remember Bridge B and Bridge C are connected to Network 1 and also send out BPDUs on their interface connected to this network—port 2 for both bridges. Bridge B sends a BPDU to Bridge C over this network segment (Segment BC). In this BPDU, Bridge B announces to Bridge C that it can reach the root bridge with a cost of 19. When this message reaches Bridge C, it adds its port 2 cost to this value, calculating that it can reach the root bridge with a total cost of 119 (100 + 19) via port 2.

Bridge C now knows that it can reach the root bridge through port 1 with a cost of 100, or through port 2 with a cost of 119. Based on these two paths, Bridge C determines that port 1 should be its root port because of its lower cost to the root.

Bridge C also sends BPDUs to Bridge B across Segment BC. In these BPDU messages, Bridge C announces a cost to the root bridge of 100. When these BPDUs are received by Bridge B, Bridge B adds this cost to the cost of its port 2 interface. Bridge B now also knows that it can reach the root bridge, via Bridge C, with a total cost of 200. Based on the two possible paths, Bridge B determines that port 1 should be its root port because of its lower-cost path to the root.

Remember, the shortest distance between two points is a straight line, or in the case of STP, the lower cost.

Designated Ports

In the small network described previously, you have determined which port(s) should be the root ports on network bridges; however, which ports will be in a blocking or forwarding mode must still be determined.

For example, Segment BC has two possible paths to the root bridge: one via port 2 on Bridge B and the other via port 2 on Bridge C. To eliminate this loop, one of these two ports must be placed in a blocking mode, as illustrated in Figure 7-7.

Figure 7-7   Bridge C with a Blocked Port

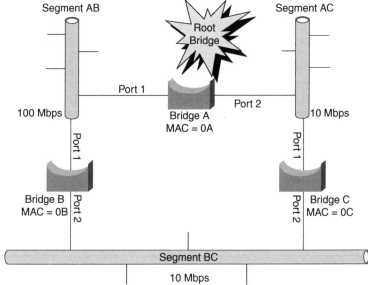

On a spanning-tree network, each network segment has one port identified as the designated port. The designated port is the port that is the single interface to forward traffic to the root bridge, and is determined via another election using BPDUs.

The network illustrated in Figure 7-7 contains three segments: Segment AC, Segment AB, and Segment BC. On each segment, one of the connected bridge ports needs to be elected as the designated port. This is always the switch port on the

segment with the lower port cost. For example, on Segment BC, two paths via port 2 on Bridge B and Bridge C are available to the root bridge, forming a loop. In this case, port 2 on Bridge B and Bridge C has a port cost of 100 on Segment BC, as illustrated in Figure 7-8.

Figure 7-8   Traffic Path from Segment BC to Segment AC

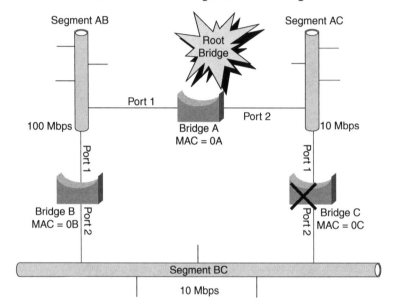

Because both bridges, Bridge B and Bridge C, have equal port costs to each other, MAC addresses are used to determine the *designated port*, making Bridge B the designated port on Segment BC because it has the lower MAC address. Therefore, port 2 on Bridge B will be placed in forwarding mode, and port 2 on Bridge C in blocking mode. When these forwarding and blocking modes are established, all traffic from Segment BC will exit the segment via Bridge B.

Convergence

After the transfer of BPDUs between systems has determined the root bridge and the root port of each bridge and switch, the network is loop free. The next topic is how the STP functions when something goes wrong in the network, such as a link failure. After the STP topology of a network has been calculated, each bridge and switch forwards BPDUs every two seconds. These BPDU messages inform the bridges and switches of which links are still active in the network, and which bridges and switches are not. For example, Bridge B in the network example illustrated in the Figure 7-9 could have failed or been powered down.

Figure 7-9   Bridge B Failure

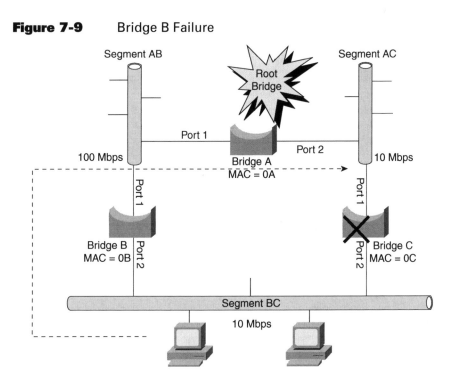

In this case, Bridge C fails to receive BPDU messages from Bridge B on Bridge C's port 2 interface. Even though Bridge C port 2 is in blocking mode, it continues receiving and analyzing BPDU messages. After 20 seconds have passed without Bridge C receiving a BPDU on port 2 from Bridge B, Bridge C assumes that Bridge B is not available and transitions into the listening state. The listening state lasts for 15 seconds and is the time when Bridge B will be listening to and

inspecting BPDUs from all other bridges. The bridge port still does not forward traffic during the listening stage.

After the 15 seconds of the listening state expire, the Bridge C port transitions into a learning state for another 15 seconds. During this time, Bridge C port 2 learns the MAC addresses of all connected hosts on the network segment. As it is with the listening state, Bridge C port 2 does not forward traffic during this learning state.

When the learning state is completed, Bridge C port 2 transitions into forwarding mode, in which it forwards traffic as the active path to the root bridge; at this point, the network is considered to be converged.

note
During the 50 seconds the network is converging on the change, no traffic is forwarded to or from any of the network bridges and switches. In today's network environment, 50 seconds can seem like an eternity. The Rapid Spanning Tree Protocol (RSTP, IEEE 802.1w) is available to address this issue (the length of time required to transition from the blocking to forwarding state); RSTP enables designated ports to change from the blocking to forwarding state in a few seconds. The exact amount of time depends on the interval between hello timers in your network. Because RSTP does not use timed intervals, as STP does, it is difficult to discuss the precise amount of time it will take an RSTP network to converge. It is because of this lack of precise timing that convergence in an RSTP network can best be measured in "a few seconds."

Chapter Summary

The purpose of the STP, standardized as IEEE 802.1d, is to prevent loops in bridged or switched networks with redundant links. Bridges or switch ports configured for STP are in one of five different states: blocking, listening, learning, forwarding, and disabled.

- **Blocking**—The port will not send or receive any data traffic across the network segment, but will listen to STP BPDU messages. When a switch or bridge running STP is powered on, all ports are in a blocking state. The port is in the blocking state for *20 seconds* before transitioning to the listening state.

- **Listening**—The port is listening to spanning-tree messages in the form of BPDUs and is determining how the network topology is configured. While in the listening state, the port is not forwarding frames. The port is in the listening state for *15 seconds* before transitioning to the learning state.

- **Learning**—The port is adding MAC addresses to its MAC address table. While in the learning state, the port is not forwarding frames. The port is in the learning state for *15 seconds* before transitioning to the forwarding state.

- **Forwarding**—The port is sending and receiving data across the network segment as normal, and after the network has converged on a topology, the port will be in either the forwarding or blocking state.

- **Disabled**—The port can be administratively disabled at any time by the network administrator and will not receive BPDUs or forward traffic across any network segments. The switch cannot put a port into the disabled state and therefore cannot take a port out of the disabled state; only the network administrator can enable or disable a port.

The calculation of a spanning-tree topology is a three-step process, and on completion of these three steps the network is loop free. The three steps are as follows:

Step 1   Elect a root bridge.

Step 2   Each device calculates the best path to the root bridge using port cost.

Step 3   Elect a root port on each nonroot bridge.

Step 4   Elect a designated port on each segment.

Step 5   All other switch interconnections are placed in blocking mode to remove loops.

The root bridge is the bridge that is continuously sending network topology information to other bridges in the network. Using the STP, the root bridge notifies all

other bridges on the network when topology changes are required. The root bridge should be located centrally in the network to provide the shortest path to other links on the network, and unlike other bridges, the root bridge always forwards frames out all of its ports.

After the root bridge is elected in the STP network, each bridge determines which port it will use to reach the root bridge; this port is called the root port.

Each LAN segment has a designated bridge and a designated port. The designated bridge has the lowest total path cost to the root bridge and the designated port through which frames are forwarded on to the network.

note

This chapter discussed the STP (IEEE 802.1d), but newer concepts for STP operation are either on the horizon or knocking on the door of current switched networks: Multiple Spanning Tree Protocol (MSTP; IEEE 802.1s), Topology Change Notification (TCN) BPDU, and Rapid STP (RSTP).

MSTP may be best if you have multiple links separating VLAN traffic. Although STP could disable some of those data paths in your network, this problem is solved by IEEE 802.1s. MSTP solves the problem by enabling multiple spanning trees within a network, allowing administrators to assign VLAN traffic to unique paths.

Topology Change Notification (TCN) works for you when there is a topology change caused by a workstation being connected or removed from a switch port. The switch sends out a TCN BPDU when a workstation is connected or removed.

RSTP, defined in IEEE 802.1w, provides for faster spanning-tree convergence after a topology change.

Chapter Review Questions

1. What is a protocol?

2. What is a bridge loop?

3. What is purpose of the Spanning Tree Protocol (STP)?

4. What is a BPDU?

5. What are the STP states? Which state can only be manually configured?

6. What is the difference between a blocked port and a disabled port?

7. What is the starting point for the Spanning Tree Protocol called?

8. What two components make up the bridge identifier, how long is the bridge identifier, and how is the bridge identifier used?

9. From the time it is powered up, how long does it take a switch to enter the forwarding state and begin forwarding LAN traffic?

10. What is convergence?

11. What does the Spanning Tree Protocol do when a new bridge is added to the network?

What You Will Learn

On completing this chapter, you will be able to:

- ✔ Describe a virtual LAN
- ✔ List three VLAN types
- ✔ Describe communications within and between VLANs
- ✔ List three VLAN modes
- ✔ List the Layer 3 switches in VLANs
- ✔ Explain the benefits of using VLANs

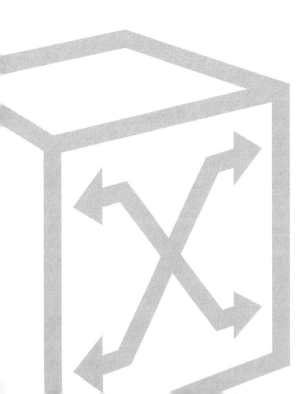

CHAPTER 8

Virtual LANs (VLANs)

This chapter takes the concept of a physical local-area network (LAN), throws it against the wall, picks up the pieces, and reassembles them. The LANs thus far discussed have all been based on physical topology and single broadcast domains with no segmentation—where there is cabling, there is a broadcast domain.

But that is all about to change. If it looks like a duck, walks like a duck, and quacks like a duck, it's a duck, right? Looks like it in Figure 8-1.

Figure 8-1   Ducks and LANs

If it looks like a LAN and talks like a LAN, it's a LAN, right? But what if it doesn't look like a LAN, but in fact has computers spread out all over; can it still talk like a LAN? In fact, it can by using a virtual LAN, or VLAN.

note

A *broadcast domain* is an area within a network topology in which information transmitted in the domain is received by all devices within the same domain. Ethernet LANs are broadcast domains because any network device attached to the LAN can transmit frames to any other network device in the shared transmission medium.

VLAN Overview

A *virtual LAN*, or *VLAN*, is a group of computers, network printers, network servers, and other network devices that behave as if they were connected to a single network.

In its basic form, a VLAN is a broadcast domain. The difference between a traditional broadcast domain and one defined by a VLAN is that a broadcast domain is seen as a distinct physical entity with a router on its boundary. VLANs are similar to broadcast domains because their boundaries are also defined by a router. However, a VLAN is a logical topology, meaning that the VLAN hosts are not grouped within the physical confines of a traditional broadcast domain, such as an Ethernet LAN.

If a network is created using hubs, a single large broadcast domain results, as illustrated in Figure 8-2.

Figure 8-2   Two Broadcast Domains Connected Across a WAN

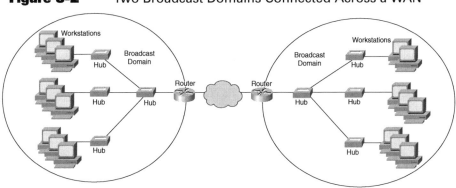

Because all devices within the broadcast domain see traffic from all other devices within the domain, the network can become congested. Broadcasts are stopped only at the router, at the edge of the broadcast domain, before traffic is sent across the wide-area network (WAN) cloud.

If the network hubs are replaced with switches, you can create VLANs within the existing physical network, as illustrated in Figure 8-3.

Figure 8-3   Two VLANs Connected Across a WAN

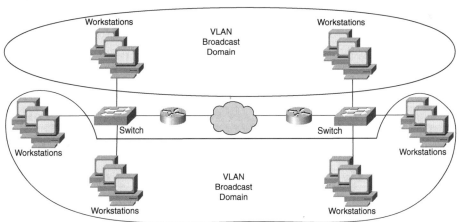

When a VLAN is implemented, its logical topology is independent of the physical topology, such as the LAN wiring. Each host on the LAN can be assigned a VLAN identification number (ID), and hosts with the same VLAN ID behave and work as though they are on the same physical network. This means the VLAN traffic is isolated from other traffic, and therefore all communications remain within the VLAN. The VLAN ID assignment made by the switches can be managed remotely with the right network management software.

Depending on the type of switching technology used, VLAN switches can function in different ways; VLANs can be switched at the data link (Open System Interconnection [OSI] model Layer 2) or the network layer (OSI model Layer 3). The main advantage of using a VLAN is that users can be grouped together according to their network communications requirements, regardless of their physical locations, although some limitations apply to the number of nodes per VLAN (500 nodes). This segmentation and isolation of network traffic helps reduce unnecessary traffic, resulting in better network performance because the network is not flooded. Don't take this advantage lightly, because VLAN configuration takes considerable planning and work to implement; however, almost any network manager will tell you it is worth the time and energy.

note

An end node can be assigned to a VLAN by inspecting its Layer 3 address, but a broadcast domain is a Layer 2 function. If a VLAN is switched based on Layer 3 addressing, it is in essence routed. There are two basic differences between routing and switching: First, the decision of forwarding is performed by the application-specific integrated circuit (ASIC) at the port level for switching versus the reduced instruction set circuit (RISC) or main processor for routing; second, the information used to make the decision is located at a different part of the data transfer (packet versus frame).

VLAN Topology

VLANs can best be defined as a group of devices on either the same or different physical LAN segments, interacting with each if they are on the physical LAN segment.

Suppose, for instance, that you work in a two-floor office building and each floor has a LAN switch providing network connectivity to every computer on that floor. The first floor is supported by Switch 1, and the second floor is supported by Switch 2. On each floor of this building, there is also a marketing staff and an engineering staff. Because of office real estate, people are sitting wherever an open desk can be found.

It is safe to say that the marketing and engineering departments have different jobs and therefore different network requirements. However, the fact that these two departments have different network requirements does not mean they cannot share the same network. Figure 8-4 illustrates how using VLANs provides virtual dedicated network resources to the marketing (VLAN 1) and engineering (VLAN 2) departments, while using the same physical network infrastructure.

If we assign all the marketing staff on the first floor (Switch 1, ports 1 and 2) and all the marketing staff on the second floor (Switch 2, ports 4, 5, 6, and 7) to a single VLAN (VLAN 1), they can share resources and bandwidth as if they were connected to the same physical network segment. Similarly, if we assign all the first-floor engineering staff (Switch 1, ports 3, 4, 5, 6, 7, and 8) and the engineering staff on the second floor (Switch 2, ports 1, 2, 3, and 8), we create VLAN 2 for the engineering staff, providing the same illusion of physical connectivity provided to the marketing staff by VLAN 1.

Figure 8-4   VLAN 1 and VLAN 2

It is important to remember that members of one VLAN cannot share the resources of any other VLAN without some sort of routing mechanism, such as a router or Layer 3 switch. For a member of the marketing staff in VLAN 1 to share resources with the engineering VLAN (VLAN 2), a router or a Layer 3 switch must be in place.

note

Communication between VLANs can occur only if there is a router or a Layer 3 switch in place enabling such connectivity.

Switches with VLAN capability can create the same division of the network into separate LANs or broadcast domains and is similar to color coding your switch ports. In Figure 8-4, ports in the light gray area can communicate with other ports in the light gray area, and ports in the dark gray area can communicate with the other ports in the dark gray area.

VLAN Operation

Several issues are involved in the operation of a VLAN:

- Who can participate in each VLAN

- How VLANs communicate among each other

- How devices within different VLANs can communicate with one another

VLAN Membership

There are three ways a network device can be assigned to a VLAN: by port, Layer 2 (MAC) address, or Layer 3 (network) address. The type of VLAN determines how a device is assigned. In a port-based VLAN, for example, you assign each switch port to a VLAN. In MAC address-based VLANs, membership is defined by the source or destination MAC address. VLANs based on Layer 3 information use the protocol type, such as the Internet Protocol (IP), and the Layer 3 (network) address in determining which VLAN the device is a member of.

Port-Based VLAN

In a port-based VLAN, such as that illustrated in Figure 8-5, each computer is assigned to its VLAN based on the port to which the computer is connected.

For example, ports 1 through 4 can be assigned to the sales VLAN, ports 6 through 10 to the engineering VLAN, and port 5 kept open as a spare port that you can assign to either VLAN. Or you can create a third VLAN with port 5 as a member. When a computer is connected to port 4, it becomes part of the sales VLAN. When that same computer is connected to port 6, however, it becomes part of the engineering VLAN.

Figure 8-5   VLAN Membership Based on Switch Port Number

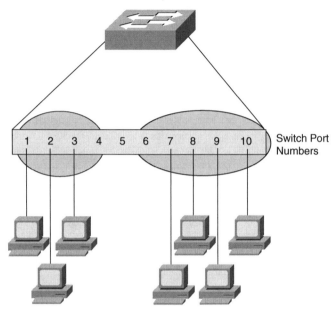

 note
On almost all switches today, all ports by default are part of VLAN 1.

The main drawback of port-based VLANs is that you must reconfigure VLAN membership when a user moves from one port to another. If you are in an environment in which people are moving around all the time, port-based VLANs can become quite the headache.

Address-Based VLAN

In an address-based VLAN, such as that illustrated in Figure 8-6, each computer is assigned to its VLAN based on the Media Access Control (MAC) address of the computer.

Figure 8-6   Address-Based VLAN

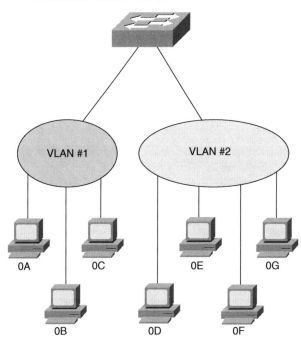

The computers with the MAC addresses 0A, 0B, and 0C are assigned to VLAN 1, and the computers with the MAC addresses 0D, 0E, 0F, and 0G are assigned to VLAN 2. (Note that these are not real MAC addresses.)

The main advantage of the address-based model is that the switch does not need to be reconfigured when a user moves to a different port, as illustrated in Figure 8-7.

The user at machine 0C changed departments, and to support this move the network administrator removed the MAC address (0C) from VLAN 1 and assigned 0C to VLAN 2 without reconfiguring any switch ports. This type of change can happen about as quickly as you can type on a keyboard.

The primary issue with MAC address-based VLANs is that a single MAC address cannot be a member of multiple VLANs without special features available on the switch enabling the multiple VLAN membership.

Figure 8-7   Machine 0C Moved to New VLAN

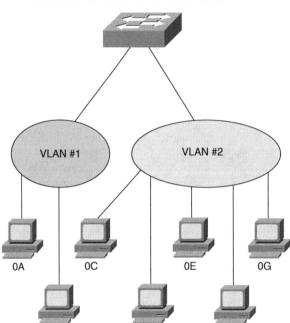

Layer 3-Based VLAN

In a Layer 3-based VLAN, such as that illustrated in Figure 8-8, each computer is assigned to its VLAN based on the OSI model Layer 3, the network layer, and the address of the computer.

The primary benefit of using a Layer 3-based VLAN is that users can physically move their workstations to any network jack without the workstation's network address being reconfigured. This might make your life as a network manager much easier because you assign a network address, or range of addresses, to a VLAN only once, instead of having to reassign a MAC address to a new VLAN. The downside of Layer 3 VLANs is the slow performance caused by additional switch processing.

Figure 8-8   Layer 3-Based VLAN

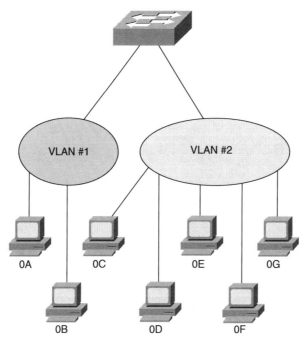

note
Because switches are Layer 2 devices, not Layer 3, additional processing
cycles are needed for the switch to manage Layer 3-based VLANs. Even
though you are using a Layer 3 address to differentiate, the device is being
assigned to a Layer 2 broadcast domain (not forwarding the packet).

Inter-VLAN Communication

We have discussed VLANs that are basically a special type of broadcast domain,
in that a VLAN is defined by a switch port rather than by traditional physical
boundaries, such as wiring hubs. Recall that when a host in one broadcast domain
wants to communicate with another, a router must be involved, and the same holds
true for VLANs.

For example, suppose that port 1 on a switch is part of VLAN 1, and port 2 part of
VLAN 17, as illustrated in Figure 8-9.

Figure 8-9   VLAN 1 and VLAN 17

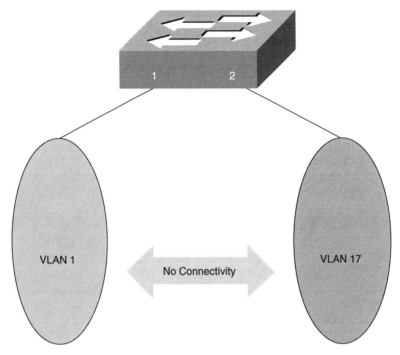

If all of the switch's ports were part of VLAN 1, the hosts connected to these ports could communicate with each other without issue. However, when the ports are made part of different VLANs, this communication is no longer possible. For a host connected to port 1 to communicate with another connected to port 2, a router must be involved, as illustrated in Figure 8-10.

Traffic leaving the host in VLAN 1 passes through the switch to the router so that the traffic can be passed back through the switch to reach the host server in VLAN 17. Instead of using a router to enable this inter-VLAN communication, a Layer 3 switch might be used.

Figure 8-10 VLAN 1 and VLAN 17 with a Router

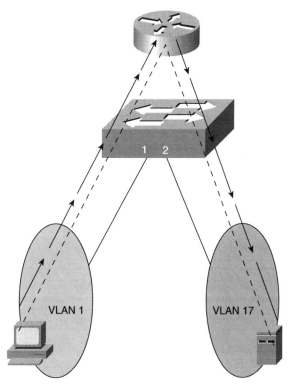

A Layer 3 switch is essentially a Layer 2 switch that can also act as a router, often through additional hardware and/or software features. If a switch is capable of Layer 3 functions, it can be configured to route traffic between VLANs defined within the switch, without the need for traffic to ever leave the switch for routing decisions. If a switch includes only Layer 2 functions, however, an external router must be configured to route traffic between the VLANs. In some cases, a packet can leave switch port 1, be forwarded to an external router, and then be routed right back to port 2 on the originating switch, as illustrated in Figure 8-10. For this reason, Layer 3 switches are popular to use throughout a corporate network.

Devices that are called Layer 3 switches track the Layer 3 addresses in and out of each port and build a table similar to a MAC address table for Layer 2. If they see the same address more than once, they forward the packet without looking at the routing table or sending it up to the main processor.

note

Regardless of the method chosen for inter-VLAN communication, either a router or Layer 3 switch, the most important point to remember is that when a host on one VLAN wants to communicate with a host on another, a routing (Layer 3) device must be involved.

Extending VLANs

To extend VLANs across different switches, a trunk link must be implemented, interconnecting the switches. This trunk link is often faster than the VLANs themselves. Think of a trunk link as being similar to an interstate highway; several small roads converge to one larger, and faster, road, as illustrated in Figure 8-11.

Figure 8-11   VLAN Trunks and Interstate Highways

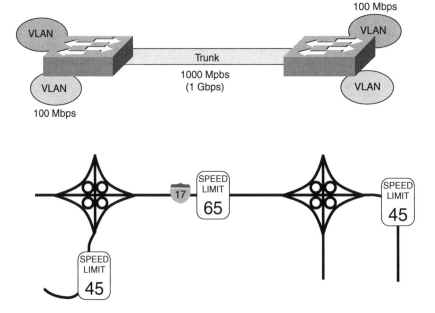

For example, you might interconnect two Gigabit Ethernet ports on different switches enabling the communication between the 100-Mbps VLANs on each switch. It is recommended that you use the fastest port available for trunk connections between switches, because this link often carries a great deal of traffic, most often for multiple VLANs.

Assume you have connected a link between the 100-Mbps ports of two switches, as illustrated in Figure 8-12.

Figure 8-12   100-Mbps Link Between VLAN 1 Ports

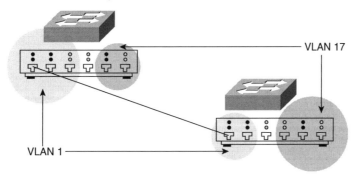

Note these ports are members of VLAN 1 on each switch. By default, without additional configuration, these ports act as a trunk link between these two switches; however, these ports pass traffic only for the VLAN associated with their port connections (in this case, VLAN 1). This type of link, in which traffic for only a single VLAN is passed, is referred to as an *access link*, as opposed to a *trunk link*, which carries traffic for multiple VLANs.

Access links get the job done in a single VLAN environment; however, multiple access links would be required if traffic from multiple VLANs were to be passed back and forth between switches. Having multiple access links between the same pair of switches would be a waste of switch ports. When traffic for multiple VLANs needs to be transferred across a single trunk link, VLAN tagging is used.

VLAN Tagging

When traffic from multiple VLANs travels across a link interconnecting two switches, you need to configure a VLAN tagging method on the ports that supply the link so that the receiving switch can identify the destination VLAN's traffic.

A number of tagging methods are in use for different technologies. The two discussed here are known as Inter-Switch Link (ISL) and 802.1q. ISL is a Cisco proprietary **VLAN tagging** method, whereas 802.1q is an *open standard*. This means that if you are connecting two Cisco switches, you could use ISL; if any non-Cisco switches are involved, however, 802.1q is your best option.

note

ISL is a Cisco proprietary VLAN tagging method; 802.1q is an open standard although both are similar in operation.

ISL tags a frame as it leaves a switch with information about the VLAN to which the frame belongs. If a frame from VLAN 17 is leaving a switch, for example, the ISL port adds information to the frame header, designating that the frame is part of VLAN 17, as illustrated in Figure 8-13.

Figure 8-13   Frames Before and After Tagging by the Switch

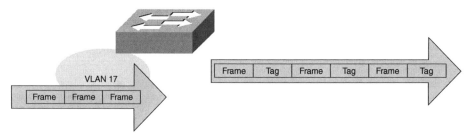

When this ISL frame reaches the port at the other end of the switch, it looks at the ISL header, determines that the frame is meant for VLAN 17, strips off the ISL information, and forwards it into VLAN 17.

One of the issues with VLAN tagging is that by adding information to an Ethernet frame, the size of the frame can move beyond the Ethernet maximum of 1518 bytes to 1522 bytes. Because of this, all non-ISL ports see frames larger than 1518 bytes as giants, and therefore invalid. As shown in Figure 8-14, this is similar to putting a jumbo-sized hot dog in a regular-sized hot dog bun. Just because the hot dog is oversized doesn't make it a bad hot dog. ISL works in much the same way, although without the mustard and relish.

Figure 8-14   ISL Frames and Hot Dogs

Because the port might see the ISL frame as a giant, the port needs to be configured for ISL so that it can understand the different frame format.

After VLAN tagging has been configured on the ports associated with the link connecting switches, the link is known as a trunk link, as illustrated in Figure 8-15.

Figure 8-15   VLAN Tagging on a Trunk Link

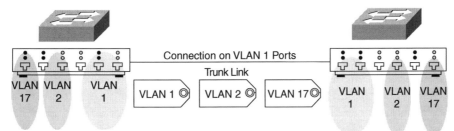

A trunk link transfers frames from many different VLANs by using Cisco ISL or the standard IEEE 802.1q.

VLAN Trunking Protocol (VTP)

Recall that the purpose of configuring VLAN tagging is to enable traffic from multiple VLANs to cross a trunk link interconnecting switches. However, VLAN tagging does not help ease the burden of configuring individual VLANs on multiple switches; this is where the Cisco *VLAN Trunking Protocol (VTP)* can help.

note
The VTP is a Cisco-proprietary protocol and is useful in large Cisco switch-based environments that include multiple VLANs.

The purpose of VTP is to provide a way to manage Cisco switches as a single group for VLAN configuration purposes. For example, if VTP is enabled on Cisco switches, the creation of a new VLAN on one switch makes that VLAN available to all switches within the same *VTP management domain*. A switch can be part of only one VTP management domain at a time, and is part of no VTP management domain by default.

Envision an environment in which you must manage 10 switches, as illustrated in Figure 8-16.

Without VTP, the creation of a new VLAN would require you to define that new VLAN individually on all necessary switches, a process that is subject to error and that is time-consuming to say the least. Instead, with VTP, you define the VLAN once and have VTP spread the information to all other switches in the same domain automatically, as illustrated in Figure 8-17.

Figure 8-16   10-Switch Network

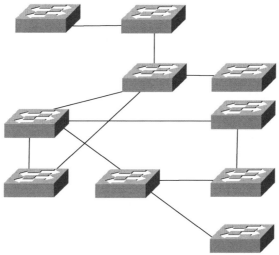

Figure 8-17   10 Switches in 1 VTP Management Domain

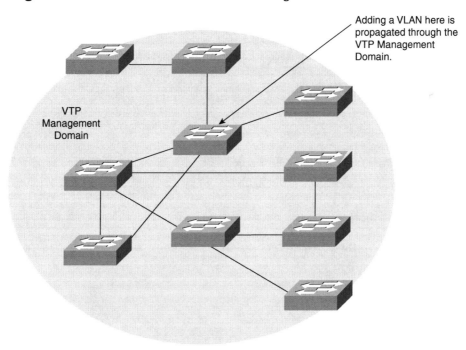

Adding a VLAN here is propagated through the VTP Management Domain.

VTP Management Domain

The primary benefit of VTP is that in large environments it facilitates adding and deleting VLANs, as well as making changes to VLAN configurations. Without VTP you would have to add a VLAN manually to each switch; with VTP you can add a VLAN to one switch and let the switches propagate the changes throughout the VTP management domain, and all before lunch!

When a VTP management domain name is defined on each switch, the switches exchange VTP information automatically and require no further configuration or day-to-day management.

VTP Modes

If you intend to make a switch part of a VTP management domain, each switch must be configured in one of four possible VTP modes: server, client, transparent, and off. The VTP mode assigned to a switch determines how the switch interacts with other VTP switches within the VTP management domain.

The following list details each of these four VTP modes:

- **Server mode**—A switch configured in server mode can be used to add, delete, and change VLANs within the VTP management domain. Server is the default mode used after a VTP has been configured on a Cisco switch. Within any VTP management domain, at least one switch must be in server mode. When in server mode, changes are passed to all other switches within the VTP management domain.

- **Client mode**—A switch configured in client mode is the recipient of any changes within the VTP management domain, such as the addition, deletion, or modification of VLANs by a server mode switch. A switch in VTP client mode cannot make any changes to VLAN information.

- **Transparent mode**—A switch configured in transparent mode passes VTP updates received by switches in server mode to other switches in the VTP management domain, but does not process the contents of these messages. When individual VLANs are added, deleted, or changed on a switch running in transparent mode, the changes are local to that particular switch only, and are not passed to other switches within the VTP management domain.

- **Off**— With the introduction of COS version 7.1.1, the option now exists to disable VTP completely on a switch.

Figure 8-18 illustrates the use of each VTP mode.

Figure 8-18   VTP Modes in Action

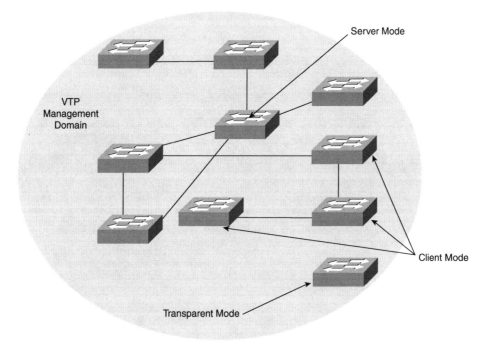

For example, think of the 10-switch network described earlier in this chapter. You could configure each switch to be in the same VTP management domain. Although each could be left in the default server mode, it might be easier to leave only one switch in server mode and configure all remaining switches for VTP client mode. When you need to add, delete, or change a VLAN, the change can be carried out on the VTP server-mode switch and passed to all client-mode switches automatically. When you need a switch to act in a relatively standalone manner, or don't want it to propagate information about its configured VLANs, transparent mode should be used.

VTP Pruning

Although the configuration of trunk links by using protocols such as ISL enables traffic from multiple VLANs to travel across a single link, this is not always the optimal choice. For example, suppose three switches are connected by two trunk links, as illustrated in Figure 8-19.

Figure 8-19   VTP Pruning

VTP Pruning prevents
VLAN 2 traffic from
crossing this trunk line.

Trunk Line   Trunk Line

Switch A   Switch B   Switch C
(VLAN 1 and 2 ports)   (VLAN 1 ports)   (VLAN 1 and 2 ports)

In this example, all three switches include ports that are part of VLAN 1, but only Switches A and C include ports in VLAN 2. Without VTP pruning, traffic for VLAN 2 will be passed to Switch B, even though it does not have any ports configured for VLAN 2.

When VTP pruning is implemented within a VTP management domain, traffic for a given VLAN is passed only to a switch across a trunk link if necessary. In Figure 8-19, for example, implementing VTP pruning in the management domain would ensure that traffic for VLAN 2 is never passed to Switch B until Switch B has VLAN 2 ports configured.

VTP advertisements are sent every 5 minutes or when a change occurs. Switches overwrite only information with a higher revision number. If a switch receives an update with VTP revision 14 but the switch is running on VTP revision 16, for example, it ignores the older revision, much as you ignore yesterday's newspaper when today's arrives on your doorstep.

IEEE 802.1q

The Institute of Electrical and Electronics Engineers (IEEE) has defined the 802.1q standard for VLANs, ensuring the interoperability of VLAN implementations between switches and network interface cards (NICs) from different vendors. Because of the various types of VLAN definitions, each vendor has developed its own unique and proprietary VLAN solution and product, such as the Cisco VTP. Without some common ground, such as an open standard, switches from one vendor will not interoperate with VLANs from other vendors.

Chapter Summary

A VLAN is a group of computers, network printers, network servers, and other network devices that behave as if they were in a single broadcast domain. To implement VLANs in a network environment, you need a Layer 2 switch that has VLAN capability. Almost all switches sold today that are described as managed switches provide the capability to configure switch ports as members of different VLANs. However, switches that don't provide any configuration function, such as many basic, lower-end switches, don't provide this capability to configure VLANs. For example, a switch you might buy at your local computer store for a home network probably wouldn't have VLAN capability.

VLANs define broadcast domains without being constrained by the physical location of the network device, such as a computer, server, or network printer. For example, instead of making all the users on the fifth floor part of the same broadcast domain regardless of their departments, you might use VLANs to make all the users in the HR department part of the same broadcast domain, separate from the users in other departments.

There are several benefits to using VLANs. Users might be spread throughout different floors of a building, so a VLAN would enable you to make all these users part of the same broadcast domain. This can also be a security feature. For example, because all HR department users are part of the same broadcast domain, you might later use security measures, such as an access list, to control which areas of

the network these users can access, or which users have access to the HR broad-cast domain. In addition, if the HR department's server were placed on the same VLAN, HR users would be able to access their server without the need for traffic to cross routers and impact other parts of the network, possibly resulting in net-work congestion and causing slowdowns.

Port-based VLANs are defined on a switch on a port-by-port basis. That is, you might choose to make ports 1 through 6 part of VLAN 1, and ports 7 through 12 part of VLAN 2. There's no need for ports in the same VLAN to be contiguous; for example, you might configure ports 1, 3, and 7 on a switch part of VLAN 1. If you want to implement VLANs, you must first configure the VLAN in the switch and then add ports to that VLAN.

Address-based VLANs are defined by the Layer 2, or the MAC, address of each device. You configure each VLAN within the switch and then assign MAC addresses to the appropriate VLAN. Address-based VLANs are port independent, which means that it does not matter to which switch port the device is connected. Its VLAN membership is determined by its MAC, or hardware, address.

Layer 3-based VLANs work in much the same fashion as address-based VLANs, but there is one exception. Although address-based VLANs use the Layer 2 (MAC) address, Layer 3-based VLANs use the Layer 3 (network) address, such as an IP address. Like address-based VLANs, Layer 3-based VLANs are port inde-pendent, and when the VLAN is defined, the membership of each device is deter-mined by its network address.

The primary reason for VLAN implementation is the cost reduction of handling user moves and changes. Any network device moved or added can be dealt with from the network-management console rather than the wiring closet. VLANs pro-vide a flexible, easy, and less-costly way to modify and manage logical groups of computers in changing environments.

Forming virtual workgroups is another advantage of VLAN. VLANs provide independence from the physical topology of the network by allowing geographically diverse workgroups, such as users on different floors or different buildings, to be logically connected within a single broadcast domain. If a department expands or relocates, VLAN implementations make it easier to add ports in new locations to existing VLANs.

VLANs can increase performance of switched networks over shared media devices by reducing the number of collision domains. Forming logical networks improves performance by limiting broadcast traffic to users performing similar functions or within individual workgroups.

VLANs can enhance network security in a shared media network environment. In a switched VLAN-based network, frames are delivered only to the intended recipients, and broadcast frames only to other members of the VLAN. This enables network managers to segment users requiring access to sensitive information into separate VLANs from the general user community regardless of physical distance.

A VLAN is not limited to a single switch if trunk links are used to interconnect switches. A VLAN might have three ports on one switch, and seven ports on another. It is the trunk link that provides the interconnection between the VLAN ports on each of these switches. The logical nature of a VLAN makes it an effective tool in large networking environments.

Chapter Review Questions

1. What is a VLAN?

2. What is the IEEE standard for virtual LANs?

3. What advantages are provided by VLANs?

4. Name the three types of VLANs and explain their differences.

5. What is a Layer 3 switch?

6. How can you communicate between VLANs?

7. How might you extend a VLAN?

8. What's the difference between an access link and a trunk link?

9. What is VLAN tagging?

10. Which VLAN tagging method is an open standard? What is the benefit of using open standards?

11. What is a VTP management domain?

12. How many VTP modes are there? What are they, and when would each be used?

13. Which VTP mode is the default mode?

What You Will Learn

On completing this chapter, you will be able to:

✔ Describe switch-based security features

✔ Explain how networks are attacked in a switched LAN environment

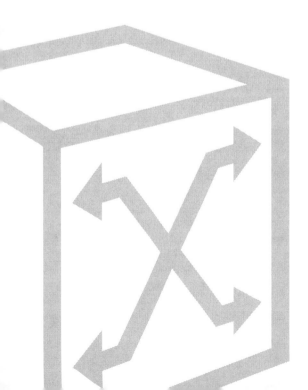

CHAPTER 9

Switching Security

There is an English proverb that states, "It is an equal failing to trust everybody, and to trust nobody," and it is the goal of network security to avoid both these failings. Network security is similar to putting your guard dog, Patches, to work for you guarding your network against any and all threats, as illustrated in Figure 9-1. This chapter focuses on establishing security for virtual local-area networks (VLANs). And as you recall from Chapter 8, "Virtual LANs (VLANs)," VLANs are a logical grouping of devices that might or might not be physically located close to each other.

Figure 9-1   Patches Guarding the Network

Just as Patches can be bought off with a steak, however, intruders can find ways into your network that you never imagined. It is best to be vigilant and protect your network and its resources as you would protect your own children.

Network Security Basic Rules

You need to keep in mind several basic rules when setting up secure Layer 2 switched VLANs:

- VLANs should be set up in such a way that the VLAN clearly separates the network's various logical components from each other, in turn segregating logical workgroups. This is the first step toward segregating those portions of your network that need more security from portions that need less.

- If some switch ports are not being used, it is best practice to disable these ports and assign them to a special VLAN that collects these unused ports. This special VLAN should have no Layer 3 connectivity, such as to a router or other Layer 3 device capable of switching.

Although devices in a particular VLAN cannot access devices in another VLAN unless a trunking or routing mechanism is available, VLANs should not be used as the single mechanism for providing network security. VLAN protocols are not designed with network security as the primary goal, and because of this VLAN protocols can be compromised rather easily. Unfortunately, VLANs enable loopholes into the network. Because VLAN protocols are not security conscious, you should use other mechanisms, such as those discussed in the next sections, to secure the network.

Because VLANs lack security, devices at different security levels should be isolated on physically separate Layer 2 devices. For example, having the same switch chassis on both the inside and outside of a firewall is not recommended, as illustrated in Figure 9-2.

Putting both the public (VLAN 46) and private (VLAN 102) VLANs on the same switch, behind the firewall, is not a good idea. The VLAN separation does not provide enough security for your private information, such as a corporate database. This is not recommended because the management of the switch is more easily compromised by having a public VLAN. In addition, this is not recommended because a simple misconfiguration or incorrect cabling could expose the management interface of the switch. Figure 9-3 illustrates the solution to this type of scenario.

Figure 9-2   Public and Private VLAN Behind the Same Firewall

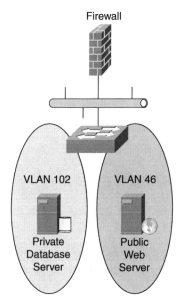

Figure 9-3   Public and Private VLANs Separated by Two Switches

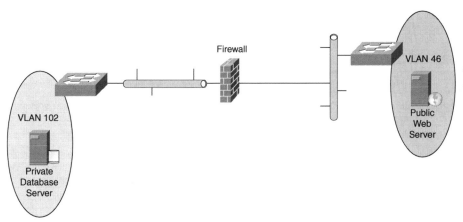

Two separate switches should be used for the *secure* and *nonsecure* sides of the *firewall*: one switch on the public side of the firewall and one switch on the private side of the firewall.

note

High-end switches can perform firewall functions without using an external firewall device.

An important point to remember is that you need to make sure VLAN trunking in your network does not become a security risk in the network switching environment. VLAN trunks should not use switch port numbers that belong to the *native VLAN*. Because the native VLAN is a VLAN that is not associated explicitly to a trunk link, the native VLAN enables network packets from the trunk port to reach other ports located in the same native VLAN, as illustrated in Figure 9-4.

Figure 9-4   When VLAN Trunking Goes Awry

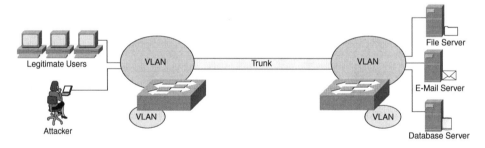

The VLAN trunk between the two switches in Figure 9-4 is part of an active VLAN. Therefore, if an attacker gains access to that VLAN, that same person now has access to all network resources inside that VLAN, such as user workstations or servers. (Aren't network attackers annoying?)

Switch ports that do not require trunking should have trunking disabled because, as illustrated in Figure 9-4, an attacker can use this trunking to hop from one VLAN to another. The attacker can do this by pretending to be another switch looking to establish a VLAN trunk with an active switch. This impersonation of a switch enables the attacker's machine to become a part of all the VLANs on the switch being attacked.

It's a good idea to use dedicated VLAN IDs for all VLAN trunks rather than using VLAN IDs that are also being used for nontrunking ports. If you don't use separate VLAN IDs, you enable an attacker to be part of a trunking VLAN pretty easily and then in turn use trunking to hop on to other VLANs as well. In other words, your attacker just bribed Patches with a steak.

note

Layer 3 interfaces between switches provide additional access control.

If one of your network users does not want his workstation to be tampered with, that user must control the physical access to that workstation, such as powering off the computer at the end of the day. In addition, it is important for any network administrator or manager to use all the proven security tools available for his or her specific platforms. These security tools range from the very basic configuration of system passwords, IP permit filters, and login banners, to more advanced tools such as ***Remote Authentication Dial-In User Service (RADIUS)***, ***Terminal Access Controller Access Control System Plus (TACACS+)***, and ***intrusion detection systems (IDSs)***.

Only after the basic security components are in place is it possible to turn attention to some of the more sophisticated security details, such as the use of port security or VLANs in your network, which are discussed in the following sections.

Port Security

When port security is enabled on a switch, any Media Access Control (MAC) address not specified for that port is denied access to the switch, and to any networks to which the switch is connected. Port security can be used to block input to an Ethernet, Fast Ethernet, or Gigabit Ethernet switch port.

The total supply, or global resource, of MAC addresses for the switch is 1024 MAC addresses. However, not all Cisco switches have 1024 MAC addresses; some have only 64 MAC addresses. In addition to this total supply, there is space for one default MAC address per port to be secured. The total number of MAC addresses that can be specified per port is limited to the global resource of 1024 MAC addresses plus one default MAC address (per port).

note
The total number of MAC addresses on any port cannot exceed 1025. Bear in mind that the switch limit is 1024 MAC addresses total for use.

The maximum number of MAC addresses for each port depends on your network configuration. The following combinations are some examples of valid allocation of MAC addresses:

- 1025 (1 + 1024) addresses on 1 port and 1 address each on the rest of the ports

- 513 (1 + 512) each on 2 ports in a system and 1 address each on the rest of the ports

- 901 (1 + 900) on 1 port, 101 (1 + 100) on another port, 25 (1 + 24) on the third port, and 1 address each on the rest of the ports

Each of these examples is listed in Table 9-1, grouped together by shades of gray. Note that the total number of allocated MAC addresses does not exceed 1024.

Table 9-1   MAC Address Allocation Examples

Number of Ports	×	Number of MAC Addresses	=	Total
1		1024		1024
2		512		1024
1		900		900
1		100		100
1		24		24
				1024

After you have allocated the maximum number of MAC addresses on a switch port, you can do one of two things:

- Manually specify the secure MAC address for the port

- Have the port dynamically configure the MAC address of the connected devices

From an allocated number of maximum MAC addresses on a port, you can manually configure all, allow all to be autoconfigured, or configure some manually and allow the rest to be autoconfigured. After the port addresses have been configured, manually or automatically, they are stored in *nonvolatile rapid-access memory (NVRAM)*.

After you allocate a maximum number of MAC addresses on a port, you specify a period of time, called the age time, during which the addresses on the specified

port remain secure. After this age time expires, the MAC addresses on the port become insecure and are no longer trusted.

note

All addresses on a port are permanently secured by default.

If a security violation occurs, you can configure the port to go into shutdown mode or restrictive mode. Shutdown mode gives you the option of specifying whether the port is permanently disabled or disabled for a specified amount of time. The default action during a security violation is for the port to permanently shut down. Restrictive mode allows port configuring to remain enabled during the security violation, only stopping packets coming in from insecure hosts.

When a secure port receives a frame, the frame's source MAC address is compared to the list of secure source addresses that were configured (manually or learned via autoconfiguration) on the port. If the MAC address of a device attached to the port is not on the secure address list, the port is shut down, either permanently or for a period of time you've configured.

Port Security Configuration Guidelines

When configuring port security, consider the following guidelines:

- You cannot configure port security on a *trunk port*.

- Port security cannot be enabled on a *Switched Port Analyzer (SPAN) port*.

- You cannot configure dynamic, static, or permanent *content-addressable memory (CAM)* entries on a secure port.

- When you enable port security on a port, any static or dynamic CAM entries associated with the port are cleared; any currently permanent CAM entries that are configured by an administrator are treated as secure.

Virtual LANs

Recall from Chapter 8 that a virtual LAN, or VLAN, is a group of computers, network printers, network servers, and other network devices behaving as if they were connected to a single, network segment.

Network attackers or malicious users often seek to gain access to the management console of a networking device, because if they are successful, they can easily alter the network configuration to their advantage.

In a VLAN switch, in addition to having a direct connection to an *out-of-band* management port (a port not used for user traffic), the network management station can use one or more VLANs for *in-band* management. The network management station can also use one or more VLANs to exchange protocol traffic with other networking devices.

Basic physical security guidelines require networking equipment to be in a controlled or locked space, such as a telephone room or communications closet. VLAN-based security's primary rule is confining in-band management and protocol traffic to a logically controlled environment, by implementing the following tools and best practices:

- Using traffic and protocol access control lists (ACLs) or filters preventing untrusted traffic from being filtered, or passed, through the switch

- Disabling Layer 2 protocols on untrusted ports, such as disabling the Cisco *Dynamic Trunking Protocol (DTP)* on switch access ports

- Configuring in-band management switch ports only in dedicated and trusted VLANs

- Not using VLAN 1 to carry user or network data traffic

There is a VLAN used for special requirements within your switch network: VLAN 1.

VLAN 1 Precautions

VLAN 1 is special because switches need to have a default VLAN to assign to their ports, including management ports, and VLAN 1 is the default VLAN. In addition, many Layer 2 protocols need to send their information across a specific VLAN on trunk links. It was for these purposes that VLAN 1 is used, and therefore VLAN 1 should not be used for user-related traffic.

As a result of this selection, VLAN 1 can sometimes end up spanning the entire network if not appropriately configured. If the diameter of VLAN 1 is large enough, the risk of instability significantly increases. Using a universal VLAN for management purposes puts trusted network devices, such as workstations and servers, at higher risk of security attacks from untrusted network devices. These untrusted network devices might gain access by switch misconfiguration, or accidentally gain access to VLAN 1 and then try to exploit this unexpected security hole in your network.

At present VLAN 1 has a bad reputation to overcome; with a little bit of help, however, VLAN 1 can redeem itself. To redeem VLAN 1, a simple security principle should be used: As a rule, the network administrator should prune any VLAN, most notably VLAN 1, from all the ports where that VLAN is not strictly needed.

note
VLAN Trunking Protocol (VTP) pruning is disabled by default.

The rule of VLAN pruning means four things to you:

- Do not use VLAN 1 for in-band or out-of-band management traffic. Instead, use a different dedicated VLAN, thereby keeping management traffic separate from user data and other necessary network protocol traffic.

- Prune VLAN 1 from all VLAN trunks and from all access ports that do not require participation in VLAN 1, including switch ports that are not connected or shut down. If a switch port is not being used for any reason, move it to a new VLAN created for this purpose. This VLAN should also be pruned.

- Do not configure the management VLAN on any trunk or access port not requiring participation in the management VLAN. This includes switch ports not connected to any network segments and ports that are shut down and not in use.

- When feasible, for near-foolproof security, use an out-of-band network management platform, separating your network management traffic from your network user, or data, traffic.

- If VLANs other than VLAN 1 or the management VLAN represent a security concern, automatic or manual VLAN pruning should be applied. When a VLAN is automatically pruned, the VLAN must be manually enabled.

Trusted and Untrusted Ports

Apart from VLAN pruning in your network, another security principle you should put into practice is this: Connect untrusted (nonsecured) devices to untrusted ports, trusted (secured) devices to trusted ports, and disable all remaining ports.

This security principle means four things to you:

- If a switch port is connected to an unknown, or foreign, device, do not try to speak the language of this unknown device because doing so could be turned to an attacker's advantage and used against you. On the switch port in question, disable any unnecessary network management protocols, such as the DTP, because you do not want to risk potentially dangerous communication with an untrustworthy neighbor.

- To prevent undesirable protocol interactions within the network-wide VLAN configuration in your network, configure VTP domains appropriately or turn off VTP. This precaution limits or prevents the risk of human error, in the form of mistakes made by a network administrator, from spreading throughout the network. Because the switch with this error would have a newer VTP revision number, the entire domain's VLAN configuration is at risk of being reconfigured with the error. Oops.

- By default, only switch ports known to be trusted should be treated as such and all other ports should be configured as untrusted. There is an adage that fits here: We trust, but verify.

- Create a VLAN to collect unused switch ports, and disable unused switch ports and put them in this unused VLAN. By not granting connectivity to this VLAN, or by placing a device into a VLAN not in use, unauthorized network access can be stopped through physical and logical barriers. In other words, while Patches (physical barrier) is enjoying his steak, the home burglar is contained in the garage because of an alarm system on the house door (logical barrier).

VLAN-Based Network Attacks

The majority of Layer 2 (data link layer) attacks exploit the inability of a switch to track an attacker, because the switch has no inherent mechanism to detect that an attack is occurring. This inability to detect an attacker means that this same attacker can perform malicious acts against the network path, altering the path and exploiting the change without detection.

note
Some of the newer switches introduced to the market can track network attackers with the implementation of firewall and IDS modules or Cisco Network-Based Application Recognition (NBAR). Firewalls are used to prevent unauthorized access to your network, and IDS sensors are used to track network attack and intrusion attempts. Cisco NBAR adds intelligent network classification to network infrastructures by using a classification engine that recognizes a wide variety of applications, including web-based applications.

Some of the most common Layer 2 attacks are as follows:

- MAC flooding attack

- Address Resolution Protocol (ARP) attacks

- Private VLAN attack

- Multicast brute-force attack

- Spanning-tree attack

- Random frame stress attack

Each of these attacks is discussed in detail in the following sections.

MAC Flooding Attack

A MAC flooding attack is not a network attack but more a limitation of the way switches and bridges work. Switches and bridges possess a finite hardware-learning table to store the source addresses of all received packets. When this table becomes full, traffic directed to addresses that cannot be learned anymore is permanently flooded. Traffic flooding is constrained within the VLAN of origin, and therefore no VLAN hopping is permitted.

On nonintelligent switches, this flooding problem arises because a sender's Layer 2 identity is not verified, and therefore the sender can impersonate an unlimited number of network devices by counterfeiting frames.

Port security, 802.1x, and dynamic VLANs are three features that you can use to limit a device's connectivity based on its user's login ID and the device's own MAC layer identification. With port security, for example, preventing MAC flooding attacks is as simple as limiting the number of MAC addresses that can be used by a single port. By using port security in this way, you tie the identification of the device's traffic to its port of origin. Dynamic VLANS enable you to dynamically assign switch ports to VLANs based on the Media Access Control (MAC) address of the device connected to the port. When you move a host from one switch port to another switch port in the network, that switch dynamically assigns the new port to the assigned VLAN for that device.

ARP Attacks

Address Resolution Protocol (ARP) is an old protocol and was developed back in the time when everyone in a network was supposed to be friendly. Because ARP was designed for a friendly environment, no security was built in to the ARP function. As a consequence, anyone can claim to be the owner of any IP address he likes. In other words, an attacker can say that his MAC address is associated to any IP address in your network. These false claims result from the fact that ARP requests and replies carry information that associates the MAC address with the IP address of a device. Because there is no way to verify these identities, anyone trying to break into your network can pretend to be someone else, such as a legitimate user of your network, and gain access to resources on your network, such as a corporate database.

ARP attacks are targeted to fool a switch into forwarding packets to a device in a different VLAN by sending ARP packets containing forged identities. Within the same VLAN, ARP attacks, also known as ARP poisoning, can fool network end nodes, such as workstations or routers, into learning these false identities. These counterfeited identities enable a malicious user to pretend to the network that she is an intermediary between two endpoints and perform a *man-in-the-middle (MiM) attack*, as illustrated in Figure 9-5.

Figure 9-5 ARP Spoofing Attack

The ARP table of PC 1.1.1.2 is compromised. All outgoing traffic will go via PC 1.1.1.3, which transparently forwards the traffic to the router.

1.1.1.1
00:0A

1.1.1.3
00::0C

1.1.1.2
00:0B

ARP message to 00::0B says "My IP address is 1.1.1.1 and my MAC address is 00:0C."

The man-in-the-middle attack occurs when one network device impersonates another network device, such as your ***default gateway***. The attacker uses the ARP packets sent to the device targeted for attack because these ARP packets are not verified by the receiver. These ARP packets poison the receiver's ARP table with forged information, injecting the attacker into your network. This attack is similar to identity theft, in which someone obtains a piece of information related to your identity and uses that information to gather more information about you. Eventually, the pretender can convince everyone he is you.

Man-in-the-middle attacks can be prevented either by blocking direct Layer 2 communication between the attacker and the attacked device or by embedding intelligence into your network, such as a Layer 3 device that can check forwarded ARP packets for identity correctness.

Private VLAN Attack

Private VLANs allow traffic to be further segmented at Layer 2, limiting the size of your broadcast domain. A private VLAN attack uses the expected behavior of a private VLAN against the VLAN itself. Private VLANs are a Layer 2 feature that is supposed to restrict traffic to Layer 2. However, recall that a router is a Layer 3 device and as such, when the router is connected to the ***promiscuous port*** of a private VLAN, the switch forwards all Layer 3 traffic received on that port to whatever destination is identified. This forwarding occurs even if the destination is in the same local network as the source, as illustrated in Figure 9-6.

note
Configuring access control lists (ACLs) on the router is a way to prevent private VLAN attacks.

Figure 9-6 Private VLAN Attack

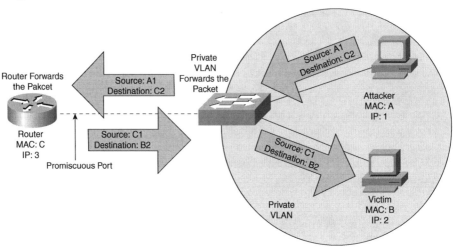

It is normal for two hosts in an isolated VLAN to fail in communicating with each other through direct Layer 2 communication but instead succeed in talking to each other using the router as a packet relay. As it is with regular routed traffic, packets relayed through a Layer 2 proxy can be filtered, if desired, by an appropriately configured ACL on the forwarding device.

Multicast Brute-Force Attack

Multicast brute-force attacks exploit the *potential vulnerability* of a switch to a storm of multicast frames. When a switch receives a significant amount of Layer 2 multicast traffic (frames) in rapid succession, the switch should limit the traffic to its original VLAN; failing to do so would leak frames to other VLANs if there is a routing mechanism in place between the VLANs.

This type of attack often proves ineffective against switches because switches should contain all the frames within their appropriate broadcast domain.

Spanning-Tree Attack

Another attack that can leverage switch vulnerability is the spanning-tree attack. Recall from Chapter 7, "Spanning Tree Protocol (STP)," that by default STP is turned on and every port on the switch both talks and listens for STP messages on the network. The spanning-tree attack consists of sniffing the network STP frames on the wire and getting the ID of the port on which STP was transmitting.

When the attacker has this port ID information, she can begin sending out STP Configuration/Topology Change Acknowledgement BPDUs (bridge protocol data units) announcing that she (the attacker) is the new root bridge with a much lower priority. This enables the attacker to listen in on all the network traffic and possibly change traffic flow.

Random Frame-Stress Attack

Random frame-stress attacks can have many incarnations but in general this attack is a brute-force attack, randomly varying several fields of a packet and leaving only the source and destination addresses untouched.

Private VLANs can be used to better isolate hosts at Layer 2 and protect these hosts from unwanted or malicious traffic from untrustworthy devices. Communities of mutually trusting hosts can be created so that a Layer 2 network can be divided into smaller Layer 2 networks where only friendly devices are permitted to communicate with each other.

Chapter Summary

Network security should be applied to all seven layers of the OSI model; however, this chapter discussed network security from a Layer 2 (data link layer) perspective. Some basic rules to keep in mind when setting up a secure Layer 2 switch-based network include the following:

- VLANs should be set up so that they clearly separate logical components of your network.

- VLANs are based on the level of security each VLAN requires.

- If any switch ports are not being used, these ports should be placed in a VLAN designed to collect these unused ports.

Using port security on your switch as a security mechanism provides a level of security because port security is based on permitted and denied MAC addresses. Because a MAC address is a hardware address, it lends itself to being a type of physical separation for your network. This differs from using VLANs, which provide more of a logical security for your network. Physical security for your network can be achieved by locking your wiring closets and preventing physical access to your network equipment.

VLANs use logical separation of network components to achieve a level of security in your network. Because VLANs are organized by assigned groups, any host that is not a member of the VLAN is denied access to any of that VLAN's resources. The switch will not recognize that host as part of that VLAN because you did not configure the VLAN to recognize that host.

Port security and VLANs are each susceptible to certain types of network attacks; when used together, however, each provides a level of network security that complements the other. No matter what your comfort level concerning network security, remember that you must take whatever precautions available to protect your network, its resources, and its users from threats both inside and outside your network.

Chapter Review Questions

1. Why and how should you separate public (external) and private (internal) VLANs?

2. What is port security?

3. What is the difference between in-band and out-of-band management and the benefit of each?

4. What are some of the common Layer 2 attacks on a network?

5. What is an ARP attack?

What You Will Learn

On completing this chapter, you will be able to:

- ✔ List the components of a switched network

- ✔ Describe flat (Layer 2) and hierarchical (Layer 3) network design

- ✔ Describe switched LAN network design

- ✔ Explain the benefits of switch, router, and VLAN implementations

- ✔ Describe network design principles

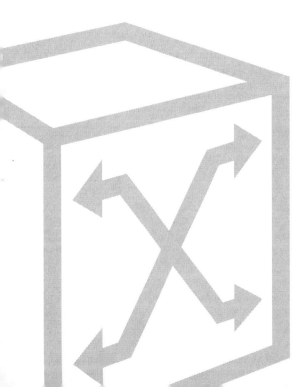

CHAPTER 10

LAN Switched Network Design

At this point in the book, all the pieces of a switched network have been discussed, but you still don't know how to put all these pieces together. This chapter revisits some of the earlier chapters and pulls the concepts together to present what a switched Ethernet LAN might look like and how it operates. You won't see any case studies here, because they are saved for Chapter 12, but there are lots of examples and figures to illustrate both Layer 2 and Layer 3 switching. So if you find yourself thinking, "My network doesn't look like the picture in the box cover yet," the similarity should become clearer by the end of this chapter.

Local-Area Network (LAN) Segments

Recall from Chapter 3, "Local-Area Networking Introduction," that local-area network, or LAN, segments are shared-media networks in which each user and device shares the network bandwidth with others on the same segment. *Microsegmentation* of the LAN through switches limits the number of users per segment, ultimately dividing the LAN so that there is a single user per-dedicated LAN segment. LAN switches can create microsegments because each switch port provides a dedicated 10-Mbps, 100-Mbps Ethernet, or Gigabit Ethernet segment to each user or network device, such as a file server or network printer.

LAN segments are connected to each other by networking devices that enable communication between these LANs while blocking other types of traffic. Switches monitor traffic between these segments and build address tables enabling them to forward frames to specific LAN ports. Switches also can provide *nonblocking* service, enabling multiple LAN conversations (traffic between two ports) to occur simultaneously.

Switch technology is the solution for most LAN traffic for the following reasons:

- Unlike hubs, which do not permit more than one data stream to pass through the hub, switches enable multiple data streams to pass simultaneously through the switch, resulting in more conversations occurring between hosts on the network.

- Switches support increased speed and bandwidth requirements of emerging technologies, which means that when you are looking at those new gadgets for your users, such as desktop videoconferencing, it is your switch that will enable the implementation of this technology.

- Switches deliver dedicated bandwidth to users because users don't like to share bandwidth. If a user has to share bandwidth with another user, that means the network connection isn't as fast as it could be, and how many times a day do you want to answer the phone and hear "The network is slow again." (I'm guessing, not many times.)

- Switches provide for a *quality of service (QoS)* capability that you can configure in your network. QoS is a defined performance level in a communications system, such as a data or voice network. To ensure that real-time voice and video are delivered without blips or static, such as with IPTV (IP television), for instance, a guarantee of bandwidth across the local- and wide-area network is required; QoS guarantees this bandwidth. Applications such as voice over IP (VoIP) rely on QoS for timely, clean delivery of voice traffic across the data network.

Switched Network Components

A switched network is made up of the following three basic components:

- Physical switch platform

- Common software infrastructure

- Network management tools and applications

Physical Switch Platform

The first component of a switched network is the physical switch itself. A LAN switch is a device that is made up of many ports connecting LAN segments, such as 100-Mbps Ethernet, and a high-speed port, such as Gigabit Ethernet. The high-speed port, in turn, connects the LAN switch to other devices in the network, as illustrated in Figure 10-1.

Figure 10-1 Physical Connection with Cable Termination Jack

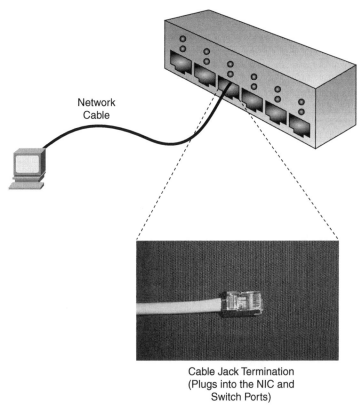

Cable Jack Termination
(Plugs into the NIC and
Switch Ports)

A LAN switch has dedicated bandwidth per port, and each port represents a different segment. For best performance, network designers often assign just one host to a port, giving that host dedicated bandwidth of 100 Mbps, as shown in Figure 10-2.

Figure 10-2 Small LAN Configuration

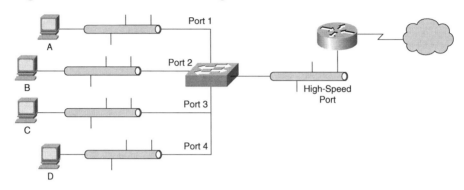

As discussed in Chapter 7, "Spanning Tree Protocol (STP)," the switch builds a table associating the Media Access Control (MAC) address of each local device with the port number through which that device is reachable. For example, referring to Figure 10-2, when Host A on port 1 needs to transmit to Host B on port 2, the LAN switch forwards frames from port 1 to port 2, thus sparing other hosts on port 3 from responding to frames destined for Host B. If Host C needs to send data to Host D at the same time that Host A sends data to Host B, it can do so because the LAN switch forwards frames from port 3 to port 4 at the same time it forwards frames from port 1 to port 2.

Whenever a device connected to the LAN switch sends a frame to an address that is not in the LAN switch's table, such as to a device not connected to the LAN switch, or whenever the device sends broadcast or multicast traffic, the LAN switch sends the frame out all ports except for the port from which the packet originated. This is known as flooding.

Because switches work like *transparent bridges*, a network built and designed with LAN switches appears as a *flat network* topology consisting of a single broadcast domain, as illustrated in Figure 10-3.

Figure 10-3　　Flat Network in a Single Broadcast Domain

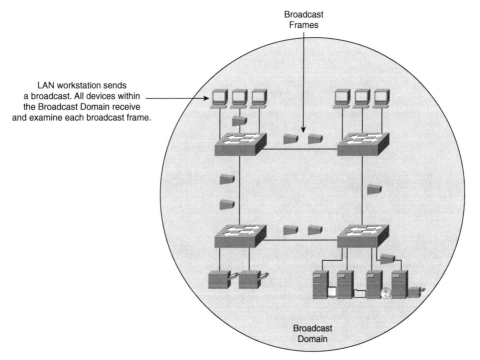

Broadcast
Frames

LAN workstation sends
a broadcast. All devices within
the Broadcast Domain receive
and examine each broadcast frame.

Broadcast
Domain

As a result, these flat networks are liable to suffer network problems, such as network congestion, because they do not scale well. Because some LAN switches can support virtual local-area networks (VLANs), however, VLAN-based networks are more scalable than traditional bridges.

Routing Platform

In addition to LAN switches, network designers often use routers as one of the components in a switched network infrastructure. Whereas LAN switches are added to wiring closets to increase bandwidth and to reduce congestion in existing shared-media networks, routers are being deployed in the network backbone. Within a switched network, routing platforms provide for the connection between disparate LANs and wide-area networks (WANs) while implementing broadcast

filters and logical firewalls. In general, if you need advanced networking services, such as a firewall and communication between LANs/VLANs using different protocols, routers are necessary in your network.

Common Software Infrastructure

The second component of a switched network model is a common software infrastructure. The function of this software infrastructure is to combine the variety of physical switching platforms such as LAN switches and multiprotocol routers.

The software infrastructure should perform the following tasks within the network:

- **Monitor the logical topology of the network**—In managing your network, you need to be able to recognize when a change in the network topology has occurred, for whatever reason, such as a link or hardware device failure.

- **Logically route traffic**—If two people are trying to talk to each other, and each is speaking a language unknown to the other person, no communication occurs. The same holds true in your network. If you have two switches, or other devices, that need to communicate and pass traffic back and forth to each other, but are not speaking the same language, or protocol, then no communication occurs.

- **Manage and control sensitive traffic**—If you send a memo through your corporate mailroom in an envelope marked "Confidential" and "Urgent," you should be able to trust that anyone handling that envelope will handle it according to those markings. In other words, no one will open the envelope because it is marked "Confidential," and the envelope will be delivered via the quickest means possible because it is marked "Urgent." This same concept holds true in your network; sensitive and high-priority traffic needs to be handled as marked from source to destination across your network, carefully and quickly.

- **Provide firewalls, gateways, filtering, and protocol translation**—Firewalls provide security for your network. Gateways provide a connection to the outside world, such as the Internet. Traffic filtering prevents unwanted traffic from being carried across the network. Protocol translation is your network language specialist, able to speak the language, or protocol, of both the sending and receiving device, if these two devices cannot do so directly. Your network might be required to provide one or more of these services, so you need to make sure that whatever switches you use have the features you need—rather like buying a car and making sure it has the options you want or need, such as heat and air conditioning.

VLANs

Recall from Chapter 8, "Virtual LANs (VLANs)," that a VLAN is a group of computers, network printers, network servers, and other network devices that behave as if they were connected to a single network segment.

In its basic form, a VLAN is a broadcast domain. The difference between a traditional broadcast domain and one defined by a VLAN is that a broadcast domain is seen as a distinct physical entity bounded by a router. VLANs are very similar to broadcast domains because their boundaries are also defined by a router. However, a VLAN is a logical topology, meaning that the VLAN hosts are not grouped within the physical confines of a traditional broadcast domain, such as an Ethernet LAN.

VLANs consist of several end systems: end-user computers, such as hosts, servers, or network printers; or network equipment, such as switches and routers. All these end systems are members of a single logical broadcast domain. VLANs do not have the physical constraints that traditional LANs have because traditional LANs are implemented based on cabling infrastructure, whereas VLANs are based on the logical infrastructure enabled by the switch, as illustrated in Figure 10-4.

Each workstation is connected to its local switch, Switch 1 or Switch 2—however, the switch determines which VLAN the workstation belongs to, VLAN 1 or VLAN 2. The VLANs here are enabled and managed by the switches. They also exchange VLAN information with each other through a VLAN trunk protocol, such as VLAN Trunking Protocol (VTP). Each VLAN supports a separate instance of the Spanning Tree Protocol (STP).

VLANs can be used to group a set of related users, regardless of their physical connectivity or proximity to each other; users can be across the building or across the country and still be a part of the same VLAN. The users might be assigned to a VLAN because they belong to the same department or team, such as an accounting or engineering department, or because data-flow patterns among them is such that it makes sense to group them together. For example, one floor of your building could be where the "top talkers" all sit.

note
Without a router, hosts in one VLAN cannot communicate with hosts in another VLAN.

Figure 10-4   VLAN Infrastructure

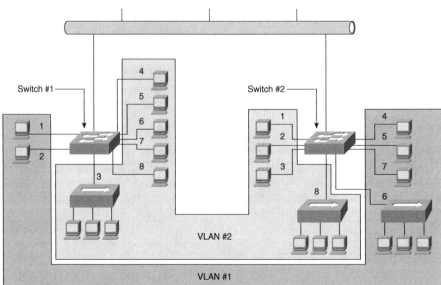

Network Management Tools and Applications

The third, and last, component of a switched network is made up of network management tools and applications. As more switches are integrated throughout the network, network management becomes vital at both the user workgroup and network backbone layers to ensure your network operates trouble free.

As part of designing a switched network, you must ensure your design takes into account network management applications needed to plan, configure, monitor, and analyze switched network devices and services. Network management applications add bandwidth to the network, some more than others, and this bandwidth needs to be accounted for in your network design.

Flat Network Topology

The typical architecture for a small LAN is workstations, printers, and servers attached to one or more hubs or to a small switch in a flat topology, as illustrated in Figure 10-5.

Figure 10-5   Flat Network Topology

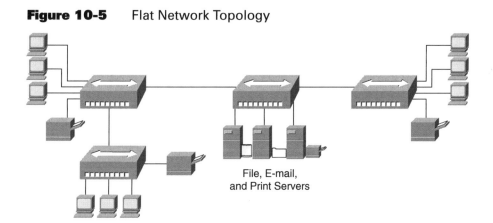

File, E-mail,
and Print Servers

The workstations, printers, and servers here use a MAC process, such as Ethernet's carrier sense multiple access collision detect (CSMA/CD), controlling access to the shared bandwidth. These devices are all part of the same bandwidth and broadcast domain and have the capability to impact the throughput of other devices and cause delay in traffic delivery.

For networks with high bandwidth requirements, caused by numerous users and/or traffic-intensive applications, network designers recommend attaching the workstations, printers, and servers to switches rather than hubs. Because hubs work at the physical layer (Layer 1) and switches work at the data link layer (Layer 2), the network is segmented into multiple smaller collision domains. This means that a small number of devices compete for bandwidth at any one time, rather than a "free-for-all" in which everyone competes for the bandwidth.

The number of nodes in a shared-medium LAN and the number of LAN segments are design parameters that should be considered when determining the use and placement of switches or hubs in your network. Because switching is a more expensive solution than using hubs in a shared-medium environment, for some organizations, hubs, or a combination of hubs and switches, might be the best solution. For organizations with high bandwidth and scalability requirements, switches should be used in place of hubs, dedicating each switch port to a single device. The use of switches in this scenario provides dedicated bandwidth to each workstation, printer, or server.

As discussed in Chapter 5, "Ethernet LANs," devices connected in a switched or bridged network are part of the same broadcast domain. Switches forward broadcast frames out all ports (in contrast to routers, which segment networks into separate broadcast domains, as illustrated in Figure 10-6).

Figure 10-6   Routers Separating Broadcast Domains

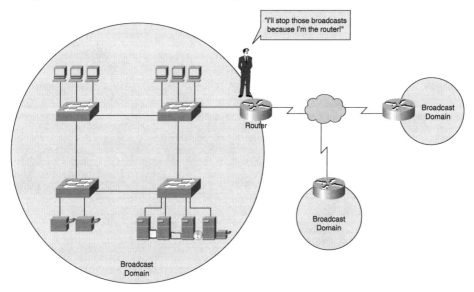

A single broadcast domain should be limited to a few hundred devices so that these devices are not overwhelmed by the processing of broadcast traffic. Introducing hierarchy into a network design by the addition of routers cuts down on the amount of broadcast traffic sent across the network.

With a hierarchical design, illustrated in Figure 10-7, networking devices are implemented in the network where each does the most good. Routers are added to a campus network design isolating broadcast traffic, and switches are added, maximizing bandwidth for high-traffic applications. Hubs can be used when simple and inexpensive network access is required; switch costs have come down over the years, however, so you should consider a small (low-end) switch rather than a hub. Getting the best performance out of your network is one of the benefits of using a hierarchical design model. Another benefit is that the modular nature of your network helps you in troubleshooting and isolating network faults.

Figure 10-7 Hierarchical Design with Campus-Area Network Core

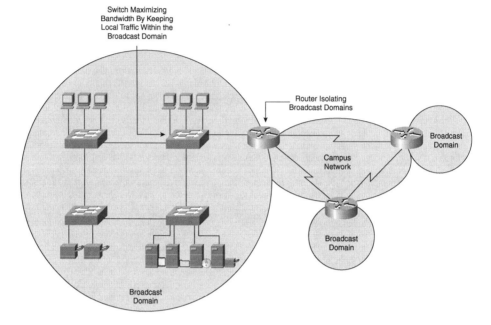

A flat network topology, as illustrated in Figure 10-8, is adequate for small networks and is implemented using Layer 2 switching. This is no hierarchy with a flat network design, and because each network device within the topology is performing the same job, a flat network design can be easy to implement and manage. The flat network topology is not divided into layers or modules and can make troubleshooting and isolating of network faults a bit more challenging than in a hierarchical network. In a small network, this might not necessarily be an issue, as long as the network stays small and manageable.

Figure 10-8   Small, Flat Network

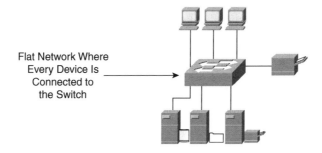

Flat Network Where
Every Device Is
Connected to
the Switch

Layer 2 Switching

Layer 2 of the Open System Interconnection (OSI model), the data link layer, provides the reliable transit of data across a physical link. The data link layer is concerned with physical addressing, network topology, line discipline, error notification, ordered delivery frames, and flow control. It is Layer 2 switching that forwards traffic based on the data link, or MAC, layer address. Layer 2 switches support simultaneous, parallel connections between Layer 2 Ethernet segments. Switched connections between Ethernet segments last only for the amount of time it takes for the frame to enter one switch port and leave through another switch port. New connections can be made between different segments for the next frame.

note

For a review of MAC addresses, see Chapter 5.

Layer 2 switches reduce network-congestion problems in Ethernet networks caused by high-bandwidth devices or a large number of users by assigning each network device to its own Ethernet collision domain. Because each LAN switch port connects to a separate Ethernet collision domain, workstations and servers can benefit from full access to the bandwidth.

Standard Ethernet operates in half-duplex mode and must contend with collisions, which are a major bottleneck. The effective solution is full-duplex communication, enabled by the LAN switch. In full-duplex mode, two stations can transmit and receive at the same time. When frames flow in both directions at the same time, Ethernet bandwidth doubles to 20 Mbps for 10-Mbps ports and to 200 Mbps for Fast Ethernet ports.

Switches operating at Layer 2 are very fast because the switch is sorting traffic based on the physical addresses, but switches are not considered "smart" in that the switch doesn't look at the datagram closely to learn anything more about where it's headed, such as to which network or user.

Hierarchical Topology

To meet your customer's business and communication goals for a corporate network design, you might need to recommend a network topology consisting of many pieces and parts—certainly a daunting venture. This venture can be made easier if you can break things down and develop the design in pieces, or layers. Breaking the design into layers is like cutting a pizza into slices instead of trying to eat the entire pizza at once; you can try designing the entire network as a whole, but tomato sauce might drip down your front.

The hierarchical network design model serves to help you develop a network topology in separate layers. Each layer focuses on specific functions, enabling you to choose the right equipment and features for the layer. For example, in Figure 10-9, high-speed WAN routers carry traffic across the enterprise backbone, medium-speed routers connect buildings at each campus, and switches and hubs connect user devices and servers within buildings.

Figure 10-9   Hierarchical Design with Routers (Core), Switches (Distribution), and Hubs (Access)

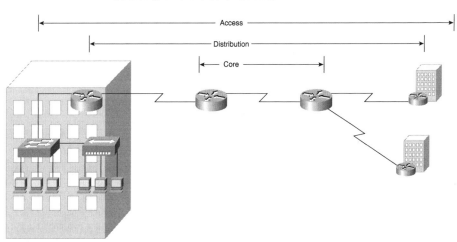

The hierarchical topology model is made up of the following:

- A core layer of high-end routers and switches optimized for network availability and performance.

- A distribution layer of routers and switches implementing forwarding decisions.

- An access layer connecting users via hubs, bridges, switches, or routers. More about the hierarchical model is discussed in the section "Hierarchical Model" later in this chapter.

Networks that grow without any plan in place tend to develop in an unstructured format. Dr. Peter Welcher, the author of network design and technology articles for *Cisco World* and other publications, refers to unplanned networks as *fur-ball networks*.

Dr. Welcher explains the disadvantages of a fur-ball topology by pointing out the problems that too many central processing unit (CPU) adjacencies cause. When network devices communicate with many other devices, the workload required of the CPUs on all the devices can be taxing. In a large flat, or switched, network, for example, broadcast frames are burdensome. A broadcast frame interrupts the CPU on each device within the broadcast domain, and demands processing time on every device, including routers, workstations, and servers.

Using a hierarchical model helps you to minimize network costs because you can buy the appropriate networking devices for each layer of the hierarchy. This in turn avoids spending money on unnecessary features for a layer, not unlike buying a home appliance with features that you are not going to use, such as a microwave with a toothbrush holder. The modular nature of the hierarchical design model also enables you to accurately plan network capacity within each layer of the hierarchy, which means you can reduce wasted bandwidth in your network. That keeps your financial people happy because you are not paying for something you're not using. Network management responsibility and network management systems can also be applied to the different layers of your network to control costs. Again, this is made possible because of the modular architecture of your network.

Network modularity enables you to keep each design element simple and easy to manage. Testing a network design is made easy because there is clear functionality at each layer. Fault isolation is improved because network transition points are easily identified.

A hierarchical design eases changes in the network environment. A Layer 3 switch helps implement a hierarchical topology. As a network requires changes, such as more users joining the network or a technology refresh/upgrade, the cost of making an upgrade to the network infrastructure is contained to a small section of the network. This is similar to putting pizza toppings on half the pizza rather than the whole. In large, flat network architectures, changes impact a large number of network devices and systems. Replacing one of the network devices in this large network can affect numerous other networks because of the interconnections between each network, as illustrated in Figure 10-10.

Figure 10-10   Replacing a Switch in a Large Network

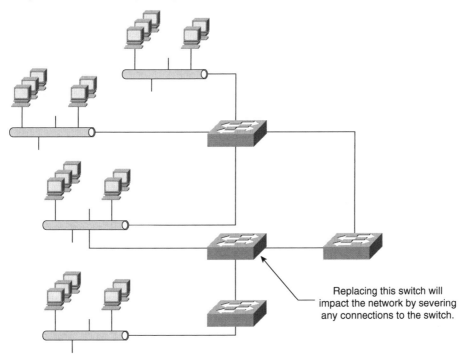

Replacing this switch will
impact the network by severing
any connections to the switch.

note

Sometimes taking all or part of the network down to make a change is
unavoidable. It is best to let your users know as soon as possible when the
network will be unavailable, and for how long.

Because scalability is often a major goal of any network design, a hierarchical
topology is recommended because modularity in the design enables you to create
design pieces that can be copied as the network grows, not unlike using a cookie
cutter to make the same cookie shape. Because each network module is the same,
network expansion is easy to plan, implement, and manage, just as it is easy to use
your cookie cutter to make 1 or 100 cookies with the same shape. For example,
planning a campus network for a new site might just be a matter of copying an
existing campus network design. If it works, why create from scratch?

Hierarchical Model

The cornerstone of any good network is the hierarchical model, which is made up of three pieces, or layers, as illustrated in Figure 10-11.

Figure 10-11   Hierarchical Model (Core, Distribution, and Access Layers)

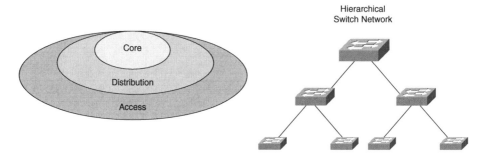

The core layer is a high-speed switching and routing backbone and should be designed to pass network traffic as fast as possible. This layer of the network should not perform any frame or packet manipulation, such as access lists and filtering, which would slow down the switching of traffic and in turn result in less than a "high-speed" environment.

The distribution layer of the network is the demarcation point between the access and core layers and helps define and differentiate the core. The purpose of the distribution layer is to define network boundaries and is the point in the network at which packet manipulation can take place. The distribution layer is where access lists and filtering (based on Layer 2 MAC or Layer 3 network addresses) will take place, providing network security. The distribution layer is also where broadcast domains are defined and traffic between VLANs is routed. If there is any media transition that needs to occur, such as between a 10-Mbps Ethernet and 100-Mbps Fast Ethernet network segment, this transition also happens at the distribution layer.

The access layer is the point at which local end users are allowed into the network. The access layer might also use access lists or filters to further meet the needs of a particular set of users. The access layer is where such functions as bandwidth sharing, filtering on the MAC (Layer 2) address, and microsegmentation can occur.

Layer 3 Switching

Layer 3 switches use the network address to identify where hosts are located on the network. Whereas Layer 2 switches read only the data link layer (MAC) address, Layer 3 switches read both the MAC and network addresses identifying where in the network a host is located from both a logical and physical topology viewpoint.

Switches operating at Layer 3 are smarter than Layer 2 devices because the Layer 3 switch incorporates routing functions calculating the best way to send traffic to its destination. However, although Layer 3 switches are smarter, they may not be as fast if their algorithms, fabric, and processor don't support high speeds. Some Layer 3 switch vendors have specialized *application-specific integrated circuits (ASICs,)* (pronounced "a-sicks") that enable Layer 3 switching to be as fast as Layer 2 switching. An ASIC is a chip that is custom designed for a specific application rather than a general-purpose chip such as a microprocessor found in a personal computer (PC) .

Switched LAN Network Designs

A good switched networking solution combines the benefits of routers and switches in every part of the network, as well as offering a flexible path to grow from shared-media to switched networks.

In general, incorporating switches in campus network designs results in the following benefits:

- **High bandwidth**—The more network bandwidth available to your users, the faster they can work, or surf the Internet. Think of a four-lane highway that enables more cars to travel than a two-lane road.

- **Quality of service (QoS)**—This is a traffic-prioritization scheme used to ensure that delay-sensitive traffic such as voice and video is given a higher priority on the network than other types of traffic that are relatively immune

to delay or changes in delay times (jitter). Often a percentage of the bandwidth is reserved for high-priority traffic, so when that type of traffic is present on the network it gets its own lane; when there is no high-priority traffic, however, all the bandwidth can be used by normal traffic. This is just like an airline ticket counter where one of the six lines is reserved for first-class passengers. The first-class passengers get a dedicated line; if there are no first-class passengers in line, however, the agent handling first class processes coach passengers.

- **Low cost**—Here is one of the mantras in the network community, quoted from RFC 1925, "The Twelve Networking Truths" by Ross Callon at http://www.faqs.org/rfcs/rfc1925.html: "Good, fast, cheap: Pick any two (you can't have all three)." Many times this is correct, but one truth is always evident to a network designer, engineer, or manager: Don't spend more money than necessary.

- **Easy configuration**—You know those "assembles in minutes" toys that don't? You do not want your network to suffer the same fate. Remember that if it is not easy to configure, it won't be easy to manage.

There are times when these solutions will not meet your requirements and some advanced network services will be required. Some of these advanced services are listed here; if you need any of these advanced networking services, then you are going to need routers in your network:

- **Firewalls**—These devices provide a way to filter out unwanted network traffic, such as broadcasts, from the reaching beyond the local network segment into the rest of the network.

- **Communication between dissimilar LANs**—If you have some users connected to an Ethernet network and some users connected to a Token Ring network, and you want these users to talk with each other, better get the router. This scenario is often seen when migrating from Token Ring to Ethernet.

- **Fast convergence**—If a failure occurs in a switched network, it takes 50 seconds for the Spanning Tree Protocol to converge on the new change. Routers can run one or more of several routing protocols, which are used to build a network map, and depending upon the routing protocol used, the routers can converge on a change in the network in as little as 1 second. Bear in mind that 802.1d STP is 50 seconds without specialized features or enhancements. In other words, worst case, 50 seconds using 802.1d STP.

- **Security**—Because routers look at the packets carried within the switched frames, you can specify that the router block traffic from certain source or destination network addresses. You can also configure the router to block all traffic from any networks to which you've not established permission to communicate, keeping potential network intruders out of your network. This is similar to requiring your network traffic to present a permission slip before it can continue on its field trip through your network.

- **Redundancy**—If one link fails, the router can determine what, if any, other links are available that provide a path from source to destination, similar to a construction worker redirecting traffic around a pothole repair. Redundancy is accomplished with the implementation of the Spanning Tree Protocol defined by IEEE 802.1d or the newer Rapid Spanning Tree Protocol (RSTP) defined by IEEE 802.1w.

- **Load balancing/sharing**—Remember that in kindergarten you were taught that it's good to share? Well, the rule applies here, too, in the form of load balancing. If you have multiple links between your source and destination, a router can be used to share the traffic across all those links, which can lead to more cost-effective use of your network. (Sharing is still a good thing.)

Switching and bridging sometimes result in the less-than-optimal path of network traffic because every frame and packet must go through the root bridge of the spanning tree if the source and destination nodes are on different branches of the spanning tree. When routers are used in your network, the routing of packets can be controlled and designed for the optimal path, providing "the quickest way out of town" for your data to get to where it needs to go (the destination network).

When designing switched LAN networks, consider the following, each discussed in more detail in the following sections:

- Comparison of LAN switches and routers

- Benefits of LAN switches in a network

- Benefits of routers in a network

- Benefits of VLANs and VLAN implementation in a network

- General network design principles

- Switched LAN network design principles

Routers and LAN Switches

The fundamental difference between a LAN switch and a router is that the LAN switch operates at Layer 2 of the OSI model and the router operates at Layer 3. It is this difference between routers and switches that affects the way that LAN switches and routers respond to network traffic. This section compares LAN switches and routers with regard to the following network design issues:

- Loops

- Convergence

- Broadcasts

- Subnetworking

- Security

- Media dependence

note
Switches implement Layer 2 functionality, and routers implement Layer 3 functionality. Because switches are beginning to implement Layer 3 functionality, in the form of multilayer switching, however, the functions of a LAN switch and a router are merging.

Loops

Layer 2-switched LAN topologies are vulnerable to loops, because the network is a flat network, as shown in Figure 10-12.

Figure 10-12 Layer 2 Loop

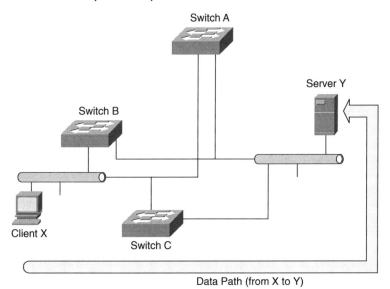

Data Path (from X to Y)

In Figure 10-12, it is possible for frames from Client X to be switched by Switch A and then for Switch B to put the same frame back on to the same LAN from where it originated. In this situation, frames loop and suffer multiple replications. To prevent this looping and replication, topologies that contain loops need to run the Spanning Tree Protocol. As discussed in Chapter 7, STP uses the spanning-tree algorithm to build topologies that do not contain loops.

note

A router can also support this design because the router would contain the broadcasts and bridge protocol data units (BPDUs) within each LAN segment.

Convergence

In transparent switching, neighboring switches make topology decisions locally based on the exchange of BPDUs. This method of making topology decisions means that converging on an alternative path can take an order of magnitude, measured in seconds, longer than in a routed environment, measured in fractions of seconds.

In a routed environment, routing protocols such as Open Shortest Path First (OSPF) maintain topological databases, or route maps, of the network, enabling the network to converge quickly in response to a change in the network topology, such as a link failure or the addition of a new network device.

Broadcasts

LAN switches do not filter broadcasts, multicasts, or unknown address frames. This lack of filtering might be a severe problem in distributed networks, which many networks are today, in which broadcast messages are used to resolve data link layer and network layer addresses and dynamically discover network resources, such as file and print servers. Broadcasts originating from each network segment are received by every computer in the switched network. Even though most network devices discard broadcasts because they are irrelevant to that device, large amounts of network bandwidth are consumed by these broadcasts. Broadcasts limit the amount of bandwidth that can be used for user data.

In some cases, the circulation of broadcasts around the network can saturate the network to the point that no bandwidth remains for application data. Imagine a roomful of people shouting for attention and leaving no "air" for a conversation between two people.

This is a situation known as a ***broadcast storm***. The problem is that new network connections cannot be established, and existing connections might be dropped. The probability of broadcast storms increases with each additional device added to the switched network. Broadcast storms are often caused by loops in the Layer 2 network and can shut down an entire network in seconds.

note

A broadcast storm is the excessive transmission of broadcast traffic within a network segment. Because routers do not forward broadcasts, routers are not subject to broadcast storms.

Subnetting

Switched networks are composed of physically separate segments, but are logically considered to be one large network, such as one Internet Protocol (IP) *subnet*, similar to grouping blocks of phone numbers together that share the same area code or exchange.

Because LAN switches operate at the data link layer (OSI Layer 2), the switches provide connectivity to the network hosts and behave as if each host were on the same cable, regardless of the logical network to which the host belongs.

note

Layer	Address Space
Layer 2	Flat address space with universally unique addresses. Each Layer 2 device is part of a single broadcast domain.
Layer 3	Hierarchical address space with identifiers within the address identifying networks and nodes within those Layer 3 networks.

Because routers operate at OSI Layer 3, they can create hierarchical addressing structures. Routed networks associate a logical addressing structure to a physical infrastructure so that each network segment has, for example, a Transmission Control Protocol/Internet Protocol (TCP/IP) subnetwork (subnet). Traffic flow on routed networks differs from traffic flow on switched networks because routed networks have more flexible traffic flow. The traffic flow in a routed network is

more flexible because routers use the hierarchy in determining the optimal path based on dynamic factors such as network congestion.

note

Routers route traffic to a destination network, not to the destination host. The router's job is to get the traffic to the destination network and let the receiving LAN determine who the host recipient is.

Security

Routers and switches each have features available that can be used to create more-secure networks. LAN switches might use custom filters providing access control to the network based on the source or destination address, the protocol type, frame or packet length, or certain bits within the frame. Routers might filter on logical source or destination network addresses and provide access control to the network based on the options available within the Layer 3 protocol being used, such as IP. For example, routers can be used to permit or deny traffic based on specific TCP/IP information for a range of network addresses, such as preventing a group of users from accessing file-sharing websites.

note

All currently shipping Cisco switches and most enterprise switch vendors have Layer 3 filtering capabilities, even in their respective Layer 2 switch product lines.

Media Dependence

Two factors need to be considered with regard to mixed-media networks, such as Ethernet and Token Ring: the *maximum transmission unit (MTU)* and the addressing scheme in the different networks.

The first factor that needs to be considered regarding mixed-media networks is that the MTU differs for various network media. Table 10-1 lists the minimum and maximum frame sizes for Token Ring and Ethernet network media.

Table 10-1   Network Media Minimum/Maximum Frame Sizes

Medium	Minimum Valid Frame Size	Maximum Valid Frame Size (MTU)
Ethernet	64 bytes	1518 bytes
Fast Ethernet	64 bytes	1518 bytes
Gigabit Ethernet (a.k.a. "Jumbo Ethernet")	64 bytes	9000 bytes
Token Ring	32 bytes	16 KB

When LANs of different media types are switched, such as between an Ethernet network and a Token Ring network, hosts must use the MTU that is the lowest common denominator of the switched LANs that make up the network. For example, look at the network in Figure 10-13.

Figure 10-13   Token Ring and Ethernet Switched Network

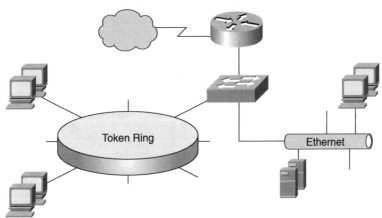

In this network, the switch recognizes that the maximum sized that can be accommodated is the 1518 bytes (1.518 kilobytes [KB]) of the Ethernet segment. If the switch allows a larger MTU, such as a 4-KB frame from the Token Ring segment, to traverse the Ethernet segment, the Ethernet segment will recognize the frame as a "giant" and discard the frame as invalid. The same holds true if a Token Ring network host sends a frame that is smaller than the minimum frame size of 64 bytes for Ethernet; however, in this case, the Ethernet segment will discard the frame as a "runt" because it is too small to be recognized as a valid frame.

This lowest common denominator requirement limits throughput and can compromise performance over a relatively fast link, such as the 100 Mbps of Fast Ethernet. Most network (OSI Layer 3) protocols can fragment, or break apart, and reassemble packets that are too large for a particular network, so networks connected with routers can accommodate the different MTU sizes, which maximizes throughput. An important consideration to remember here is high-speed routers use special hardware to route frames, which often limits the fragmenting and reassembling of packets.

The second factor that needs to be considered regarding mixed-media networks is that because switches operate at Layer 2, these switches must use a translation function to switch between different media. The translation function can result in serious problems such as converting the MAC (hardware) address from Token Ring to Ethernet. One issue with moving data from a Token Ring to an Ethernet network is the Layer 2 addressing; Token Ring network devices read the Layer 2 MAC address from left to right, whereas Ethernet network devices read the Layer 2 MAC address from right to left.

Because routers work at Layer 3, routers are independent of the properties of any physical media. Furthermore, because routers work at Layer 3, they can use a simple address-resolution protocol resolving differences between Layer 2 and Layer 3 addresses. An example of an address-resolution protocol is IP's *Address Resolution Protocol (ARP)*, which can determine the Layer 2 address if you have the Layer 3 address, as illustrated in Figure 10-14.

Figure 10-14   The Adventures of ARP

note

Whereas ARP is used in IP to determine the Layer 2 (data link) address if you know the Layer 3 (network) address, Reverse ARP (RARP) does the opposite; if you know the Layer 2 address, Inverse ARP (InARP) or RARP can give you the Layer 3 address. RARP is the more common term used when discussing reverse address resolution.

Benefits of a Layer 2 Switch in a Network

Layer 2 switches in your network might offer some, or all, of the following benefits to you:

- **Bandwidth**—Using a technique called microsegmentation, LAN switches provide increased performance for individual users because the switch allocates dedicated bandwidth to each switch port for each network segment.

- **VLANs**—Recall from Chapter 8 that VLANs are created by LAN switches that group individual ports into logical switched workgroups. Communication between these ports requires a router.

Benefits of a Layer 3 Router in a Network

Because routers use Layer 3 addresses, which often have structure to the address, routers can use techniques, such as address summarization, in building networks that maintain performance and responsiveness as they grow in size. By imposing a hierarchical structure on a network, routers can efficiently use redundant paths and determine optimal routes in a constantly changing network environment.

This section describes router functions that are vital in a switched LAN design:

- Broadcast and multicast control

- Broadcast segmentation

- Media transition

Broadcast and Multicast Control

If your user applications require broadcast and/or multicast support, such as videoconferencing, IPTV, or streaming data, such as a stock ticker, you should manage the broadcasts and multicasts that can cause network congestion. Routers are best suited to control these broadcasts and multicasts in your network by performing the following functions:

- **Caching the addresses of remote hosts**—When hosts send a broadcast packet determining the address of a remote host that the router already knows about, the router responds on behalf of the remote host and filters the packet from leaving the local network by dropping the broadcast packet.

- **Caching advertised network services**—When a router learns of new network services, the router caches the necessary information and does not forward the broadcasts related to the new service. When a client of that network service sends a broadcast locating that service, the router responds on behalf of the new service and filters the broadcast from the rest of the network by dropping the broadcast packet, sparing other network hosts from having to respond. For example, Novell *Internetwork Packet Exchange (IPX)* clients use broadcasts to find local services; and in a network without a router, every server responds to every client broadcast by multicasting its list of services. Routers manage these Novell broadcasts by collecting services not local to the switch and sending out periodic updates describing the services offered on the entire network.

- **Providing special protocols**—Special multicast protocols, such as the *Internet Group Multicast Protocol (IGMP)* and *Protocol Independent Multicast (PIM)*. These new multicast protocols enable multicasting applications to "negotiate" with routers, switches, and workstations to determine which devices belong to a multicast group. This negotiation helps limit the range and impact of the multicast stream on the network.

A good network design contains a mix of appropriately scaled switching and routing implementations. Given the effects of broadcast radiation on CPU performance, well-managed switched LAN designs must include routers for broadcast and multicast management to keep your network from being saturated and crippled with unnecessary traffic.

Broadcast Segmentation

In addition to preventing broadcasts from radiating throughout the network, spreading uncontrolled, routers are also responsible for providing services to each LAN segment. The following list identifies some examples of these services provided in a network environment:

- **Address Resolution Protocol (ARP)**—Rather than a workstation's ARP request flooding the network forcing every host to respond, the router can respond to the ARP request on behalf of the owner.

- **Dynamic Host Configuration Protocol (DHCP)**—With this protocol, an IP address is automatically assigned to a workstation on a TCP/IP network. DHCP saves you from having to manually assign permanent IP addresses to each workstation, a daunting task if you have hundreds of workstations to support. Routers can provide DHCP services to the network, preventing the DHCP broadcast from wandering the network waiting for a DHCP server to respond to the request.

- **Simple Network Management Protocol (SNMP)**— This protocol is a widely used for network monitoring and management. Network monitoring and management information is passed from SNMP agents to the workstation console used to oversee the network. Routers can act as SNMP agents for devices connected to their LAN or WAN interfaces, avoiding the addition of costly network probes on each network segment.

In a flat network, a single router would be bombarded by myriad requests needing responses, in turn taxing the router processor. Therefore, you need to consider the number of routers that can provide reliable services to a given subset of VLANs and that some type of hierarchical design needs to be considered for your network.

Media Transition

Routers are used to connect networks of different media types, such as Ethernet and Token Ring, translate the OSI Layer 3 network addresses, and fragment packets as necessary. Routers perform these same functions in switched LAN designs. Most switching is done within like media, such as Ethernet and Token Ring switches, with some capability of connecting to another media type, as discussed in the section "Media Dependence" earlier in this chapter. If a requirement for a switched network design is to provide high-speed connectivity between unlike media, however, routers will be required in your network design.

VLAN Design Considerations

In a flat, bridged network, all broadcast frames and packets generated by any host in the network are sent to and received by all other hosts in the same network. The ambient level of broadcasts generated by the higher-layer protocols in the network, known as ***broadcast radiation***, restricts the total number of nodes that the network can support. In severe cases, the broadcast radiation effects can be such that a workstation spends all of its CPU power on processing broadcasts, and not on any other applications, such as your e-mail, web browser, or Solitaire game.

Designing and implementing VLANs solves some of the scalability problems of large, flat networks by breaking the single broadcast domain into several smaller domains, each of which is its own VLAN. It is insufficient to solve the broadcast problems inherent to a flat, switched network by overlaying VLANs on top of the network. This reduces the size of each broadcast domain, but it in turn increases the number of domains, thus introducing a different problem with management and design.

VLANs without routers do not scale well into larger campus environments. Routing is instrumental to the building of scalable VLANs and is the only way you can impose hierarchy on your switched VLAN network.

VLANs enable the following features to be implemented in your network:

- **Broadcast control**—Switches isolate collision domains for attached hosts and only forward appropriate traffic out a particular switch port; VLANs refine this isolation concept further by providing complete isolation between VLANs. A VLAN contains all broadcast and multicast traffic within itself.

- **Security**—VLANs can provide security in two ways:

  — High-security users can be grouped into a VLAN, and no users outside of that VLAN can communicate with them.

  — Because VLANs are logical groups that behave like physically separate entities, inter-VLAN communication is enabled through the use of a router. When a router is used in your network, security and filtering functionality is then available to you because routers look at OSI Layer 3 information.

- **Performance**—The logical grouping of users allows, for example, engineers using networked computer-assisted design/computer-assisted manufacturing (CAD/CAM) workstations or testing a multicast application to be assigned to a VLAN containing just those engineers and the servers they need. When you separate the engineering group traffic into its own VLAN, their work does not affect the rest of the network users, resulting in improved network performance for both groups. The engineering team has

dedicated bandwidth, and the rest of the users are not slowed down by the engineering team's use of the network.

■ **Network management**—The logical grouping of users, separated from their physical or geographic locations, allows for easier management of the network. It is not necessary to pull cables if you are moving a user from one network to another, such as moving to a new floor in the building. Network moves, additions, and changes are achieved by configuring the switch port into the appropriate VLAN.

VLAN Implementation

The two primary methods of creating the broadcast domains that make up the various types of VLANs you can implement are as follows:

■ **By port**—Also known as a segment-based VLAN, each port on the switch can be part of only one VLAN. With port-based VLANs, no network (OSI Layer 3) address recognition occurs within the switch, so IP and Novell IPX networks must share the same VLAN definition. This means that all traffic within the VLAN, regardless of the network protocol used, will share the broadcast domain. All traffic within the VLAN is switched, and traffic between VLANs is routed by an external router or by a router within the switch.

■ **By protocol**—Also known as a virtual-subnet VLAN, protocol-based VLANs are based on network (OSI Layer 3) addresses. Protocol-based VLANs can differentiate between different network protocols, such as IP and IPX, enabling the definition of VLANs to be made on a per-protocol basis, somewhat like grouping people together at a party based on the language each speaks so that they can communicate with each other. With Layer 3-based VLANs, it is possible to have a different virtual topology for each protocol in use within the network, with each topology having its own set of transmission and network security policies. Switching between protocol-based VLANs happens automatically when the same protocol is used within each VLAN. Communication between VLANs on different Layer 3 subnets needs an external router or router card in the switch.

When using Layer 3-based VLANs, a switch port can be connected to more than one VLAN.

note

VLANs are often differentiated by assigning each VLAN a "color," or VLAN ID. For example, engineering might be the "blue" VLAN, and manufacturing might be the "yellow" VLAN.

For a refresher on VLANs, review Chapter 8.

General Network Design Principles

For network design, there is no one "good network design," and there is certainly no "one size fits all." A good network design is based on many concepts, some of which are summarized by the following key general principles:

- **Examine for single points of failure carefully**—There should be redundancy in your network, so that a single link or hardware failure does not isolate any portion of the network resulting in those users losing access to network resources. The amount of redundancy required varies from network to network. Some networks might require a backup link between two sites, and some networks might require redundant links, routers, and switches. The amount of redundancy depends on how much money you want to spend on the extra equipment and what level of risk you are willing to accept by not having the redundancy.

  — Two aspects of redundancy need to be considered: backup and load sharing. A backup path should be available as an alternative to the primary path so that if the primary path fails, traffic will automatically run across the backup path; sort of like a detour in your network. Load sharing happens when two or more paths to a destination exist and both can be used to share the network load.

- **Characterize application and protocol traffic**—The application data flow profiles the client/server communication across your network and this profile is essential to allocate sufficient resources for your users. Some examples might be reducing the number of workstations using a particular server or the number of client workstations on a segment.

- **Analyze available bandwidth**—There should not be significant difference in available bandwidth between the different layers of the hierarchical model. It is important to keep in mind that the hierarchical model refers to conceptual layers providing functionality in your network, not an actual physical separation. In a small network, for example, a single switch might provide both core and distribution layer services; the switch backplane would be the core layer and the switch port being the distribution layer, and the network segment itself being the access layer.

- **Build networks using a hierarchical or modular model**—Hierarchy in your network enables separate segments to be networked together. A hierarchical network design gives you three conceptual layers in your network—core, distribution, and access with each layer providing different functionality.

Switched LAN Network Design Principles

When designing switched LAN campus networks, the following factors must be considered:

- **Broadcast storms**—Broadcast storms can be fatal to a network. When nearly 100 percent of host CPU cycles on a device, such as a switch or users computer, are consumed by processing broadcast and multicast packets, the network is crippled and unusable. Because of delays inherent in carrier sense multiple access collision detect (CSMA/CD) technologies, such as Ethernet, any more than a small amount of broadcast traffic impacts the operation of devices attached to a switch. Although VLANs reduce the effect of broadcast radiation in LANs, there is still a scaling issue as to how many hosts should reside within a given VLAN. A router provides for larger network designs because a VLAN can be segmented depending on traffic patterns within the VLAN. In a network design where traffic is not logically segmented, however, a single router can be burdened with large amounts of traffic where the destination LAN is the same as the origination LAN.

- **Well-behaved VLANs**—A well-behaved VLAN is not just a VLAN that behaves itself when company is visiting the parents, but it once meant a VLAN in which 80 percent or more of the traffic is local to that VLAN. The 80 percent rule is violated when a user in one VLAN reads mail from a second VLAN, reads and writes to file servers from a third VLAN, and sends print jobs to network printers in a fourth VLAN. In current network environments the 80/20 rule has given way to the implementation of *server farms*, which are a collection of application servers in a network-centric location. The 80/20 rule carried more weight back in the days of slower network connections than what are available today. When you had 10 Mbps available to you for user data, for example, you tried to keep as much local traffic off the line as you could. In today's environment of 100-Mbps and 1-Gbps network links, however, there is often enough available bandwidth that the 80/20 rule has lost its usefulness in network design.

- **Available bandwidth supporting routing functions**—Inter-VLAN traffic must be routed. The network design needs to account for this traffic and allocate enough bandwidth to move inter-VLAN traffic from the source, through the router, to the destination. The amount of bandwidth used between switches needs to be monitored to ensure there is adequate trunk bandwidth between switches. EtherChannel provides incremental trunk speeds between Fast Ethernet, Gigabit Ethernet, and 10Gigabit Ethernet by combining multiple Fast Ethernet up to 800 Mbps, Gigabit Ethernet up to 8 Gbps, and 10 Gigabit Ethernet up to 80 Gbps.

- **Appropriate placement of administrative boundaries**—Switching flattens networks. The deployment of switches outside of your administrative boundary can impact the network within your administrative boundary. If this is the case, your network traffic will be traveling across other networks,

essentially trying to find its way on its own rather than being directed by your switches.

Network designs are evolving with the deployment of switching from the user desktop to the network backbone. Three topologies have emerged as generic, switched campus network designs:

- Scalable switching

- Large switching/minimal routing

- Distributed routing/switching

Scalable Switching

A scalable switched network deploys switching at all hierarchical layers (core, distribution, and access) of the network without the use of routers. In this design, each layer consists of switches, with the devices in the access layer providing slower-speed connection to end users. A scalable switching design is illustrated in Figure 10-15.

Figure 10-15   Scalable Switch Design

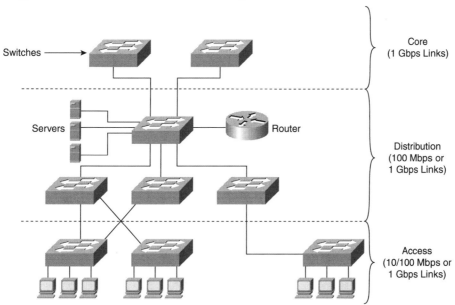

A scalable switch network design is a low-cost and easy-to-install solution for a small campus network. This design does not require knowledge of network address structure, is easy to manage, and enables all users to communicate with one another.

However, you do need to remember that a scalable switch network makes up a single broadcast domain, which can lead to network congestion if the amount of broadcasts increases, such as with additional users being added to the network. If a scaled switched network needs to grow beyond the broadcast domain, then VLANs should be used to create multiple smaller broadcast domains.

note

When VLANs are used, end users in one VLAN cannot communicate with end users in another VLAN unless routers are deployed within the network to enable this inter-VLAN communication.

Large Switched/Minimal Routing

The large switched/minimal routing design deploys switching at the access, distribution, and core layers of the network, as illustrated in Figure 10-16.

Figure 10-16   Large Switched Network with Minimal Routing

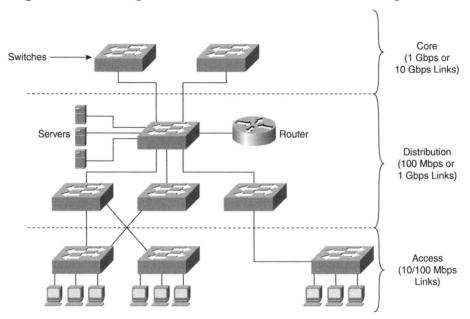

In the case of LAN switching in the distribution layer, the following issues need to be considered when designing your network:

■ Support for VLAN trunking technology in each enterprise-class LAN switch you use in the network. (Remember, some low-end switches do not support VLAN trunking.)

■ The switches in the distribution layer must run the Spanning Tree Protocol (STP) to prevent network loops. Running STP means that some connections will be blocked and load sharing will not be available for you to use in your network. However, you can load balance by having some VLANs block on one port and other VLANs block on the other port when using trunking.

If you want to scale the large switched with minimal routing network design, you must use a logical hierarchy. The logical hierarchy is made up of VLANs and routers enabling communication between the VLANs. In this topology, routing is used only in the distribution layer, and the access layer depends on bandwidth through the distribution layer to gain access to high-speed switching functionality in the core layer. The large switched/minimal routing design scales well when VLANs are used such that the majority of resources are available in the VLAN. If this topology can be designed so that 80 percent of traffic is inside the VLAN and 20 percent of traffic is external to the VLAN, the bandwidth needed for communication between VLANs is not a concern. If there is more than 20 percent communication required between VLANs, however, access to routing or Layer 3 switching in the core becomes a scalability issue, at which point you should take another look at how your VLANs are designed, possibly segmenting the VLANs even further or regrouping your users and servers.

Distributed Routing/Switching

The distributed routing/switching design uses switching in the access layer, routing in the distribution layer, and high-speed switching in the core layer, as shown in Figure 10-17.

Figure 10-17 Distributed Routing and Switching Design

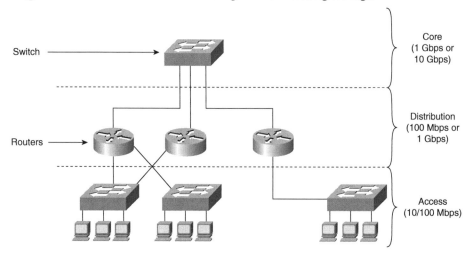

The distributed routing/switching design follows the classic hierarchical network model in both physical and logical fashions. Because this design provides high bandwidth for access to routing functionality, the distributed routing and switching design scales very well. This design is ideal for networks that do not have the 80/20 rule consideration, such as a server farm implementation.

Chapter Summary

There is no "one size fits all" network design; there are only models to which you, like other network designers, engineers, and managers, adhere. Given the right tools, you can design, build, and manage your network; and this chapter has discussed the essential tools that you will need to design, build, and manage a switched network.

These are the components of a switched network: the physical switch platform itself; a common infrastructure, to implement features on your switches; and a network management platform, so that you can monitor and manage your network's performance.

There are two types of switched networks in your design toolkit: a Layer 2 (flat) switched network and a Layer 3 (hierarchical) switched network. Layer 2 switched networks are flat networks made up of switches to create a single broadcast domain. These networks use the data link layer, or MAC, address in making filtering and forwarding decisions. Layer 3 switched networks add a hierarchical component to the network through a routing element, which uses the network layer address in making filtering and forwarding decisions. It is this same router element that also filters broadcasts from the rest of the network and thus creates a boundary for the broadcast domain.

LAN designs use switches to replace traditional hubs and use a mix of routers to minimize broadcast radiation in your network. By using the right pieces of software and hardware, and by adhering to good network design, you can build network topologies that can be robust and adapt to nearly any change in network conditions, such as a link or hardware failure, or changes in requirements, such as adding more users and devices.

Regardless of whether you use Layer 2 switching, Layer 3 switching or routing, VLANs, or a combination of all these elements, you should still abide by some general network design principles. You should examine your network design and implementation for single points of failure, adding redundant hardware or links when necessary. Look at the applications that are using your network and the protocol traffic these applications create. Watch the bandwidth usage on your network to ensure there is enough bandwidth available for all network users. When you build your network, use a hierarchical or modular model so that as your network grows, you add on the necessary parts (instead of undertaking a major redesign effort).

note

Network design case studies are discussed in Chapter 12, "Switching Case Studies."

Chapter Review Questions

1. What is microsegmentation?

2. What are the three basic components of a switched network?

3. What is a flat network?

4. Name the most significant problem inherent in a flat network?

5. What are some of the features available to you in a VLAN implementation?

6. What are some of the issues you need to address in a mixed-media environment, such as mixing Token Ring and Ethernet LANs?

7. What are some general principles of network design?

8. What are some principles of switched LAN design?

9. What are some of the network services offered by routers that are not available with switches alone?

10. What is the difference between ARP and RARP?

11. Is there a "one size fits all" concept for network design?

What You Will Learn

On completing this chapter, you will be able to:

✔ Describe the FCAPS model and its use

✔ List various methods used to monitor and manage a network

✔ Describe some network management protocols used for the monitoring and management of a network, such as SNMP and RMON

✔ Explain the functions of the Switch Port Analyzer (SPAN) for switch network management

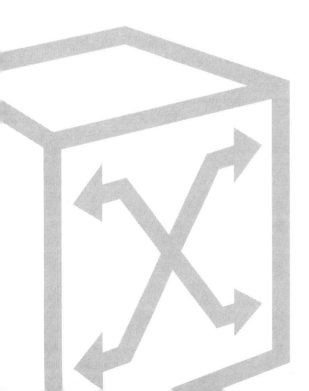

CHAPTER 11

Switch Network Management

You might have been tasked to design and implement a switched network out of a number of pieces, not unlike putting together a jigsaw puzzle, and you've succeeded in doing so. Congratulations! However, you might be looking at the network and thinking to yourself, "My network looks like the box cover. What can I do to make sure it stays that way?" This chapter helps you answer that question through a discussion of the monitoring, management, and maintenance of a switched LAN.

Before discussing the management of a Layer 2 or Layer 3 switched network, the chapter discusses the concepts behind network management. Although a full discussion of network management is beyond the scope of this book, the chapter presents important network management fundamentals and how they are applied in a switched environment.

Network Management Model

The principles of network management resemble the principles of network communications; both use a layered approach. The layered approach of the FCAPS model for network management is like the Open System Interconnection (OSI) model used for internetworking, as shown in Figure 11-1.

Figure 11-1   FCAPS and OSI Models

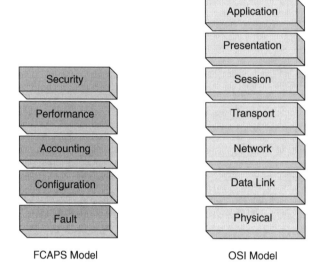

FCAPS Model   OSI Model

note

The correlation between the FCAPS layers and the layers of the OSI model is not direct.

FCAPS Model

FCAPS is an acronym for the network management model, or framework, and is made up of five layers, as follows:

- **(F)ault management**—Network faults and problems are found and fixed.

- **(C)onfiguration management**—The network is monitored and controlled, often from a central point, such as a network operations center, or NOC. Configuration management includes keeping track of hardware and software on the network and any modifications to this hardware and software.

- **(A)ccounting management**—Network resources are distributed and departments are charged for their end users' network use, such as long-distance or bandwidth usage per user.

- **(P)erformance management**—Network congestion and bottlenecks are minimized.

- **(S)ecurity management**—Only people who need access to specific network resources are allowed to see and use these resources. Security management applies equally to both outside intruders and internal users; not all network hackers are from outside an organization.

Each of these layers is discussed in more detail in the following sections.

note
Whereas the OSI model works in a service-based mode, meaning that each layer provides services to the layer above and depends on the layer below, the FCAPS model works in a more isolated fashion; each layer can operate independently of the other layers.

Fault Management

Fault management detects, logs, and notifies network managers of any network issues. If possible, fault management can automatically fix network issues, such as rerouting traffic around the fault, much like detouring traffic around an accident on the highway, as illustrated in Figure 11-2.

If a network has redundancy (backup path) built in to its topology, fault management can be configured to occur automatically. The fault is not corrected automatically, but rather the recovery of network connectivity happens automatically. Would you rather troubleshoot a network problem while your users are up on a backup path or while your phone is ringing off the hook? With fault management, your network can automatically detour the network traffic to the good path.

Most network management systems poll the managed devices for error conditions, such as failed links or network congestion, and present this information to the network manager in a manner that is usable, such as an alarm at a network management console or the automatic sending of an e-mail or text page to the network manager, as illustrated in Figure 11-3.

Figure 11-2   Network and Highway Detours

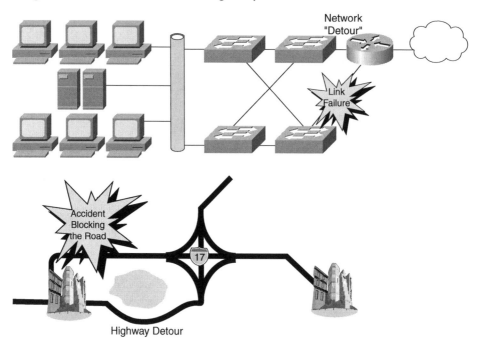

Figure 11-3   Fault Management in Action

note

Fault management takes care of events and traps as they occur within your network. A *trap* is an event that occurs when certain triggers happen. This is similar to your being notified of an overdue bill payment because the billing system "trapped" the event that the payment was not received in time; the trigger is the billing system recognizing the overdue payment, and the trap is the automatic notice sent to you in the mail. Network management traps work in the same fashion. When an event happens within the network that you have set a trap for, such as a failed link, an event notification is sent to the destination you have defined: a network management station, e-mail, or even your pager.

Figure 11-4 illustrates the basic process of fault management.

Figure 11-4   Fault Management Flowchart

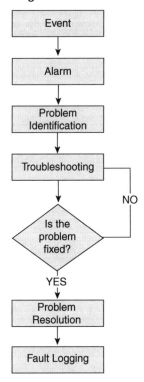

When a network event occurs, an alarm is sounded. When the network manager (you) detects the alarm, you begin to identify what the problem is in the network. After you've identified the problem, such as a device or link has failed, you begin to solve the problem; this is called ***troubleshooting***. You continue to troubleshoot the problem until you have found a resolution that works and fixes the problem. After you have applied this fix, you log the initial fault and what you did to correct it, so that if it happens again you don't have to re-create your efforts. In other words, if that little red light lights up again, you'll know what to do because you did it before.

Configuration Management

The purpose of configuration management is to monitor network, system hardware, and system software configuration information so that the network operation impact of various hardware and software components can be tracked and managed. Changes, additions, and deletions from the network must be coordinated with the network manager or network management personnel, often in a ***network operations center (NOC)***.

Before any change is made to the network, it is good practice to have all parties involved in the change discuss what will change, how it will be changed, who will make the change, when the change will occur (often during off-hours when network users are minimally impacted), and, most important, what to do if the change doesn't work, as illustrated in Figure 11-5.

Generally it is not a good idea to effect many changes at one time, because that can be a recipe for disaster. If you need to make several changes to your network, it is best, if possible, to make one change at a time to ensure the network remains up and stable. If you make several changes simultaneously and something goes wrong, you might not know what caused the problem, making fault management your new goal.

Figure 11-5   Configuration Management in Action

The *configuration management* comprises a number of elements:

- **Inventory hardware**—An inventory of active and spare network hardware.

- **Inventory software**—An inventory of software in use and its associated license keys.

- **Configuration information**—A baseline of hardware firmware updates and software patches that have been applied within your network, and the function of each update and patch. The baseline is often used in the installation of new devices as a template or standard.

- **Change control**—A process whereby network hardware and software changes are managed in a controlled environment without back-out procedures in place, in case an update does not take or goes bad, and the network is down as a result. You can think of change control as the Reset button on your network.

Accounting Management

Accounting management is intended to measure network utilization so that individuals or group users on a network can be regulated to prevent one person, or group of people, from using all the network bandwidth and keeping others from using the network to its full capacity. Accounting management also provides the network manager a means to bill network usage back to customers or internal departments, as illustrated in Figure 11-6.

Figure 11-6   Accounting Management in Action

Accounting management provides a mechanism for the Information Technology (IT) department to bill network usage back to internal departmental users so that no one department gets "stuck" with the bill.

Accounting management and performance management share some characteristics. These are the functions they have in common:

■ Monitoring and measuring of network bandwidth utilization.

- Analysis of usage patterns and the trend of those usage patterns. Is usage decreasing, increasing, or holding steady?

- Ongoing measurement of network bandwidth. This measurement can result in bandwidth utilization and billing information, helping you ensure there is enough network bandwidth for all your users.

Performance Management

Similar to accounting management, *performance management* is intended to measure various aspects of network performance. Performance management makes available these network performance aspects so that the network can be maintained at an acceptable threshold, not over- or underutilized, as illustrated in Figure 11-7.

Figure 11-7   Performance Management in Action

"This is where we upgraded our switches to the newest firmware. You can see the difference because the number of network errors decreased to zero and enabled us to reduce our utilization baseline because we are not having to resend all the errored traffic."

Performance management provides you the tools and methods to collect and analyze network statistics, enabling you to "paint a picture" of your network and how it behaves. Performance management also provides you reporting mechanisms so that network performance can be measured against *service level agreements (SLAs)* that you might have contracted with a service provider.

note

An overutilized network can result in contention for network bandwidth, which can be identified by users complaining of a slow network. An underutilized network can result in your paying for network bandwidth you are not using (and might never use).

Figure 11-8 illustrates the performance management process.

Figure 11-8   Performance Management Process

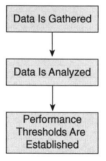

First you must gather the interesting performance data. "Interesting" does not mean that the data makes for lively reading, but that it pertains to the network segment you are measuring. After you've gathered this data, you must analyze it and determine the baselines. The average network usage might be a more useful baseline for you than the peak usage data, for example, because the average utilization helps you determine whether your usage is going up or down. After you've established your baseline—in this case, our baseline is average utilization—you need to establish the performance thresholds, the points at which you consider the network to be over- and underutilized. What you use for a baseline depends on your situation and what information you are looking for, such as average utilization, minimum/maximum utilization, peak utilization hours, and so on.

Aside from reactive-based processes, performance management enables you to proactively monitor and manage your network in the form of network simulation or trend analysis. The data collected can be used to create reports justifying network upgrades or to support projects that have been started. Often the technical details are important for political and financial purposes, not just for your own group.

Performance management baseline and trend analyses examine the following network characteristics:

- **Network-capacity planning**—The total amount of network bandwidth.

- **Availability**—The total amount of time your network is up and available to its users.

- **Response time**—The total amount of time it takes for a transaction to complete (for example, a frame being sent from an end user to its destination).

- **Throughput**—The average network bandwidth your network is capable of sustaining. If you have a 100-Mbps Fast Ethernet local-area network (LAN), but your users can use only about 50 kbps of it, there is likely a throughput issue.

- **Utilization**—The average amount of bandwidth and time your network is being used by the network end users.

Security Management

Security management controls access, in accordance with your organization's security guidelines, to network resources.

Most network management systems address security regarding network hardware—for example, someone logging in to a router or switch.

Security management systems perform the following functions:

- The identification of sensitive network resources

- The establishment of maps between sensitive network resources and user sets, mapping out which users can access which resources

- The monitoring of sensitive network access points and the logging of inappropriate or failed access to these resources

When applied, a good network security management system adds several safe-guards to prevent unauthorized network access; however, the only safe computer is a standalone computer (one that is not connected to any network). If we all used standalone computers, it would certainly make doing business in today's world challenging, but would be a boon for carrier pigeon breeders. Because carrier pigeons are not always our best choices for a network transport, we accept certain risks when deploying a network, and security management mitigates these risks.

note

Different aspects of security management in an Internet Protocol (IP) network are combined with the implementation of the AAA model. *AAA* is the acronym for authentication, authorization, and accounting. AAA is a system in IP networks that controls what resources users have access to and tracks user activity over a network.

- *Authentication* is the process of identifying an individual, often based on a username and password combination. Authentication is based on the assumption that each individual user has unique information setting that person apart from other users on the network.

- *Authorization* is the process of granting user access to network resources once the user has been authenticated. The amount of information and the number of services the user has access to depend on the user's authorization level.

- *Accounting* is the process of tracking a user's activity while accessing network resources, including the amount of time spent in the network, services accessed while there, and the amount of data transferred during the session. Accounting data can be used for trend analysis, capacity planning, billing, auditing, and cost allocation.

- AAA services often require a server that is dedicated to providing the three services.

Security management is not just about prevention, but also about detection. Security management includes alerting the network manager when an unauthorized user tries to gain access to network resources, as illustrated in Figure 11-9.

Figure 11-9   Security Management in Action (Detecting a Network
Intruder)

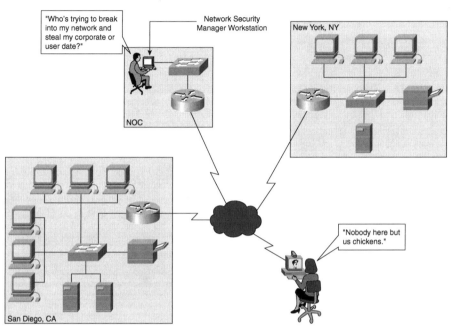

In Figure 11-9, an alarm at the NOC is alerting the network manager that someone
is attempting to gain access to network resources, such as a router, a switch, a
server, or even a user's workstation. As a network manager, you don't care what
this person is going after or why, only that it's happening and you have security
management policies already in place that address what to do in this case.

The components of security management are as follows:

- **Policy**—The organization has a security policy on user access to certain network resources. The policy spells out who can access what and what happens when a security compromise occurs.

- **Authority**—An individual is identified who has the authority to grant access
  to sensitive network resources so that users cannot provide themselves
  access to certain information.

- **Access level**—Sensitivity level of information is identified as well as user access to these levels. Information can be categorized as confidential, secret, or top secret.

- **Exceptions**—Any exceptions to the security policy or access level must be documented to prevent accidental compromises.

- **Logging**—All activities are logged, whether users logging in to their own machines or someone attempting to log in to a network switch.

Protocols

Just as several network protocols are implemented using the OSI model, several network management protocols are implemented using the FCAPS model. The two network management protocols discussed in this chapter are the Simple Network Management Protocol (SNMP) and the Remote Monitoring Protocol (RMON).

Simple Network Management Protocol (SNMP)

SNMP is a popular network management protocol used in today's network environment. SNMP was defined by the Internet Engineering Task Force (IETF) for Transport Control Protocol/Internet Protocol (TCP/IP) networks and is referred to as the "Internet-standard management framework." SNMP defines both a protocol and architecture for managing networks, and the SNMP framework is used when building network management applications or management devices.

SNMP has evolved into three versions; SNMPv1, SNMPv2, and SNMPv3.

- **SNMPv1** reports only whether a device is up (working) or down (not working).

- **SNMPv2** includes security and a Remote Monitoring (RMON) Management Information Base (MIB). The RMON MIB provides continuous feedback without having to be queried by the SNMP console.

- **SNMPv3** provides message-level security. SNMPv3 also includes an MIB for remotely monitoring/managing the configuration parameters for this message-level security.

SNMP is based on the manager/agent model consisting of a manager and an agent, a management information database, managed objects, and the network management protocol, as illustrated in Figure 11-10.

Figure 11-10   SNMP Manager and Agent

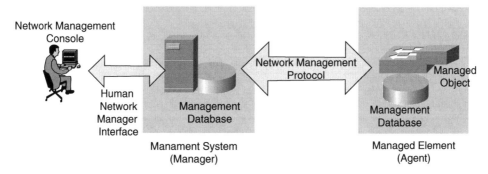

The SNMP manager provides the interface between the human network manager through a network management console and the management system. The SNMP agent provides the interface between the manager and the network device being managed.

Both the SNMP manager and SNMP agent use the *Management Information Base (MIB)* and a small set of commands to exchange information. The MIB is organized in a tree structure with individual variables, such as point status or description, being represented as leaves on the branches. (MIBs are further discussed later in this chapter.)

Network management information is exchanged between the SNMP manager and agent through SNMP messages.

SNMP Messages

SNMP uses five messages when communicating between the manager and the agent: GET, GET-NEXT, GET-RESPONSE, SET, and TRAP.

- The **GET** and **GET-NEXT** messages enable the SNMP manager to request information for a specific variable, such as the status of a switch port: Is the port up or down?

- When the GET or GET-NEXT message is received by the SNMP agent, the agent issues a **GET-RESPONSE** message back to the SNMP manager with the requested information, such as identification of the switch responding with the port status.

- The **SET** message enables the SNMP manager to request that a change be made to a specific variable, such as changing an alarm threshold on a port or device. The SNMP agent responds with a GET-RESPONSE message indicating the change has been made or an error indication as to why the change cannot be made.

- The **TRAP** message enables the agent to alert the SNMP manager of an event, such as a link failure.

The SNMP agent sends information contained in an MIB to the SNMP manager. The MIB is a data structure defining what information is gathered from the device. An MIB might be compared to a job application; only certain information can be asked for and will be provided.

note

In MIB and SNMP messages, a numeric tag called the object identifier (OID) differentiates each variable from another. An OID is made up of a series of numbers separated by decimal points and might look like this: 1.3.5.1.6.4.1.2.7.1.

SNMP, for all its worth, does have some limitations. SNMP can store a limited amount of information, such as traffic counters or the number of link errors. Another limitation is that SNMP is a polled system, meaning agents respond only to manager requests for information (not including traps, and therefore a sizable amount of network traffic can result from the constant "Is everything okay/Everything is okay" conversations between the SNMP manager and agent.

The RMON protocol was developed to overcome these SNMP limitations and can provide more detailed information.

Remote Monitoring (RMON)

The RMON protocol was developed to overcome the limitations of SNMP. As mentioned, SNMP can store only limited amounts of information (for example, counters for overall traffic and number of errors), and because SNMP is a polled system, additional network traffic is carried, possibly putting more load on the network. RMON provides more detailed information than SNMP and provides for a more simplified data-collection mechanism than SNMP.

RMON uses a client such as a network management console or a network analyzer, and the RMON client gathers the statistics from one or more RMON agents. These agents can be standalone RMON probes that are located in strategic spots in the network, such as network concentration points, or embedded RMON agents in routers and switches, as illustrated in Figure 11-11.

Figure 11-11   Network Management Console and RMON Client (Probe)

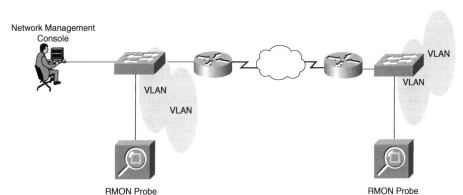

RMON specifies 10 services called RMON groups; 9 groups are for Ethernet, and 1 group is Token Ring. Not all devices have to support all RMON services (because some of the RMON groups require extensive device memory and processor power). Most standalone RMON probes support all 10 services, but embedded RMON might be limited to only a few groups.

Table 11-1 lists the RMON groups.

Table 11-1 RMON Groups

Technology	RMON Groups		
	Group Number	**Group Name**	**Group Description**
Ethernet	1	Statistics	General traffic utilization and error count, including collisions.
	2	History	Long-term statistics history and is used for baselining.
	3	Alarm	Alarms triggered when events occur, similar to SNMP traps, and enable the setting of alarm thresholds.
	4	Host	Individual statistics from transmitters (senders) and receivers on the network segment.
	5	Host "Top n"	"Top n" of the host statistics, such as the "top 10 hosts reporting errors" or the "top 10 network users"; also known as the "top talkers."

Table 11-1   RMON Groups (continued)

Technology	RMON Groups		
	6	Matrix	Packet and error counts for each conversation on the network.
	7	Filter	Definition of which packets will be analyzed in statistics or packet-capturing operations. The filter group is required if you are using the capture group.
	8	Capture	Capture and storage of packets in the agent prior to transmission to the RMON client. If you are using the capture group you must also use the filter group.
	9	Event	Log file of what happened.
Token Ring	10	Token Ring	Specific Token Ring data, such as beaconing errors on the ring.

note
Cisco switches support the following RMON groups: statistics group, history group, alarm group, and the event group.

RMON clients communicate directly to the RMON agent, and RMON collects only data at the OSI Layer 2 (data link) level. If you want information about what the frames are carrying, such as the higher-layer protocols (for example, IP or TCP), you must decode the frames using a protocol analyzer.

RMON2 was developed to provide data on the higher-level protocols, such as IP and Internetwork Packet Exchange (IPX), and through the rest of the OSI model stack, up to and including the application layer (OSI Layer 7). RMON2 provides information on which protocols are being used on the network and the mix between them, standard RMON host and matrix information for the network and applications layers, and a history function that might be used for baselining your network.

RMON is not vital for network testing; however, it makes your life easier and enables you to access the network statistics from wherever you are, such as from the NOC.

Switch Port Analyzer (SPAN)

Switched Port Analyzer (SPAN), sometimes called port mirroring or port monitoring, copies switch network traffic and forwards it out the SPAN port for analysis by a network analyzer. By enabling the SPAN, you can monitor traffic on a switch port by forwarding incoming and outgoing traffic to another port for data collection and analysis. You can use a network analyzer on this monitor port to troubleshoot network problems by examining traffic on other ports or segments without taking the network out of service.

Suppose, for instance, that you want to examine traffic flowing in and out of a port, or within a virtual local-area network (VLAN). In a shared network, such as Ethernet, you would attach a network analyzer to an available port on the hub and your analyzer would listen to all traffic on the segment, as illustrated in Figure 11-12.

The analyzer decodes the frames and provides you with an analysis of the frame contents, such as the packets and other higher-layer protocol information.

In a switched network, however, this is not as simple as in a shared network. In a switched network, the switch filters frames from transmitting out a port unless the bridge/switch table believes the frame's destination is on that port, or the frame needs to be flooded, such as during a spanning-tree update. This is not going to work for you because you want to see all the switch traffic, from all the VLANs. The SPAN switch feature enables you to attach an analyzer on a switch port and capture traffic from other ports in the switch, as illustrated in Figure 11-13.

Figure 11-12   Network Analyzer in a Shared Network

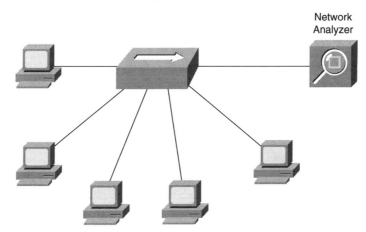

Figure 11-13   Network Analyzer in a Switched Network

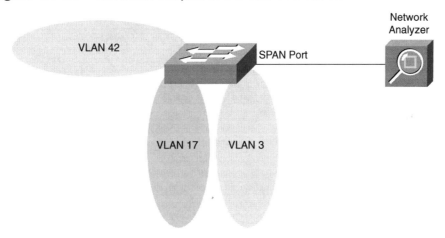

The SPAN port mirrors traffic from one or more source interfaces on any VLAN, or from one or more VLANs to a destination port for analysis. The network analyzer attaches to the SPAN port and examines the traffic as it passes through the switch. The network analyzer enables you to dig into the details of your network traffic. For SPAN configuration, the source interfaces and the destination interface must be on the same switch.

note

SPAN does not affect the switching of network traffic on source interfaces; copies of the frames received or transmitted by the source interfaces are sent to the destination interface.

Chapter Summary

FCAPS is the acronym for a model of network management and consists of five levels: fault management, configuration, accounting, performance, and security.

At the fault management level, network problems are found and corrected and potential future problems are identified and prevented, minimizing network downtime.

At the configuration management level the operation and configuration of the network is monitored and controlled. Hardware and software changes and updates, including new equipment configurations and software patches, are coordinated, including a back-out plan. If anything should go wrong during a hardware or software update the back-out plan provides for an "undo" function. Configuration management also provides for an inventory of network hardware and software, including spare equipment.

At the accounting management level, network resources are distributed appropriately among network users, making the most effective use of the network and minimizing network costs by not maintaining more network bandwidth than is necessary. The accounting management level is also responsible for ensuring that organizations, departments, or end users are billed correctly and appropriately for their network usage.

The performance management level involves overall performance of the network. Performance is a measurement of several variables, including, but not limited to, network uptime, available bandwidth, and maximum throughput per user, average bandwidth per user, and average bandwidth per protocol. The goal of performance management is to minimize network bottlenecks, or choke points, where users can experience network slowdowns resulting in poor application performance. Performance management also provides for a method to identify and analyze improvements that might exist, now or in the future, that will provide the best overall network performance.

The security management level protects the network resources and its users from the following: outside intruders (such as malicious hackers), unauthorized users (internal or external), and physical or electronic sabotage. Security management also involves the confidentiality and integrity of user information. The security systems enable network managers to control what authorized users can (and cannot) do within the network and its systems.

The Simple Network Management Protocol, or SNMP, is a widely used network management and monitoring protocol. Network management and monitoring data is passed from SNMP agents to the network management console overseeing the network. The SNMP agents are either a hardware or software process reporting activities that reside in each network device, such as routers or switches. The network management consoles are often located in network operations centers, or NOCs. The SNMP agents send information contained in a Management Information Base, or MIB, back to the SNMP manager. The MIB is a data structure defining what data can be collected from the device and what can be managed, such as, the turning on or off of a router or switch port interface.

SNMPv1 provides basic information regarding the managed device, such as "Is the device up or down?"

SNMPv2 provides enhancements to SNMPv1 such as security and a RMON MIB. The RMON MIB provides continuous feedback from the managed device without having to be queried by the SNMP management console.

SNMPv3 builds on the enhancements of SNMPv2 by adding a security component to the data being sent back to the network management console.

RMON provides extensions to SNMP, providing more in-depth network monitoring capabilities. With SNMP, the management station queries the network devices for information; RMON is proactive and can set alarms based on traffic condi-

tions, such as network errors or failures. RMON2 can monitor the application traffic flowing through the network and provide information regarding this traffic. Devices can generate traps without a specific query issued from a management station, even without RMON.

SPAN, sometimes called port mirroring or port monitoring, copies switch network traffic and forwards the frames out the SPAN port for analysis by a network analyzer or probe. With SPAN you can monitor an individual switch port, multiple ports on the local switch, local traffic for a single VLAN, or local traffic for multiple VLANs. With SPAN you cannot monitor traffic from a remote switch, such as a switch on the other side of a trunk link; SPAN enables you to monitor only traffic on the local switch.

Chapter Review Questions

1. What is the FCAPS model used for?

2. What are the layers of the FCAPS model?

3. What is a NOC? What purpose does a NOC serve?

4. What are the six steps in the fault management process?

5. Why is configuration management important to a network manager?

6. What do the accounting and performance management functions provide to a network manager?

7. Why is security in your network important?

8. What are some of the differences between SNMPv1, SNMPv2, and SNMPv3?

9. What are some of the differences between SNMP and RMON?

10. What benefits does SPAN provide you in a switched environment?

What You Will Learn

This chapter examines case studies for the following:

- ✔ Hub-based networks

- ✔ Bridge-based networks

- ✔ Small switch-based networks

- ✔ Medium and large switch-based networks

- ✔ VLANs

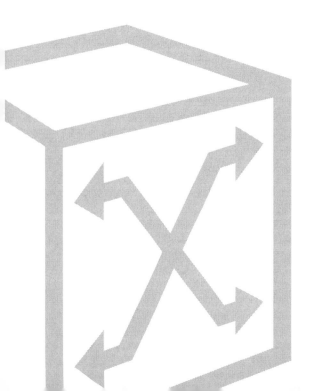

CHAPTER 12

Switching Case Studies

Before examining the case studies of this chapter, consider the following rules of thumb regarding switch design:

- When designing a network, you should follow some basic steps, such as assessing the network's existing (if any) network, notational and technical drawings, test plans, and implementation plans.

- Remember that switches break up collision domains, whereas routers break up broadcast domains.

- When implementing Ethernet, there is a design rule called the "5-4-3 rule" for the number of repeaters and segments on shared-access Ethernet backbones in a tree topology. The 5-4-3 rule divides the network into two types of physical segments: populated (user) segments and unpopulated (link) segments. User segments have users' systems connected to them, and link segments connect network repeaters together. The rule mandates that between any two nodes on the network, there can be only a maximum of five segments, connected through four repeaters (hubs), and only three of the five segments can contain user connections.

By this point in the book, you might be asking yourself, "How have other people handled the issues raised in this book?" Because there is no "one size fits all" for network architecture, this chapter presents some scenarios you might come across in your networking adventures.

Hub-Based Networks

Nowadays hubs are inexpensive devices that you can use in your network to provide port or connection sharing for your users. For example, you might use a hub in your home to share an Internet connection among multiple computers or in your office to share a switch port with multiple users grouped together in a room.

Hubs in a Home Network

Suppose that you have a computer at home, with a printer, and are using a cable modem or digital subscriber line (DSL) for access to the Internet, as illustrated in Figure 12-1.

Figure 12-1   Home Computer, Modem, and Internet

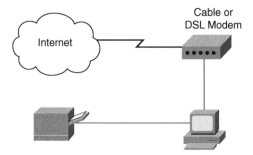

The network shown in Figure 12-1 is a basic network configuration typical for home use. It uses the minimum number of devices to provide you a connection to the Internet: the computer, the cable/DSL modem, and the Internet access line itself.

Now suppose that your office issues you a laptop, and you want to be able to telecommute (work from home) at times. Because you already have an Internet connection to your home, you might want to share that connection, rather than install a second connection for your laptop; a small hub enables you share this connection, as illustrated in Figure 12-2.

Figure 12-2 Hub-Based Network

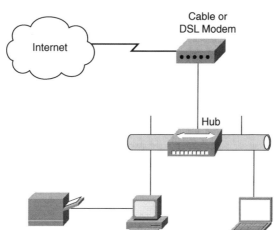

With the addition of a small hub from your local computer or office-supply store, you can share your dedicated Internet connection with multiple computers, and you are limited only by the number of ports on the hub, such as a four- or eight-port hub.

When you look at the network illustrated in Figure 12-2, it is obvious that there is little provided in the way of network security. Okay, let's be blunt: There is no network security in this architecture! Recognizing this lack of security, it is advisable to install a software-based firewall on each device (computer) connected to the hub, because as you might recall, the hub is a multiport repeater and takes whatever signal is received on one port and repeats it out all ports—not the most secure model.

It is worth mentioning that within 24 months of the time of writing this book, it is expected that all hub-component vendors will stop making hubs and make only low-end switches. With this said, it would be perfectly reasonable for you to go to your local computer store and buy a small low-end switch rather than a hub for this same scenario. The purpose here is to show where a hub might be used today.

Hubs in an Office Network

Suppose you share an office with a few people, each in his or her own workspace, with the exception of a control desk with multiple computers, as illustrated in Figure 12-3.

Figure 12-3 Control Desk and Cubicles

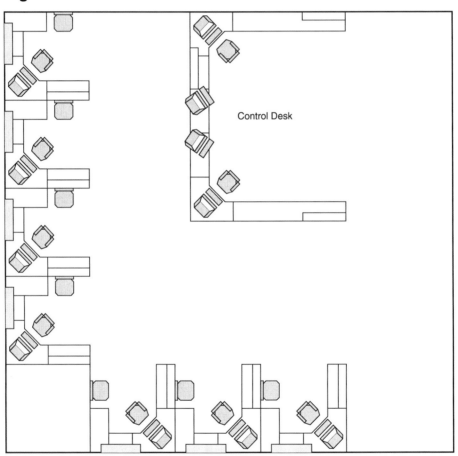

Figure 12-3 shows a control desk with four computers and seven cubicles, each with its own computer. In this setup, 11 computers are sharing a single network connection, such as to the Internet. However, you might have recognized a pattern in that the number of ports on a hub, bridge, or switch is a multiple of two. (This chapter doesn't go into the specifics because such specifics are beyond the scope of this book.) Suffice it to say that the number of ports available on a hub, bridge, or switch are numbered in this way: 4-ports, 8-ports, 16-ports, 24-ports, and so on. However, the office pictured in Figure 12-3 needs 11 ports. So although it might be easy to say, "Drop in a 16-port hub and call it a day," life is not that easy.

note

Using hubs is not the only possible solution for this scenario. This chapter presents another possible solution, using switches, in subsequent sections.

You could use both an eight- and four-port hub, creating a daisy chain, as illustrated in Figure 12-4. This architecture enables you to share a port on the eight-port hub with the four-port hub, which has the three control-desk computers connected to it. Keep in mind that one of the ports of your four-port hub is being used to provide the uplink to the eight-port hub, so you have only three usable ports for workstations available on the four-port hub.

Figure 12-4   Small Hub-Based Daisy Chain

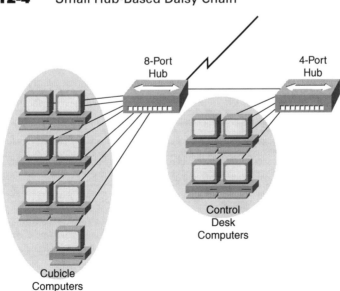

Recall from Chapter 5, "Ethernet LANs," that hubs create both a single broadcast and collision domain, meaning that all devices connected via the hubs can recognize traffic from all other devices. In a small network, this is not significant; with every device you add to the network, however, you are adding more traffic that all other devices must contend with for bandwidth, as illustrated in Figure 12-5.

Figure 12-5   Large Hub-Based Daisy Chain

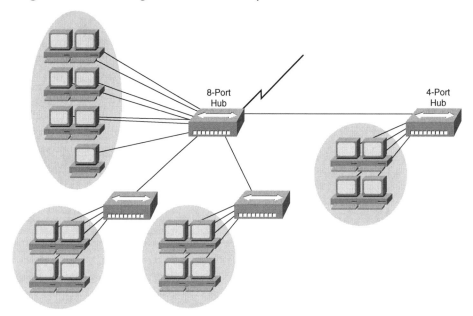

Although the network architecture shown in Figure 12-5 might work, be aware of the single collision domain you've created, and the subsequent complaints from your users: "The network is slow." If your users are using the network for e-mail and web surfing, the issue of the large collision domain probably won't arise. If your users are using more network-intensive applications, such as computer-assisted design/manufacturing (CAD/CAM) applications, however, consider segmenting your network, with switches alone, for example, or switches with virtual local-area networks (VLANs) configured.

Bridge-Based Networks

You've just been informed by your boss that your sales office is moving to another city, and you need to figure out a way to keep operations in both offices running as if it they were a single entity while your users move. Figure 12-6 illustrates what your network looks like today, before the moving company shows up at the office.

Figure 12-6   Office Before Relocation

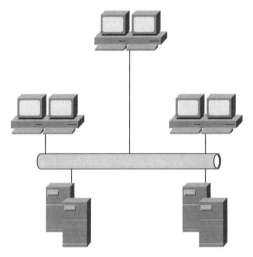

In your sales office today, you have four servers and six computers sharing the same Ethernet local-area network (LAN) segment. Two of these servers and two of the computers will be the first in the network to be relocated. Now, before you break out the "So, You're Relocating" brochures, let's figure out a way to link the old and new offices together. You could use a LAN bridge, as illustrated in Figure 12-7.

At this point you have two LANs, one in the old office and one in the new. These two LANs are connected across a wide-area network (WAN) connection of some type, such as a Frame Relay or private-line connection, with a bridge on each side. The bridges here are transparent in that they supply a transparent connection between the two LANs. To your users and servers, it will seem as if nothing has changed, except maybe the scenery.

Figure 12-7   Office During Relocation

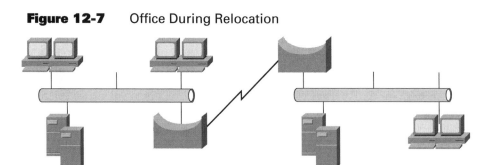

When all your network equipment from the old office has moved to the new office, you no longer need the bridge link to be up and can therefore disconnect the bridges. However, you could leave the bridge as a permanent connection, if some of the people are not moving.

This solution works only if the bridges have WAN interfaces. If not, you need to use a router as well. If you encounter this scenario, it would be more cost-effective to implement a router to enable the WAN connection between the two offices, as illustrated in Figure 12-8.

Figure 12-8   Using a Router with a WAN Connection

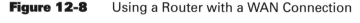
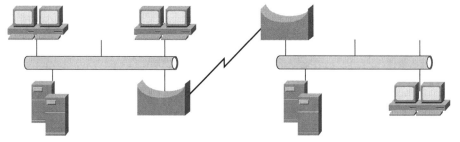

Small Switch-Based Networks

You were just hired to manage a network for a small company and arrive on the scene to find the current network a mess. You have daisy-chained hubs everywhere, people keep moving around, and your users are complaining that the network is slow. You've locked yourself in a room with a whiteboard to diagram your network, and you've come up with what is shown in Figure 12-9.

Figure 12-9   Whiteboard Drawing of Your Current Network

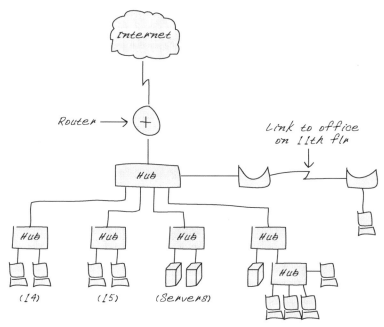

When looking at an existing network or designing a new network, remember that it's best to break it down into pieces. Take a look at what you have here:

- An Internet connection and a router.

- Hanging off that router is a hub with five connections.

- Four of these connections are going to other hubs, and one of those hubs has another hub hanging off it with additional attached workstations.

- The fifth connection is going to another floor in the building and is connected with a bridge.

You have four groups of users spread throughout the office: a sales team, a marketing team, an engineering team, and a human resources team. Each user community has unique demands on the network in terms of bandwidth and availability. For example, the sales team needs the network so that they can communicate via e-mail with their clients, and the engineering team needs the network so that they can test how their new applications operate across the Internet.

At this point it might be worthwhile deploying a switch and segmenting the network into more manageable pieces, such as giving the sales and engineering teams their own segments so that they are not contending with each other for the network bandwidth. Because hubs are used everywhere, your current network is one large collision domain. This is not a bad thing, unless you have users complaining. You can improve network performance by implementing a small switch, as illustrated in Figure 12-10.

Figure 12-10 Small Switch-Based Network

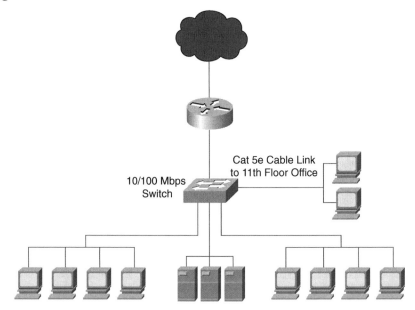

To implement the configuration shown in Figure 12-10, you bought a small switch, with 48 or 96 ports on it (because you don't have many users, but you want to leave some room to grow). You removed all the bridges and hubs from the network and connected everyone directly to the switch. You thought about using VLANs here but have decided to wait and see whether VLANs are necessary—because this is still a small network (fewer than 50 ports are being used), but you are going to keep an eye on things and see whether performance has improved and if the user complaints drop.

The small switch design, illustrated in Figure 12-11, shows another option in which multiple switches are used to create a hierarchical design.

Figure 12-11 Small Hierarchical Switch-Based Network

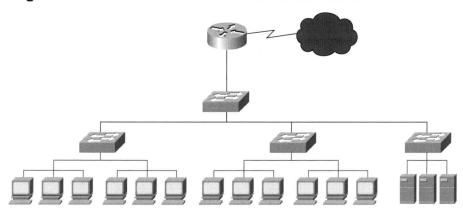

This switch-based hierarchical design enables you to better manage your network by controlling the flow of traffic rather than using hubs, which repeat all traffic to all users. Using switches in this hierarchical design also provides you more usable ports for end users than hubs provide.

Medium and Large Switch-Based Networks

You find yourself in an office-park scenario, or a university campus, where buildings are spread around within a defined perimeter or fence line. Suppose you are managing a network spread across five buildings, for instance, as illustrated in Figure 12-10.

Figure 12-12   Campus LAN

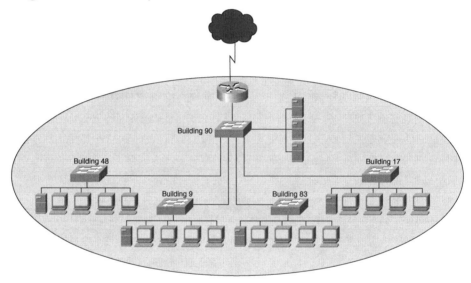

This network is made up of the following:

- The switch in Building 90 is the network core providing access to the Internet and a server farm, made up of e-mail, file, and web servers. The Building 90 switch also provides interconnectivity for the switches in the remaining buildings.

- Buildings 48, 9, 83, and 17 are offices spread across a corporate office park.

- Each building houses sales, engineering, administrative, marketing, and customer service agents.

Each building has a dedicated switch providing connectivity back to the switch in Building 90. For the users in each of these buildings to access resources from another building, their traffic will be switched through the core switch in Building 90. You might use Layer 2 or Layer 3 switching in this scenario, depending on how much of your network is being consumed by broadcasts.

VLANs are another solution that you might implement in a campus scenario.

VLANs

Your network is humming along with no issues and all is well with the world when you meet a friend for lunch. Over sandwiches and salads, your friend asks for your help with their network because users are screaming and performance could be better. Your friend draws the network diagram in Figure 12-13 on a napkin.

Figure 12-13   Network on a Napkin

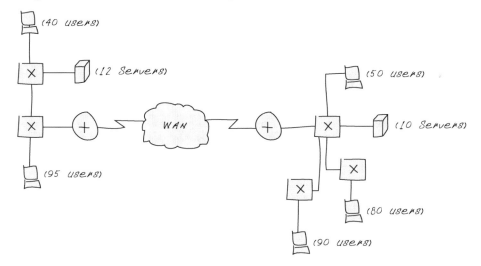

Your friend explains that there are three user communities spread across the two offices, and they are connected by a Frame Relay WAN link, which is always congested and causes users to suffer long delays in transferring files back and forth. You explain to your friend the concept of VLANs, and how implementing VLANs here will help cure the network congestion by putting each user community into its own virtual LAN, so that it doesn't have to share LAN resources with users outside its community, as illustrated in Figure 12-14.

Figure 12-14   VLANs

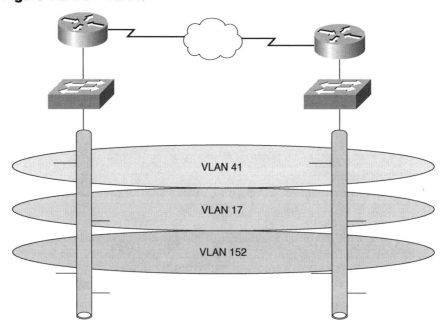

You show your friend that by using VLANs, each user community has its own broadcast domain that does not interfere with the broadcast domains belonging to the other user communities. Because what you've suggested breaks up the broadcast domains, your friend's users should see a noticeable improvement in network response time, because each LAN is not being saturated with local broadcasts; only the users within each VLAN will see their respective broadcasts.

After you've explained VLANs, your friend thanks you and buys you lunch.

Figure 12-15 illustrates a larger-scale switch-based network with the following characteristics:

- The router provides connectivity to the Internet for all connected users.

- The Ethernet segment connected to the router is connected to two switches and a wireless access point (WAP). The WAP provides wireless access to the computers capable of wireless LAN (WLAN), such as a user laptop.

- One of the two switches connected to the Ethernet segment supports users located in the same building as the router and segment where the other switch supports a campus-area network (CAN). The CAN connects switches housed in different buildings, each switch supporting either end users or servers.

Figure 12-15 Complex Switch-Based Network

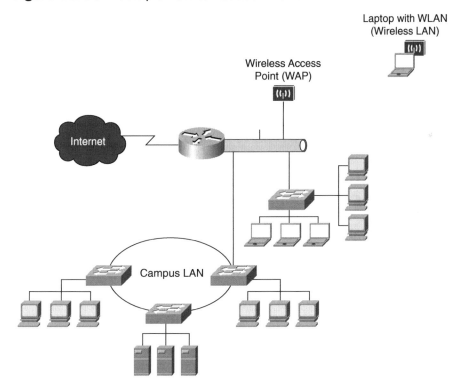

Chapter Summary

"Do you use a hub, bridge, or a switch in your network?" That is the question. Although this question might not rival Shakespeare's "To be, or not to be" (*Hamlet*, Act I, Scene I), it is still a question for the ages, albeit the network age. The truth of the matter is that the answer to this question lies in the statement that applies to all network design questions: "It depends."

I realize that "It depends" might leave you a bit despondent, but rest assured, you have more tools available to you today than those before you, and many people have contributed to figuring out what to do when faced with these types of questions.

You might use a hub, bridge, or switch in your home network of 2 computers and Internet connection, or you might use a hub, bridge, or switch in your office network of 20 computers and a WAN connection. Would a hub work in these environments? Sure. Would a bridge or switch work in each of these environments? Of course, because as discussed in this book, bridges and switches work at the same layer of your network, the data link layer (Open System Interconnection [OSI] Layer 2). The question you need to answer is not "Do I use a hub, bridge, or a switch?" The question is actually, "What is the best choice for the operation of my network today and in the future?"

There is no easy answer, and if there were, I would share it with you here. When faced with a situation with which you are unfamiliar or not sure what to do, talk about it with others who might know. Remember, a standalone computer is not a network, and a standalone engineer is not a network engineer.

We're all in this together.

Chapter Review Questions

1. Should you use a hub, bridge, or switch?

2. What are some basic steps in designing a network?

3. What breaks up a collision domain?

4. What breaks up a broadcast domain?

5. When might you use switches rather than hubs?

6. When might you use a router rather than a switch?

7. What is the number-one rule of a network?

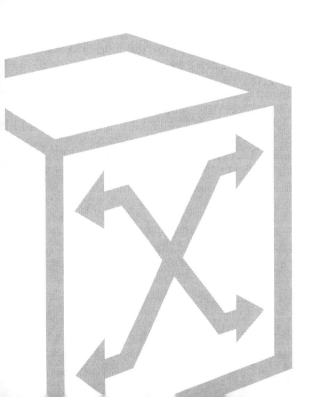

Answers to Chapter Review Questions

Chapter 1

1. What is the definition of a network?

    Answer: A network is a system of lines or channels that cross or interconnect, or a group or system of electrical components and connecting circuitry designed to function in a specific manner.

2. What are network models?

    Answer: Network models provide the guiding principles behind the development of network standards.

3. What is a network standard, and why are there network standards?

    Answer: Network standards define the rules of network communication and are like laws that must be followed for different equipment vendors to work together.

4. What is a proprietary feature?

    Answer: If a vendor implements a feature that does not adhere to any network standards, it is called a proprietary feature.

5. What are the three data transmission modes, and how do they operate?

    Answer: Simplex mode, half-duplex mode, and full-duplex mode. Simplex mode is one-way communication only. Half-duplex mode is two-way communication, but not at the same time. Full-duplex mode is simultaneous two-way communication.

6. List the major characteristics of a LAN.

   Answer: The primary characteristic of a LAN is its geographic coverage. LANs are found in a small geographic area where there is a short distance between connected computers, as in small offices or on each floor of a larger office building. LANs enable the sharing of office resources, such as file servers for file sharing among users or print servers for shared printers.

7. List the major characteristics of a MAN.

   Answer: MANs are found in a metropolitan, or citywide, geographic area, interconnecting two or more office buildings in a broader geographic region than a LAN would support, but not so broad that a WAN would be required.

8. List the major characteristics of a WAN.

   Answer: WANS are found in broad geographic areas, often spanning states and countries, and are used to connect LANs and WANs together.

9. What are the three parts of a frame? What is a function of each part?

   Answer: Header, data (or payload), trailer. The header is the beginning of the frame, significant in that the frame's source and destination are found in the frame header. The payload is the data part of the frame, the user's information. The trailer identifies the end of the frame.

10. What function in a network does cabling provide?

    Answer: Cabling provides the physical interconnection between network devices and nodes.

11. List some examples of user data.

    Answer: Examples of user data include e-mail, web-browsing traffic, word-processed documents, spreadsheets, database updates.

12. What is the best definition of network topology?

    Answer: Network topology refers to the physical or logical geometric arrangement of interconnected network devices.

13. What is the best definition of network protocol?

Answer: A network protocol is the communication rules and formats followed by all interconnected devices on a network requiring communication with one another.

14. What is the definition of network media?

Answer: Network media refers to the physical component of a network. Communication signals traverse network media from source to destination. Some examples of network media are copper and fiber-optic cabling.

15. What is a network origination point?

Answer: A network connection has two ends: the origination and termination points. The origination point is the source of the data—the location from which the data is being sent.

16. What is a network termination point?

Answer: A network connection has two ends: the origination and termination points. The termination point is the destination of the data—the location to which the data is being sent.

Chapter 2

1. What is ANSI, and what does it do?

Answer: ANSI is the acronym for the American National Standards Institute and is a U.S. governmental body responsible for approving U.S. standards in several categories, including computers and communications.

2. What is the ITU-T, and what does it do?

Answer: The ITU-T is the telecommunications standardization sector of the ITU (International Telecommunication Union) and is responsible for technical recommendations about telephone and data communications systems telecommunications carriers.

3. What is the IEEE, and what does it do?

Answer: The IEEE is the Institute of Electrical and Electronics Engineers and is the leading technical authority in several technology fields, such as computer engineering and electronics.

4. What does OSI stand for, and what is the OSI model?

Answer: OSI stands for Open System Interconnection. The OSI model is a model of network architecture and of the protocol suites across the network architecture. The OSI model was developed as a framework for international standards in various and diverse computer network architectures to be developed and implemented.

5. Describe and name the layers in the OSI model.

Answer: There are seven (7) layers in the OSI model: (7) application, (6) presentation, (5) session, (4) transport, (3) network, (2) data link, and (1) physical.

6. What are some advantages of a layered model approach to networking?

Answer: Whether it is the OSI model layers or the Hierarchical Design Model layers, the layered approach provides the same advantages: the compartmentalization of network functions. This compartmentalization enables vendors to develop and produce a specific product set, such as network hardware (routers, switches) or software (computer or network operating system). This same compartmentalization provides the network administrator a step-by-step approach to troubleshooting a network fault, and to isolating the failure from the rest of the network, such as implementing a failover path or replacing the hardware

7. What is the network standard for 10-Mbps Ethernet? 100-Mbps Ethernet? 1000-Mbps/Gigabit Ethernet? 10Gigabit Ethernet?

Answer: 10-Mbps Ethernet—IEEE 802.3

100-Mbps Ethernet—IEEE 802.3u

1-Gbps 1000-Mbps—IEEE 802.3z

10,000-Mbps/10-Gbps Ethernet—IEEE 802.3ae

8. What is encapsulation, and how does it work (in reference to the OSI model)?

Answer: Encapsulation is the process by which each layer of the OSI model wraps protocol information around the information received from the layer above. Each layer of the OSI model performs a specific function, adding that layer's information; based on this information, the receiving side knows what to do upon receipt of the data.

Chapter 3

1. What the three components of a frame?

Answer: Header, payload, and trailer.

2. What is a bit?

Answer: Bit is short for "binary digit" and is the smallest unit of information that can reside on a computer or be carried by a network communications device.

3. What are the main characteristics and differences between a LAN and a WAN?

Answer: LANs are networks confined to relatively small geographic areas, such as within a building, or a house. LANs use hubs, bridges, switches, and routers to connect LAN segments together. WANs are networks spanning across broad geographic areas, such as between cities across a state, country, or the world, interconnecting LANs from these locations. WANs use routers to connect these LANs together.

4. How does a repeater work?

Answer: A repeater is a communications device that amplifies or regenerates a signal extending the transmission distance of the signal across the network.

5. How does a hub work?

Answer: A hub is a multiport repeater; when a signal is received on one port, it is forwarded out all ports on the hub. It is up to each network device attached to the hub to determine whether it is the intended recipient of the signal traffic.

6. How does a bridge or switch work?

Answer: A bridge or switch learns the MAC addresses of devices on the respective sides of the two interfaces. The information helps keep frames that are destined for the local subnet from passing over the bridge and wasting bandwidth on the other side. If it knows that a specific MAC address is on one side, the bridge drops the frame. Bridges forward broadcasts out all ports, as well as forward frames destined for a MAC for which the bridge has no entry in its table.

7. What is the difference between a bridge and a switch?

Answer: A bridge is considered a multiport hub, whereas a switch is considered to be a multiport bridge with multiple network segments that might, or might not, communicate with each other. Switches also build tables based on the MAC address received on each switch port and forward frames based on these tables.

8. What is the difference between a physical topology and a logical topology?

Answer: Physical topology is the actual physical, or real, arrangement of network devices via some sort of media, such as copper or fiber-optic cabling. Logical topology is the virtual arrangement of network devices, made possible by the physical topology. The logical and physical topologies might look similar when laid out, but the logical topology is based on user communication requirements. For example, because a frame passes through a switch does not mean it must stop at that switch on its way to its destination.

Chapter 4

1. What determines the category of a cable?

Answer: The cable category is determined by the number of twists per inch.

2. Describe a star topology.

Answer: In a star topology, all network devices are connected to a central point such as a hub or a switch.

3. Describe a ring topology.

Answer: In a ring topology, all network devices are connected to each other in the shape of a loop, or ring, so that each device is directly attached to two other devices.

4. Describe a tree topology.

Answer: In a tree topology, several star topologies are connected to a single linear backbone, such as a single switch.

5. Which LAN topologies usually use switches?

Answer: Switches are commonly used in star and tree topologies.

6. When would you use a star (hub-and-spoke) or a ring topology?

Answer: Due to its centralized nature, a star (hub-and-spoke) topology is somewhat easier to install and manage than a ring topology. Centralization, however, creates a single point of failure. If the central hub or switch fails, the entire network is down. A ring topology does not have this central point of failure but can be more difficult to install than a star topology. The determining factor is the choice between ease of management and simple redundancy.

7. When would you use a tree topology?

Answer: In a larger LAN environment, such as in an office building, a single star topology can become cumbersome to maintain and manage because all users are essentially on the same network segment. Using a tree topology can physically segment users by their location, such as the first or second

floor, making it easier to maintain and manage the network. Each tree branch, or floor, can either use resources on the same branch (switch) or share resources with users from other branches (such as those on another floor), within the same tree.

Chapter 5

1. What is a MAC address?

   Answer: A MAC address is the physical address of a network device and is 48 bits (6 bytes) long. MAC addresses are also known as the physical addresses and hardware addresses.

2. What are the components of a MAC address?

   Answer: A MAC address is made up of two parts: the organizational unique identifier (OUI) and the vendor assigned serial number, or address.

3. How is a MAC address represented?

   Answer: A MAC address is represented in hexadecimal format, specifically as six pairs of hexadecimal numbers separated by hyphens.

4. How does Ethernet operate?

   Answer: Ethernet is a shared media LAN operating at 10-Mbps, 100-Mbps, 1000-Mbps (Gigabit) or 10000-Mbps (10 Gigabit) modes. 10/100 Ethernet and Gigabit Ethernet can operate in either half-duplex or full-duplex mode. 10 Gigabit Ethernet operates in full-duplex mode only. When in half-duplex mode, Ethernet operates in a CSMA/CD environment, whereas in full-duplex mode each device has dedicated access to network bandwidth.

   Carrier sense multiple access collision detect (CSMA/CD) enables half-duplex Ethernet operation, in that each device listens to the line before sending its data. If the line is in use, meaning the device senses a carrier on the line, it holds off transmitting. If the line is not in use, meaning no carrier is sensed on the line, the device begins transmitting.

5. What is a collision, and what happens when a collision occurs on an Ethernet network segment?

Answer: A collision occurs when two or more devices attached to an Ethernet network segment send traffic across the line at the same time. When a collision occurs, each affected device waits a random amount of time before resending the data. The length of the wait is determined by a backoff algorithm.

6. Describe a repeater and how it operates.

Answer: A repeater repeats incoming signals from one interface and regenerates, or resends, the signal out all other interfaces.

7. Describe a hub and how it operates.

Answer: A hub is a central device in a network that joins lines together in a star configuration. Ethernet hubs are multiport repeaters often with 4, 8, 16, or 24 ports. A signal received on one port is repeated out all ports to all connected devices; it is up to each device to determine by the destination MAC address if it is the intended recipient of the transmission.

8. Describe a bridge and how it operates.

Answer: A bridge is a multiport hub and is used to connect two or more LAN segments together. A bridge uses a filtering table to determine whether a frame received from one LAN segment is to be filtered (dropped) or forwarded to another LAN segment connected to the bridge.

9. Describe a switch and how it operates.

Answer: A switch is a multiport bridge that cross connects two LAN nodes together, giving each sender/receiver pair the full network bandwidth rather than the shared bandwidth environment created by hubs. Switches separate collision domains by filtering and forwarding frames based on the source and destination hardware, or MAC, addresses. When a switch receives frames destined for an unknown address, the switch broadcasts these frames out all ports.

10. Describe a router and how it operates.

Answer: Routers are devices that forward data packets from one local-area network (LAN) or wide-area network (WAN) to another LAN or WAN. Routers forward these packets based on their routing tables, which are built using certain routing protocols. Routers read the network address from the packet within each transmitted frame and select a transmission method for the packet based on the best route available. Routers also drop packets destined for an unknown address. An unknown address is an address that is not found in the routing tables.

11. What is a backoff algorithm?

Answer: The backoff algorithm is a random amount of time each station waits after a collision has occurred on the network segment before attempting data retransmission.

12. What Ethernet technologies operate in half-duplex mode? Full-duplex mode?

Answer: Half-duplex: 10 Mbps (10BASE-T), 100 Mbps (100BASE-T), 1000 Mbps (Gigabit Ethernet). Full-duplex: 10 Mbps (10BASE-T), 100 Mbps (100BASE-T), 1000Mbps (Gigabit Ethernet), 10000 Mbps (10 Gigabit Ethernet). 10-Mbps and 100-Mbps Ethernet can operate in either half- or full-duplex mode depending on the network interface card and switch port capability.

13. Given the MAC address 00-aa-00-62-c6-09, identify the OUI and vendor-assigned serial number.

Answer: OUI: 00-aa-00

Serial number: 62-c6-09

14. How does a bridge determine whether a frame is forwarded or filtered?

Answer: Bridges determine whether to forward a frame based on the entries in its filtering table. If a frame is received from a port and the frame is destined for the network segment on that same port, the bridge filters (drops) the frame from its memory because the intended recipient is on the same network segment and would have received the frame. If the destination network segment is on a different bridge port, the bridge forwards the frame out that intended port.

15. What is the difference between cut-through and store-and-forward switching?

    Answer: Cut-through switching forwards an incoming data frame before the frame is completely received by the switch. Store-and-forward switching stores the complete incoming frame before forwarding the frame on to its intended destination.

16. In what LAN environment are routers most commonly used?

    Answer: In a local-area network (LAN) environment a router is commonly used to connect LANs together across a wide-area network (WAN) or to connect a LAN to the Internet.

Chapter 6

1. What is unicast and how does it work?

    Answer: Unicast is a one-to-one transmission method. A single frame is sent from the source to a destination on a network. When this frame is received by the switch, the frame is sent on to the network, and the network passes the frame to its destination from the source to a specific destination on a network.

2. What is multicast and how does it work?

    Answer: Multicast is a one-to-many transmission method. A single frame is sent from the source to multiple destinations on a network using a multicast address. When this frame is received by the switch, the frame is sent on to the network and the network passes the frame to its intended destination group.

3. What is broadcast and how does it work?

Answer: Broadcast is a one-to-all transmission method. A single frame is sent from the source to a destination on a network using a multicast address. When this frame is received by the switch, the frame is sent on to the network. The network passes the frame to all nodes in the destination network from the source to an unknown destination on a network using a broadcast address. When the switch receives this frame, the frame is sent on to all the networks, and the networks pass the frame on to all the nodes. If it reaches a router, the broadcast frame is dropped.

4. What is fragmentation?

Answer: Fragmentation in a network is the breaking down of a data packet into smaller pieces to accommodate the maximum transmission unit (MTU) of the network.

5. What is MTU? What's the MTU for traditional Ethernet?

Answer: MTU is the acronym for maximum transmission unit and is the largest frame size that can be transmitted over a network. Messages longer than the MTU must be divided into smaller frames. The network layer (Layer 3) protocol determines the MTU from the data link layer (Layer 2) protocol and fragments the messages into the appropriate frame size, making the frames available to the lower layer for transmission without further fragmentation. The MTU for Ethernet is 1518 bytes.

6. What is a MAC address?

Answer: A MAC address is the physical address of a network device and is 48 bits (6 bytes) long. MAC addresses are also known as physical addresses or hardware addresses. (Give yourself a pat on the back if you recognize this question from Chapter 5. The repetition shows how important it is to understand MAC addresses and how they are used in your switched network.)

7. What is the difference between a runt and a giant, specific to traditional Ethernet?

   Answer: In Ethernet a runt is a frame that is less than 64 bytes in length, and a giant is a frame that is greater than 1518 bytes in length. Giants are frames that are greater than the MTU used, which might not always be 1518 bytes.

8. What is the difference between store-and-forward and cut-through switching?

   Answer: Cut-through switching examines just the frame header, determining the output switch port through which the frame will be forwarded. Store-and-forward examines the entire frame, header and data payload, for errors. If the frame is error free, it is forwarded out its destination switch port interface. If the frame has errors, the switch drops the frame from its buffers. This is also known as discarding the frame to the bit bucket.

9. What is the difference between Layer 2 switching and Layer 3 switching?

   Answer: Layer 2 switches make their forwarding decisions based on the Layer 2 (data link) address, such as the MAC address. Layer 3 switches make their forwarding decisions based on the Layer 3 (network) address.

10. What is the difference between Layer 3 switching and routing?

   Answer: The difference between Layer 3 switching and routing is that Layer 3 switches have hardware to pass data traffic as fast as Layer 2 switches. However, Layer 3 switches make decisions regarding how to transmit traffic at Layer 3 in the same way as a router. A Layer 3 switch cannot use WAN circuits or use routing protocols; a router is still required for these functions.

Chapter 7

1. What is a protocol?

   Answer: A protocol is the agreed-upon rules governing transmitting and receiving of data between two network devices, such as computers, switches, or routers. Protocols determine the type of error checking to be used, how the sending device indicates it has finished sending a message, and how the receiving device indicates it has received a message; however, not all protocols indicate the completion or reception of a message.

2. What is a bridge loop?

Answer: A bridge loop occurs when two or more active paths exist between network segments.

3. What is purpose of the Spanning Tree Protocol (STP)?

Answer: The Spanning Tree Protocol provides path redundancy in a bridged or switched network while preventing undesirable loops created by multiple active paths between hosts.

4. What is a BPDU?

Answer: BDPU is the acronym for bridge protocol data unit and is a Spanning Tree Protocol message frame describing the attributes of a switch port. These attributes include the port's MAC address, priority, age of message, timers, and cost to reach. BPDUs enable switches participating in an STP to gather information about each other and build a topology map so that each switch has a path to forward network traffic.

5. What are the STP states? Which state can only be manually configured?

Answer: Blocking, listening, learning, forwarding, and disabled. The only state that can be manually configured is the disabled state.

6. What is the difference between a blocked port and a disabled port?

Answer: A blocked port does not send or receive any traffic, but listens to the Spanning-Tree BPDU messages, whereas a disabled port is manually shut down by the administrator and can be enabled only in the same fashion.

7. What is the starting point for the Spanning Tree Protocol called?

Answer: The Spanning Tree Protocol reference point is called the root switch or port.

8. What two components make up the bridge identifier, how long is the bridge identifier, and how is the bridge identifier used?

Answer: The bridge identifier is made up of the bridge priority (2 bytes) and the MAC address (6 bytes). The bridge identifier is used to elect the root bridge or switch port in a LAN.

9. From the time it is powered up, how long does it take a switch to enter the forwarding state and begin forwarding LAN traffic?

   Answer: 50 seconds. The switch port starts in the blocking state at power up and transitions to the listening state. It takes 20 seconds for the switch port to transition from the blocking to the listening state, 15 seconds to transition from the listening to learning state, and another 15 seconds for the switch port to transition from the learning to the forwarding state.

10. What is convergence?

   Answer: Convergence is the process by which network devices, such as bridges, switches, or routers, learn of a change in network topology and then agree on what the new topology looks like after the change.

11. What does the Spanning Tree Protocol do when a new bridge is added to the network?

   Answer: Adding a bridge to the network changes the topology and thereby causes each bridge and switch to converge on the change by means of the Spanning Tree Protocol. STP puts all bridges and switches that are new or changed into a blocking state, listening for BPDUs, learning what the network looks like, and forwarding traffic through each port as determined by the Spanning Tree Protocol.

Chapter 8

1. What is a VLAN?

   Answer: A virtual LAN, or VLAN, is a group of computers, network printers, network servers, and other network devices behaving as if they were connected to a single network segment. A VLAN might also be considered a broadcast domain.

2. What is the IEEE standard for virtual LANs?

   Answer: IEEE 802.1q.

3. What advantages are provided by VLANs?

Answer: VLANs provide the following advantages:

— Help make Layer 2 networks scalable

— Isolate problems within a small part of the network

— Remove the physical network boundaries, enabling users and servers to be located anywhere.

— Enhance network security through logical segmentation of users and groups

— Increase performance by containing broadcast traffic

4. Name the three types of VLANs and explain their differences.

Answer: Port based, address based, and Layer 3 based. Port-based VLAN membership is based on the switch port. Address-based VLAN membership is based on the MAC, or hardware, address of the connecting device. Layer 3-based VLAN membership is based on the network address of the connecting device.

5. What is a Layer 3 switch?

Answer: Switches work at Layer 2 of the OSI model, the data link layer, using MAC addresses to the determine source and destination of the network traffic. Routers work at Layer 3 of the OSI model, the network layer, using Layer 3 (network) addresses, such as an IP address, to determine the source and destination of the network traffic. The difference between a Layer 3 switch and a router is that the switch uses a different algorithm to decide how to forward packets across the network. In contrast, routers forward packets based on algorithms that are determined by the routing protocol.

6. How can you communicate between VLANs?

Answer: Because direct communication between VLANs is not possible within a switch, a Layer 3 device is required to forward the traffic between VLANs. Each VLAN is a broadcast domain and uses Layer 2 (MAC) addressing to determine the source and destination of each frame, whereas a Layer 3 device, such as a router or Layer 3 switch, uses the network address to determine the source and destination of the traffic. Traffic can be forwarded between VLANs because Layer 3 looks beyond the broadcast domains.

7. How might you extend a VLAN?

Answer: You can extend a VLAN beyond the switch by using a trunk link.

8. What's the difference between an access link and a trunk link?

Answer: Access links are interfaces that belong to only one VLAN, whereas trunk links transport traffic from multiple VLANs between switches.

9. What is VLAN tagging?

Answer: VLAN tagging is used to identify the VLAN to which frames belong as they are received by a switch from across the trunk link connecting two switches together.

10. Which VLAN tagging method is an open standard? What is the benefit of using open standards?

Answer: The open standard for VLAN tagging is IEEE 802.1q. The benefit of using open standards is that it ensures interoperability between differing vendor equipment, such as a switch from ABC Company and a switch from XYZ Corporation.

11. What is a VTP management domain?

Answer: A VTP management domain is a group of switches sharing VTP information with each other.

12. How many VTP modes are there? What are they, and when would each be used?

Answer: Four: Server mode, client mode, transparent mode, and off.

Server mode might be considered the master switch in that all changes within the VTP management domain originate from a switch in server mode.

Client mode forwards updates to other devices, even though it cannot make changes.

Transparent mode receives VTP management domain, such as additions, deletions, and other changes, from the server mode switch. Switches configured for transparent mode do not process these updates; instead, the switch just passes the updates along. Off mode disables VTP completely on the switch.

13. Which VTP mode is the default mode?

Answer: Server mode.

Chapter 9

1. Why and how should you separate public (external) and private (internal) VLANs?

Answer: You should separate public (external) and private (internal) VLANs because separating your internal and external networks provides a measure of security in the network by not exposing internal resources to the outside world. You should do so by using two switches and a firewall in the network: one switch on the public, or outer, side of the firewall and one switch on the private, or inner, side of the firewall.

2. What is port security?

Answer: Port security is used to deny access to a switch or a network connected to that switch's port. When port security is enabled on a switch, any MAC address not specified for that port is denied access to the switch and any networks to which the switch is connected.

3. What is the difference between in-band and out-of-band management and the benefit of each?

Answer: In-band management means that network management traffic is carried to the network management workstations and managers across the same network as the data traffic. This includes the same devices and consumes the same bandwidth as the user data traffic. Out-of-band management means that network management traffic is carried to the network management workstations and managers across a separate network from the user data traffic.

The benefit of in-band management is that little additional money is spent in building the network management infrastructure. The accompanying drawback of in-band management is that it uses network resources designed for your users. The benefit of out-of-band management is that the network management traffic does not impact the data traffic and therefore does not consume network bandwidth. The drawback of out-of-band management is the cost of building a second network infrastructure to carry your network management traffic.

4. What are some of the common Layer 2 attacks on a network?

Answer: Some of the most common Layer 2 attacks are MAC flooding attacks, ARP attacks, private VLAN attacks, multicast brute-force attacks, Spanning-Tree attacks, and random frame stress attacks.

5. What is an ARP attack?

Answer: ARP attacks can occur on the same VLAN as well as different VLANs and can fool a switch into forwarding packets to a network device in a different VLAN by sending ARP packets containing forged identities. ARP attacks require the attacker to spoof the MAC address of a legitimate member of a VLAN by pretending to be that legitimate member. ARP spoofing, or ARP poisoning, is an effective attack because the switch does not know that someone has stolen the legitimate MAC address.

Chapter 10

1. What is microsegmentation?

Answer: Microsegmentation is the capability of treating a small number of hosts, or nodes, as a single physical segment or collision domain. Microsegmentation can be accomplished with a switch, because a switch treats each port as its own segment.

2. What are the three basic components of a switched network?

Answer: A switched network is composed of three basic components: physical switching platforms, a common software infrastructure, and network management tools.

3. What is a flat network?

Answer: A flat network is one Layer 2 network segment. It is a network in which all attached devices can reach each other without going through any intermediary hardware devices, such as a router. A VLAN is an example a flat network.

4. Name the most significant problem inherent in a flat network.

Answer: A flat network is a single broadcast domain, and because every host on the network must process every frame it receives, each host must process each broadcast frame it receives to determine whether it is the intended recipient. In a larger network with numerous broadcasts, this results in wasted processor time on each host, and contention for network bandwidth, because while the broadcasts are using the network, no one else can.

5. What are some of the features available to you in a VLAN implementation?

Answer: VLANs provide you a means to extend a LAN beyond its local geography. VLANs also enable you to group users together based on function, such as creating a virtual LAN for different departments within an organization, regardless of their physical proximity to each other.

6. What are some of the issues you need to address in a mixed-media environment, such as mixing Token Ring and Ethernet LANs?

Answer: Two factors need to be addressed in a mixed-media environment. The first factor is the minimum and maximum frame size each media is capable of supporting, and determining the lowest common denominator for each medium used. The second factor that needs to be considered regarding mixed-media networks is that switches must use a translation function to switch between different media, and this translation function can result in problems such as converting the MAC address among the different media.

7. What are some general principles of network design?

Answer: Some general network design principles are as follows:

— Examine your network for single points of failure, implementing redundant hardware or links when necessary.

— Characterize the applications that are using your network and the protocol traffic these applications create.

— Analyze the bandwidth usage on your network, ensuring there is enough available bandwidth for all network users.

— Build your network using a hierarchical or modular model, so that as your network grows, you can add the necessary parts, rather than undertaking major redesign effort.

8. What are some principles of switched LAN design?

Answer: Switched LAN design principles include the following:

— Contain broadcast radiation containment.

— Ensure your VLANs are moving network traffic in an efficient manner, minimizing hops between source and destination network segments.

— Ensure you have enough available bandwidth to support routing functionality in your network.

— Ensure you have placed administrative boundaries in the appropriate place(s) within the network.

9. What are some of the network services offered by routers that are not available with switches alone?

Answer: Routers provide broadcast and multicast control and segmentation in the network by filtering messages from being forwarded to any other network. Routers also provide the following functions: media transition, such as between Token Ring and Ethernet; transition between the different media types of each network; determination of where traffic goes based on the network (OSI Layer 3) address, not the MAC (OSI Layer 2) address.

10. What is the difference between ARP and RARP?

Answer: Reverse Address Resolution Protocol (RARP) allows a physical machine in a local-area network to request its IP address from a gateway server's Address Resolution Protocol (ARP) table or cache. (RARP is confined to a broadcast domain, as opposed to Bootstrap Protocol [BOOTP], which can cross routers.)

11. Is there a "one size fits all" concept for network design?

   Answer: No. Network designs are unique based on several factors and, as such, there is no "one size fits all" network design.

Chapter 11

1. What is the FCAPS model used for?

   Answer: The FCAPS model is used as the framework for network management platforms.

2. What are the layers of the FCAPS model?

   Answer: Fault management, configuration management, accounting management, performance management, and security management.

3. What is a NOC? What purpose does a NOC serve?

   Answer: A network operations center, or NOC, is a central network management location. The focus of a NOC is the implementation of the FCAPS model. A NOC functions as a control center for network fault management (troubleshooting), configuration, accounting, performance monitoring, and security.

4. What are the six steps in the fault management process?

   Answer:

   Step 1 A network event triggers an alarm.

   Step 2 The alarm prompts the network manager to identify the cause of the alarm (the problem).

   Step 3 The network manager identifies the cause of the alarm, such as a failed link or device.

   Step 4 The manager begins to troubleshoot the problem.

   Step 5 The problem is resolved.

   Step 6 The network manager documents the fault and the fix in a log, such as in a trouble ticket.

5. Why is configuration management important to a network manager?

Answer: Configuration management is important because it is the process for recording all network moves, adds, changes, or deletions. Configuration management accounts for hardware and software updates, and what each update does to the network, ensuring the most recent versions are running in the network. Configuration management also provides for a back-out plan—a plan to be executed if an update causes problems or network failure, not unlike an Undo button for your network. Configuration management also helps create a template or standard configuration for new device implementation.

6. What do the accounting and performance management functions provide to a network manager?

Answer: Performance management enables you to monitor and analyze network statistics trends, such as total network usage or network usage per user. Accounting management works in a fashion similar to performance management, but provides a mechanism for you to monitor and bill network usage to the appropriate organization or department. Accounting management also supplies a mechanism to ensure you are not overpaying for the network, such as paying for more network bandwidth than you use or need.

7. Why is security in your network important?

Answer: Security is important because it enables you to protect your network resources and network users. Security affords protection from both inside users and outside intruders trying to harm the network. Culprits could be trying to cause a network failure or to steal corporate information, such as internal documents or customer data (for example, personal credit information).

8. What are some of the differences between SNMPv1, SNMPv2, and SNMPv3?

Answer: SNMPv1 reports whether a device is up (working) or down (not working). SNMPv2 includes security and an RMON (Remote Monitoring) MIB (Management Information Base). SNMPv3 provides message-level security and includes an MIB for remotely monitoring/managing the configuration parameters for this message-level security.

9. What are some of the differences between SNMP and RMON?

   Answer: SNMP works in a poll/response model in which the SNMP manager polls the SNMP agent for information; whereas RMON works in a one-way model, in which network management information is sent from the RMON probe to the RMON client, often the network management console.

   RMON can also provide more-detailed information than SNMP in the form of network analysis and trending.

10. What benefits does SPAN provide you in a switched environment?

   Answer: SPAN enables you to monitor local switch traffic, from one or multiple ports or from one or multiple VLANs. The benefit of SPAN is that you can monitor the switch network traffic without taking the switch, or any of its users, out of service.

Chapter 12

1. Should you use a hub, bridge, or switch?

   Answer: It depends.

2. What are some basic steps in designing a network?

   Answer: Some of the steps include assessing the network and developing technical drawings, testing plans, and implementation plans.

3. What breaks up a collision domain?

   Answer: Bridges and switches.

4. What breaks up a broadcast domain?

   Answer: Routers.

5. When might you use switches rather than hubs?

Answer: When you are concerned about scaling network growth without having to replace equipment or needing to break up collision domains because of the impact collisions are having on your network.

6. When might you use a router rather than a switch?

Answer: When you need to connect to a wide-area network, such as a Frame Relay or Internet network, or when you need to break up broadcast domains.

7. What is the number-one rule of a network?

Answer: It has to work!

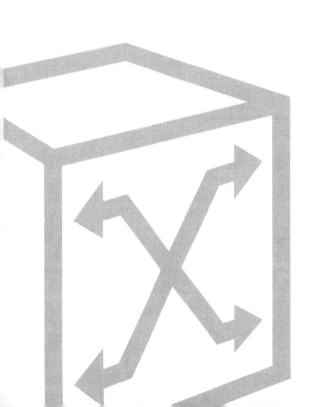

Glossary

5-4-3 rule   This rule refers to the number of repeaters and segments on shared-access Ethernet backbones in a tree topology. The 5-4-3 rule divides the network into two types of physical segments: populated (user) segments and unpopulated (link) segments. User segments have users' systems connected to them. Link segments are used to connect the network's repeaters together. The rule mandates that between any two nodes on the network, there can only be a maximum of five segments, connected through four repeaters, or concentrators, and only three of the five segments may contain user connections.

access link   An access link is only part of one VLAN and is the connection between the node and the VLAN. Any devices attached to an access link are unaware of VLAN membership.

Address Resolution Protocol (ARP)   A TCP/IP protocol used in learning a node's physical, or MAC address, by broadcasting the network address of the device in question. The Address Resolution Protocol, or ARP, is a TCP/IP protocol used to determine a network node's data-link, or MAC, address.

application-specific integrated circuit (ASIC)   Pronounced "a-sick." An ASIC is a chip that is custom designed for a specific application rather than a general-purpose chip such as a microprocessor found in a personal computer (PC).

ARP table   A table of IP addresses and their corresponding MAC addresses.

authentication, authorization, and accounting (AAA)   AAA is an architectural framework for configuring a set of three independent security functions (authentication, authorization, and accounting) in a consistent manner.

back-off algorithm   The formula built in to a contention-based local-area network device, such as an Ethernet NIC, that is used after collision by the media access controller to determine when to try again to get back on to the LAN.

bit bucket   Slang for the virtual waste bucket into which bits are thrown.

bridge   A data communications device connecting two or more network segments. Bridges forward frames between these network segments.

broadcast   To send information to two or more devices simultaneously over a communications network. Broadcast involves sending a transmission simultaneously to all members of a group.

broadcast radiation   The ambient or background level of broadcasts carried in the network.

broadcast storm   A pathological condition that can occur in a TCP/IP network. Broadcast storms are caused by a large number of broadcast packets propagated unnecessarily across a network, thereby causing network overload.

ciphertext   Normal text that has not been encrypted and is readable by anyone.

carrier sense multiple access with collision detect (CSMA/CD)   The LAN access method used in Ethernet. For a device to gain access to the network, it checks to see whether the network is quiet (senses the carrier). If it is not, it waits a random amount of time before retrying. If the network is quiet and two devices access the line at exactly the same time, their signals collide. When the collision is detected, they both back off and each waits a random amount of time before retrying.

collapsed backbone network   The backbone network connecting all network segments is collapsed (shortened considerably), and contained within a hub, or switch chassis.

collide   See *collision*.

collision   The result of two workstations (or PCs) trying to use a shared-transmission medium (cable) simultaneously. For example, in a local-area network, the electrical signals, which carry information, bump into each other. This ruins both signals and both must retransmit their information. In most systems, a built-in delay ensures that collisions do not occur again. The whole process takes fractions of a second. Collisions in LANs make no sound. Collisions do, however, slow down a LAN.

collision detection   The process of detecting that simultaneous (and therefore damaging) transmission have taken place. Typically, each transmitting worksta-tion that detects the collision waits some period of time to try again. Collision detection is an essential part of the CSMA/CD access method. Workstations can tell that a collision has taken place if they do not receive an acknowledgement from the receiving station within a certain amount of time (fractions of a second).

collision domain   A group of nodes in an Ethernet network that compete with each other for access. If two or more devices try to access the network at exactly the same time, a collision occurs. In a switched Ethernet environment, each transmitting-receiving pair of nodes is essentially its own collision domain, except that no collisions can occur, because there is no sharing of bandwidth.

congestion   A condition that arises when a communications link, path, or net-work experiences an offered traffic load (that is the amount of traffic offered) that exceeds the network's capacity. For example, consider a 10-Mbps link connected to a switch port. If the switch end station offers to the port a traffic load in excess of 10 Mbps, a congestion condition arises, often in the throttling back (slowing down) of traffic being sent to the switch.

Content Addressable Memory (CAM) entries   Entries in a MAC table. See also *MAC tables*.

convergence   The point at which all the internetworking devices share a com-mon understanding of the routing topology. The slower the convergence time, the slower the recovery from link failure. The convergence time is the time it takes for all network devices, such as a bridge, switch, or router, to update their tables and be in agreement with all the other devices.

cut through   In a network switch, the connecting of one circuit to another.

cut-through switch   A switching device that begins to output an incoming data packet before the packet is completely received.

cyclic redundancy check (CRC)   A process used to check the integrity of a block of data. A CRC character is generated at the transmission end. Its value depends on the hexadecimal value of the number of 1s in the data block. The transmitting device calculates the value and appends it to the data block. The receiving end makes a similar calculation and compares its results with the added character. If there is a difference, the recipient requests retransmission. CRC is a common method of establishing that data was correctly received in data communications.

cyphertext   See *ciphertext*.

data   The AT&T Bell Labs definition: "A representation of facts, concepts, or instructions in a formalized manner suitable for communication, interpretation, or processing." If it's not voice or video, it's data.

delay   Also referred to as "latency." The wait time between two events, such as the time from when a signal is sent to the time it is received. There are all sorts of reasons for delays, such as propagation delays caused by weather conditions (affecting radio signals), satellite delays caused by the distance the signal must travel to the satellite in space and back, and or serialization delay caused by the amount of time it takes the signal to enter/exit a port interface. The additional time introduced by the network in delivering a packet's worth of data compared to the time the same information would take on a full-period, dedicated point-to-point circuit.

default gateway   The default gateway of a network is the router used to forward all traffic not addressed to a network host within the local network.

demarcation point   The point of separation and/or interconnection where the lines from the telephone company network service provider connect to the customer's lines.

demodulate   The reverse of modulate.

designated port   The designated port is the port that is the single interface to forward traffic to the root bridge.

designated switch   The closest switch to the root switch through which frames are forwarded to the root.

destination   The receiving side or ending point of a transmission across a network.

distant end   The far end of a network connection. Also referred to as the circuit or route destination.

DIX   DEC, Intel, Xerox standard. An earlier Ethernet standard that was superseded by IEEE 802.3. Network protocols often use the Ethernet frame from this specification.

Dynamic Trunking Protocol (DTP)   A Cisco proprietary protocol that enables a switch port to automatically negotiate and configure a VLAN trunk with another switch port.

encryption   The reversible transformation of data from the original (the plaintext) to a difficult-to-interpret format (ciphertext) as a mechanism for protecting the confidentiality, integrity, and authenticity of the original data. Encryption uses an encryption algorithm and one or more encryption keys.

error correction   Routines in a system that correct for errors during transmission. Error correction detects errors in received transmissions and corrects those errors before delivering the transmitted data to the user.

error handling   Routines in a system that respond to errors. The effectiveness of an error-handling response is measured in how the system informs the user of such error conditions and what alternatives it provides for dealing with them.

FCAPS   An acronym for the network management model that is made up of five layers: fault (F), configuration (C), accounting (A), performance (P), and security (S) management.

file server   A high-speed computer in a network that stores the programs and data files shared by users. A file server acts like a remote disk drive.

firewall   A firewall is a device that implements security policies designed to keep a network secure from network intruders. A firewall can be a single router filtering out unwanted packets, a combination of routers and servers each performing some type of firewall processing, or a dedicated hardware device examining each packet and determining whether the packet is allowed to enter the network the firewall is protecting.

flat network topology   A flat network is one Layer 2 network segment. It is a network in which all attached devices can reach each other without going through any intermediary hardware devices, such as a router. A VLAN is a flat network. A nonblocking switch has enough paths available that all traffic can pass through the switch without being blocked or dropped.

flooding   A network switching method whereby identical frames are sent in all directions to ensure that they reach their intended destination.

fragment-free switching   A hybrid of cut-through and store-and-forward switching.

frame   Generic term specific to a number of data communication protocols. A frame of data is a logical unit of data, which is commonly a fragment of a much larger set of data, such as a file of text or image information.

full-duplex connection   A circuit connection that can send and receive data simultaneously. In pure digital networks, this is achieved with two pairs of wires. In analog networks or in digital networks using carriers, it is achieved by dividing the bandwidth of the line into two frequencies, one for sending and the other for receiving.

fur-ball networks   A network that grows in all directions without any structure and often results from poor (or no) network planning.

half-duplex connection   A circuit connection that can send data in both directions, but only one direction at a time. Example: Two-way radio was the first to use half duplex—while one party spoke, the other party listened.

header   In network communications, a temporary data set added to the beginning of the user data in order to transfer the user data across a network. The header contains source and destination addresses as well as data that describe the content of the message.

hexadecimal   This base-16 numbering system is used as shorthand for representing binary numbers. Each half byte (4 bits) is assigned a hex digit as shown in the following. Hex values are identified with an *H* or dollar sign; thus $3E0, 3E0h, and 3E0H all stand for the hex number 3E0.

host-based intrusion detection system (HIDS)   See *intrusion detection system (IDS)*.

hub   A central connecting device in a network that joins communication lines together in a star configuration. Passive hubs are connected-only units that add nothing to the data passing through them. Active hubs (sometimes called multiport repeaters) regenerate the data bits to maintain a strong signal. Intelligent hubs provide added functionality.

in-band   In-band exchanges between devices give each other control information on the same channel as the data transmission.

interconnected   To be attached to another entity. For example, one device is attached to another device, or one user to another user.

Internet Group Multicast Protocol (IGMP)   The protocol governing management of multicast groups in a TCP/IP network.

Internet Protocol (IP)   The network layer protocol in the TCP/IP communications protocol suite (the *IP* in TCP/IP). IP contains a network address and allows messages to be routed to a different network or subnet. IP does not ensure delivery of a complete message, and the TCP transport layer is used to provide this guarantee.

Internetwork Packet Exchange (IPX)   See *Novell Internet Protocol (IPX)*.

intrusion detection systems (IDS)   An intrusion detection system or IDS (pronounced "eye-dee-ess") is a software or hardware platform that detects an attack on a network or computer system. A network-based IDS, or NIDS, is designed to support multiple hosts, whereas a host-based IDS, or HIDS, detects illegal actions within the host. Most IDS programs typically use signatures of known cracker attempts to signal an alert. Others look for deviations from an established normal routine (baseline) as an indication of an attack.

latency   See *delay*.

MAC tables   A table of MAC addresses and their associated bridge/switch ports.

man-in-the-middle (MiM) attack   Also known as a replay attack. A MiM attack is a breach of security in which information is stored without authorization and then retransmitted to trick the receiver into unauthorized operations, such as false identification or authentication or a duplicate transaction. For example, in a poorly designed authentication system, it is possible to record the output from a valid fingerprint using wiretapping and make it a substitute when an invalid fingerprint is presented for analysis. MiM attacks can be prevented using strong digital signatures that include time stamps and unique information from the previous transaction, such as the value of a constantly incremented sequence number.

managed object   The single piece of information that is created by the individual components in a network architecture. See *Management Information Base (MIB)*.

Management Information Base (MIB)   A MIB is a collection of managed objects residing in a virtual information store. Collections of related managed objects are defined in specific MIB modules. See *managed object*.

maximum transmission unit (MTU)   The largest possible unit of data that can be sent on a given physical medium. Example: The MTU of Ethernet is 1500 bytes. The MTU is the largest frame size that can be transmitted over the network. Messages larger than the MTU are broken down, or fragmented, into smaller frames.

media   The conduit or link that carries transmissions. Examples: coaxial cable, copper wire, radio waves, waveguide, and fiber. Plural of medium.

Media Access Control (MAC) address   A MAC address is in the form of a 48-bit number unique to each LAN (local-area network) NIC (network interface card). The MAC address is programmed into the card at the time of manufacture. The IEEE registration authority administers the MAC addresses scheme for all LANs that conform to the IEEE Project 802 series of standards. These LANs include both Ethernet and Token Ring. The MAC address comprises two distinct identifiers (IDs), which are programmed into ROM (read-only memory) and cannot be changed. The first address is a unique 24-bit manufacturer's ID, also known as the organizational unique identifier (OUI), which is assigned by the IEEE to the manufacturer of the NIC. The second address is a 24-bit extension ID, assigned by the manufacturer.

medium   Any material substance that can be used for the sending and receiving of signals from one point to another, such as radio, light, or acoustic waves. Examples: optical fiber, cable, wire, dielectric slab, water, air, and free space. Singular of media.

microsegmentation   The capability of treating a small number of hosts, or nodes, as a single physical segment or collision domain. Microsegmentation can be accomplished with a switch because a switch treats each port as its own.

modem   Acronym for modulator/demodulator. Conventional modems are equipment that convert digital signals to analog signals and vice versa. Modems are used to send digital data signals over the analog Public Switched Telephone Network (PSTN).

modulate   The changing or converting of a signal from one type to another, such as converting a signal from analog to digital.

multicast   The broadcast of messages to a selected group of workstations on a LAN, WAN, or the Internet. Multicast is communication between a single device and multiple members of a device group.

multistation access unit (MAU)   A central hub in a Token Ring local-area network (LAN).

native virtual LAN   A native virtual LAN is a VLAN that is not associated explicitly with a trunk link.

network   A system of interconnected lines. A system that sends and/or receives any combination of voice, video, and/or data between users.

network address translation (NAT)   An Internet standard that enables a local-area network (LAN) to use one set of IP addresses for internal traffic and a second set of addresses for external traffic. NAT enables a company to shield internal addresses from the public Internet.

network-based intrusion detection system (NIDS)   See *intrusion detection system (IDS)*.

network interface card (NIC)   A printed circuit board that plugs into the PCI bus of both the client machines and servers in a network. The network adapter controls the transmission and receiving of data at the OSI model physical and data link layers.

network latency   Network latency is the delay introduced when a frame or packet is temporarily stored, analyzed, and then forwarded on to the network. Network latency is measured in milliseconds (ms).

network operations center (NOC)   A network operations center, or NOC, is a central network management location. A NOC functions as a control center for network fault management (troubleshooting), configuration, accounting, performance monitoring, and security.

network segmentation   The division of a single network into multiple smaller segments.

NIC   See *network interface card (NIC)*.

node   A network junction or connection point. Every terminal, computer, hub, and switch is a node.

nonblocking switch   A nonblocking switch has enough paths available that all traffic can pass through the switch without being blocked or dropped.

nonsecure   The segment(s) of a network that are not protected from intrusion or attacks by an outside, or public, entity are considered nonsecure. Nonsecure network segments are "open to the world."

nonvolatile RAM (NVRAM)   Nonvolatile RAM is memory that retains its contents even when powered off.

Novell Internet Protocol (IPX)   The Internetwork Packet Exchange, or IPX, protocol is the network layer protocol in the Novell NetWare operating system. Similar to the IP layer in TCP/IP, IPX contains a network address and enables messages to be routed to a different network or subnet.

out-of-band   Out-of-band devices exchange control information on a dedicated channel, separate from that used by the active data transmission channel. An out-of-band port is not part of an active domain and does not carry network data but rather network management data. Out-of-band ports are used when you do not want to add bandwidth to the active network data channel.

packet   A block of data that is transmitted over the network in a packet-switched system. The terms *frame*, *packet*, and *datagram* are often used synonymously, although erroneously, in network discussions. Packets are found at the OSI model network layer and frames are found at the OSI model data link layer.

payload   The data-carrying capacity of some structure, typically referring to a part of a packet or frame in a network system. The payload holds the message data generated from the user.

PIM-DM   See *Protocol Independent Multicast (PIM)*.

PIM-SM   See *Protocol Independent Multicast (PIM)*.

plaintext   Normal text that has not been encrypted and is readable by text editors and word processors.

port cost   The cost of a switch port is based on the number of network segments the frame crosses before reaching its destination.

port monitoring   See *SPAN*.

potential vulnerability   A potential vulnerability in a software platform is better known as a bug (as in software bug). A bug, which is a code error, can be exploited.

print server   A computer hardware device that controls one or more printers and enables a printer to be located anywhere in the network.

promiscuous mode   Promiscuous mode is the condition in which a network node, or a port on a network node, recognizes and accepts all incoming packets, regardless of protocol type or destination. If a network device is in promiscuous mode, it might have been compromised.

promiscuous port   A port configured for promiscuous mode.

proprietary   With regard to hardware and software, the term *proprietary* specifies that the property in question was developed by and is currently owned by a vendor organization or individual.

Protocol Independent Multicast (PIM)   PIM is a multicast routing protocol endorsed by the Internet Engineering Task Force (IETF) and is used in conjunction with an existing unicast routing protocol. PIM comes in two flavors: dense mode (PIM-DM) and sparse mode (PIM-SM). Dense mode is used when recipients in the target group are in a concentrated area. Sparse mode is more efficient when members are scattered across the network.

quality of service (QoS)   A defined level of performance in a data communications system.

RADIUS   Remote Authentication Dial-In User Service, or RADIUS, is an access-control protocol using a challenge/response method for authentication. Challenge/response is an authentication method used to verify the legitimacy of users logging on to the network. When a user logs on to the network, the server uses account information to send a challenge number back to the user. The user enters a defined response, which is then sent back to the server.

registered jack (RJ)   Any of the RJ series of jacks, described in the *Code of Federal Regulations*, Title 47, part 68. Used to provide interface to the public telephone network.

repeater   The simplest type of LAN interconnection device. A repeater moves all received packets or frames between LAN segments. The primary function of a repeater is to extend the length of the network media (cable).

Reverse Address Resolution Protocol (RARP)   Reverse ARP is a low-level TCP/IP protocol used by a workstation (typically diskless) to query a node for purposes of obtaining its logical IP address.

route   The path a message takes across a network.

router   Intelligent devices that connect like and unlike LANs. They connect to MANs (metropolitan-area networks) and WANs (wide-area networks). Routers can be X.25, Frame Relay, and Asynchronous Transfer Mode (ATM). Routers are protocol sensitive, typically supporting multiple protocols.

runtless switching   See *fragment-free switching*.

secure   The segment(s) of a network that are protected from intrusion or attacks by an outside, or public, entity are considered secure.

server farm   A room of PCs that are acting as servers and are arranged in racks along walls. These PCs may include file servers, database servers, print servers, e-mail servers, and web servers. Powerful PCs containing databases and other information that they dispense to thousands of PCs connected to them from across the network.

service level agreement (SLA)   Between the provider and the user, a contract that specifies the level of service expected during the term of the agreement. SLAs are used by vendors and customers as well as internally by IT shops and their end users.

simplex connection   A circuit connection that can send information in one direction only. One-way transmission.

source   The sending side or starting point of a data transmission across a network.

SPAN   The Cisco Switched Port Analyzer (SPAN) feature, sometimes called port mirroring or port monitoring, selects network traffic for analysis by a network analyzer such as a SwitchProbe device or other Remote Monitoring (RMON) probe.

SPAN port   A configured switch port that selects network traffic for analysis by a network analyzer. Also known as port mirroring.

Spanning Tree Protocol (STP)   Spanning Tree Protocol (STP) is a link-management protocol that prevents the formation of logical loops in the LAN and is standardized in IEEE 802.1d.

steady-state condition   A network in a steady-state condition is a network that has few changes and is considered static in nature. This is not to say that there cannot be change in a steady-state network; it means that changes are few and far between.

store-and-forward switching   The temporary storage of a message for transmission to its destination at a later time, such as when the entire frame is received into the switch buffers.

subnet   A subnet is a division of a network into an interconnected, but independent, segment, or domain. The division is accomplished to improve performance and security.

switch   A mechanical or electronic device that directs the flow of signals, either electrical or optical, from one side to the other.

T1   A 1.544-Mbps point-to-point dedicated, digital circuit provided by the telephone companies. The monthly cost is typically based on distance. T1 lines are widely used for private networks as well as interconnections between an organization's private branch exchange (PBX) or LAN and the telephone company (telco).

TACACS+   Terminal Access Controller Access Control System, or TACACS, is an access-control protocol that authenticates a user logging on to the network. TACACS is a simple username/password system. TACACS+ adds encryption and a challenge/response option to the TACACS operation.

TIA/EIA-568   Standards for wiring buildings for telecommunications.

topologies   The pattern of interconnection between nodes, such as in a star or ring topology.

trailer   In network communications, a data code or set of codes that make up the last part of a transmitted message.

transceiver   A device that both transmits and receives data.

transparent bridge   A nonblocking switch has enough paths available that all traffic can pass through the switch without being blocked or dropped.

trap   To test for a particular condition in a running program. For example, to "trap an interrupt" means to wait for a particular interrupt to occur and then execute a corresponding routine. An error trap tests for an error condition and provides a recovery routine. A debugging trap waits for the execution of a particular instruction in order to stop the program and analyze the status of the system at that moment.

troubleshooting   The art and science of figuring out why something does not work and fixing the problem.

trunk link   A trunk link carries multiple VLANS between devices and is often supported on Fast Ethernet or Gigabit Ethernet links.

trunk port   The originating or terminating port of a communications trunk.

unicast   The communication from one device to another device over a network. In other words, a point-to-point communication.

virtual LAN (VLAN)   A VLAN is a networking technology that enables networks to be logically segmented without having to be physically segmented or wired.

virtual LAN (VLAN) tagging   VLAN tagging is used by the receiving switch to identify the VLAN to which frames belong as they are received from across the trunk link that connects the two switches together.

VLAN Trunking Protocol (VTP) pruning   VLAN Trunking Protocol (VTP) pruning maximizes network bandwidth use by reducing unnecessary flooded traffic, such as broadcast, multicast, unknown, and flooded unicast packets from being sent across the network.

VTP management domain   A VTP management domain is a group of switches that share VTP information.

wide-area network (WAN)   A communications network that covers a wide geographic area, such as a state or country.

wirespeed   The bandwidth of a particular transmission or networking system. For example, the wire speed of 10BASE-T Ethernet is 10 Mbps. When data is said to be transmitted at wire speed, this implies there is little or no software overhead associated with the transmission and that the data travels at the maximum speed of the hardware.

workstation   A terminal or desktop computer in a network. A generic term for a user's machine.

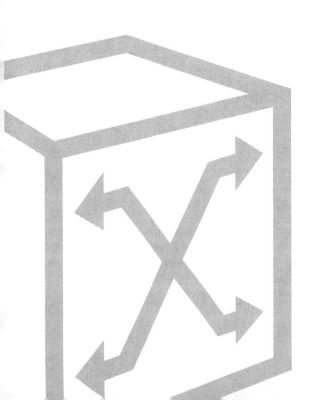

INDEX

E

V

vendor-assigned addresses (MAC), 90, 118

virtual circuits, 31

virtual LANs. *See* **VLANs**

VLAN Trunking Protocol. *See* **VTP**

VLANs (virtual LANs), 225–226

80/20 rule, 255

address-based VLANs, 178–181

advantages of, 174

assigning end nodes, 174

assigning network devices, 177

benefits, 251

broadcast control, 251

broadcast domains, 172

campus networks, 303

case study, 303–305

communicating with other VLANs, 176

designing, 250–252

differentiating, 253

Ethernet, 40

extending, 184–185

hubs, replacing with switches, 173

identification numbers, 174

IEEE 802.1q, 193

implementing, 252–253

infrastructure, 225

inter-VLAN communication, 181, 184

inter-VLAN traffic, routing 255

Layer 3-based VLANs, 180

limiting node numbers, 174

logical hierarchy, 259

membership, 177–179, 181

network management, 252

node numbers, limiting 174

operation, 177–187

overview, 172–174

performance, 251

port-based VLANs, 177–178, 252

routers (required), 181, 226

routing inter-VLAN traffic, 255

routing mechanisms, 176

scalability, 223

security, 200–203, 207–215, 251

ARP attacks, 212–213

MAC flooding attacks, 211

multicast brute-force attacks, 214

private VLAN attacks, 213–215

random frame-stress attacks, 215

spanning-tree attacks, 215

trunking security, 202

segment-based VLANs, 252

segmenting, 296, 304

server farms, 255